THE FOREIGN OFFICE

THE FOREIGN OFFICE

OFFICE

AN ILLUSTRATED HISTORY OF
THE PLACE AND ITS PEOPLE

ANTHONY SELDON

with photographs by Kim Sayer

HarperCollins*Illustrated*

First published in 2000 by
HarperCollins*Illustrated*
an imprint of HarperCollins*Publishers*
77-85 Fulham Palace Road
London W6 8JB

The HarperCollins website
address is: www.**fire**and**water**.com

Text © Anthony Seldon 2000

A CIP catalogue record for this book
is available from the British Library.

ISBN: 0 00 710118 X

Designer: Louise Dick
Copy Editor: Caroline Taylor
Indexer: Susan Martin

04 03 02 01 00
9 8 7 6 5 4 3 2 1

Colour reproduction by
Colourscan Pte.
Printed and bound in the UK by Bath
Press Colourbooks Ltd.

 ARCHITECTS

INTRODUCTION &
ACKNOWLEDGEMENTS

This book is the second in a series on the principal public buildings in British history. The aim of this volume is to provide an account of the history and present use of the Foreign Office, as well as, to a lesser extent, of those other buildings and offices associated with it over the years.

The history told in these pages is highly selective: there is no attempt to be comprehensive, or even representative. Only a small proportion of overseas embassies and, indeed, buildings within Britain connected with foreign affairs, can be covered within the confines of this book. Nevertheless, I hope that I have provided a sense of place as well as history.

I still remember standing on the bridge in St James's Park, just after coming down to London from Oxford, a city not without its own architectural triumphs, and gazing across the lake. My breath was taken away. Nowhere had I seen such an inspiring, uplifting, even magical, vista. The Foreign Office dominates that view. Years later I read Christopher Hussey, who had stood on the same spot:

'Seen from the Park, down the lake, the dramatic mass of black and white Portland stone enriched with countless statues composes, in conjunction with the towers of Westminster, Kent's Horse Guards, and the pinnacles of Whitehall Mansions, one of the most grandly picturesque urban landscapes in the world.'

A short while after contemplating that first, never-to-be-forgotten view, I was walking along Horse Guards Road past the building, with an old friend who had just entered the Foreign Office. Pointing up, he said in awed tones, 'that room was the Foreign Secretary's'. And those are the windows, I mused, through which Edward Grey stared bleakly in the summer of 1914. I had become smitten, but it would be another twenty years before I would come to write the story of the Foreign Office. That friend, Sherard Cowper-Coles, is now the Foreign Secretary's Principal Private Secretary, in which capacity he has played a key part in facilitating this book's passage.

Many others helped in the book's production. First and foremost I thank the Secretary of State, Robin Cook, and the Permanent Under Secretary at the FCO, John Kerr, for allowing the book to be written. Many have given unstintingly of their time. In the Foreign Office, I would like to thank in particular Kate Crowe, as well as Keith Hamilton, Heather Yasamee and Richard Bevins of the Records and Historical Department for their knowledge and superlative help

throughout. Jim Hoare gave generously of his unrivalled knowledge of British embassies. In the Library Helen Glass was a key figure throughout and I also much appreciated the help of all the Library staff, especially Paul Thorpe. Neil Cooke and John Denny from architects Cecil Denny Highton provided invaluable information on the buildings. Together with Ian Toplis, the author of the definitive book on the Foreign Office's architecture, they gave me the best possible advice.

I would like to thank the following diplomats and former diplomats for their help: Leonard Appleyard, John Coles, Ewen Fergusson, Richard Gozney, John Graham, David Hannay, Nicholas Henderson, John Kerr, Donald Maitland, Ian Samuel, David Wilson, Oliver Wright and Patrick Wright. My appreciation also to Douglas Hurd and Geoffrey Howe for their enthusiasm and continuing support.

Colonel Brook, David Brown, Josie Buckwell, Colonel Clements, Mike Cook, John Gallehawk, Malcolm Harris, Linda Hudson, John Kimmins, Matthew Kirk, Jean Monro, Angie Moore, Teri Osborne-Gomez, Chris Rainsford, Pranay Sanklecha, Juliet Smith, Peter Snowdon and Tony Whitestone all gave invaluable help and support, as did my GCSE History set at Brighton College.

Finally, my thanks go to Fiona Screen, my ever patient publisher, and to Victoria Alers-Hankey, for her considerable work on picture research, to Polly Powell, for getting the book off the ground, to Teresa Goudie for her four months of tireless and outstanding work as my researcher, to Mary Anne Brightwell and Anne-Marie Weitzel, who typed from near-illegible drafts, to all my wonderful colleagues, especially Mary-Ann Collins, Simon Smith, Philip Robinson and John Bone at Brighton College, and to John Barnes, Professor Hugh Berrington and Joanna Seldon, for reading over the text. Any errors that remain are entirely my own.

The book was written over the Easter holidays in Newton Ferrers, Walberswick and West Buckland. My thanks to my family and friends, and to my governors at Brighton College.

NOTE: IN THIS BOOK THE TERM 'FOREIGN OFFICE' IS USED TO MEAN 'FOREIGN AND COMMONWEALTH OFFICE' WHEN THIS IS AFTER 1968; 'FOREIGN SECRETARY' DENOTES THE 'SECRETARY OF STATE FOR FOREIGN AFFAIRS', AND PEOPLE ARE MENTIONED IN THE TEXT WITHOUT THEIR TITLES, ALL FOR REASONS OF BREVITY.

CONTENTS

INTRODUCTION &
ACKNOWLEDGEMENTS 5

RAISING THE FLAG

10

THE BUILDING IN HISTORY

34

THE BUILDING TODAY

72

THE GREAT & THE GOOD

108

CARLTON GARDENS

132

HOME AND ABROAD

142

DORNEYWOOD & CHEVENING

182

A SECRET WORLD

198

LOWERING THE FLAG

218

FORMER FOREIGN SECRETARIES 233

BIBLIOGRAPHY 234

PICTURE CREDITS 235

INDEX 236

British Imperial Territories, 1850

British rule

NORTHWEST TERRITORIES

RUPERT'S LAND

BRITISH COLUMBIA

VANCOUVER ISLAND

CANADA WEST

CANADA EAST

PRINCE EDWARD ISLAND

NEWFOUNDLAND

NOVA SCOTIA

NEW BRUNSWICK

BERMUDA

WEST INDIES (see inset)

JAMAICA

BRITISH HONDURAS

BRITISH GUIANA

PITCAIRN ISLAND

FALKLAND ISLANDS

SOUTH GEORGIA

SOUTH SANDWICH ISLANDS

ASCENSION

ST HELENA

TRISTAN DA CUNHA

UNITED KINGDOM

HELIGOLAND

GIBRALTAR

IONIAN ISLANDS

MALTA

THE GAMBIA

SIERRA LEONE

GOLD COAST FORTS

CAPE COLONY

NATAL

BRITISH KAFFRARIA

ADEN

SEYCHELLES

MAURITIUS

INDIA

LOWER BURMA

HONG KONG

PENANG

MALACCA

SINGAPORE

LABUAN

SARAWAK

NEW ZEALAND

WESTERN AUSTRALIA

NORTHERN TERRITORY

SOUTH AUSTRALIA

QUEENSLAND

NEW SOUTH WALES

VICTORIA

VAN DIEMEN'S LAND (TASMANIA)

WEST INDIES

THE BAHAMAS

CAYMAN IS.

JAMAICA

TURKS & CAICOS IS.

BRITISH VIRGIN IS.

ANGUILLA

ST CHRISTOPHER-NEVIS

MONTSERRAT

BARBUDA

ANTIGUA

DOMINICA

ST LUCIA

ST VINCENT

BARBADOS

GRENADA

TRINIDAD & TOBAGO

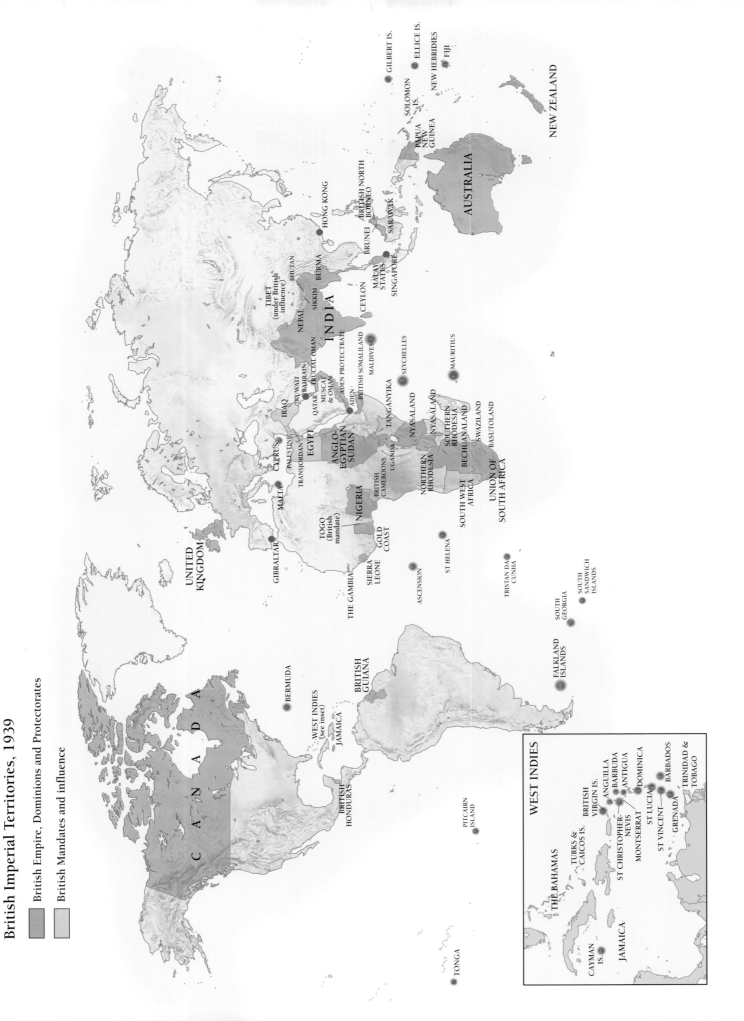

British Imperial Territories, 1939

British Empire, Dominions and Protectorates

British Mandates and influence

GILBERT IS.

ELLICE IS.

FIJI

NEW HEBRIDES

SOLOMON IS.

PAPUA NEW GUINEA

NEW ZEALAND

AUSTRALIA

BRITISH NORTH BORNEO

HONG KONG

SARAWAK

BRUNEI

MALAY STATES

SINGAPORE

BHUTAN

BURMA

SIKKIM

NEPAL

TIBET (under British influence)

INDIA

CEYLON

MALDIVES

SEYCHELLES

MAURITIUS

TRUCIAL OMAN

BAHRAIN

KUWAIT

QATAR

MUSCAT & OMAN

ADEN PROTECTORATE

ADEN

BRITISH SOMALILAND

IRAQ

TANGANYIKA

NYASALAND

NYASALAND

SOUTHERN RHODESIA

SWAZILAND

BASUTOLAND

CYPRUS

PALESTINE

TRANSJORDAN

EGYPT

ANGLO-EGYPTIAN SUDAN

UGANDA

NORTHERN RHODESIA

BECHUANALAND

SOUTH WEST AFRICA

UNION OF SOUTH AFRICA

MALTA

GIBRALTAR

UNITED KINGDOM

BRITISH CAMEROONS

NIGERIA

TOGO (British mandate)

GOLD COAST

SIERRA LEONE

THE GAMBIA

ASCENSION

ST HELENA

TRISTAN DA CUNHA

SOUTH GEORGIA

SOUTH SANDWICH ISLANDS

FALKLAND ISLANDS

BERMUDA

WEST INDIES (see inset)

JAMAICA

BRITISH GUIANA

BRITISH HONDURAS

C A N A D A

PITCAIRN ISLAND

TONGA

WEST INDIES

THE BAHAMAS

TURKS & CAICOS IS.

BRITISH VIRGIN IS.

ANGUILLA

ST CHRISTOPHER-NEVIS

BARBUDA

ANTIGUA

MONTSERRAT

DOMINICA

ST LUCIA

ST VINCENT

GRENADA

BARBADOS

TRINIDAD & TOBAGO

CAYMAN IS.

JAMAICA

RAISING THE FLAG

FLAG

NO COUNTRY IN HISTORY has wielded as much power across the globe as Great Britain at the height of its power. No country has had as much influence over the way the world has evolved, nor possessed a larger nor a more far-flung empire. Language, culture, sport, even the adoption of Greenwich as the meridian for longitude, and as the base line for the world's time zones, all testify to Britain's impact on the globe. This book will explore the history since 1868 of the building that was at the nerve centre of that power, and study some of the people and outposts which wielded that power at its height, and during its long decline. How did a relatively small country on the northern fringes of Europe come to acquire such influence? And how did Britain's diplomatic structures adapt to its changing position in the world?

THE STATE OF BRITAIN IN 1660

By 1500 leadership in Europe was being taken over by nation states, notably Spain, France and England. After the Wars of the Roses (1455–85) England's strength and cohesion was to grow under the Tudor monarchs. Henry VII and his son Henry VIII consolidated the power of the government and centralised power in the crown. The break with Rome gave the monarchy new power and wealth, and created a sovereign country independent of overseas jurisdiction. In the early 1540s Wales became fully integrated into the English system of government, and gained the right to parliamentary representation. The reign of Elizabeth I saw England defeat Spain, the great military power of the sixteenth century, in the battle of the Spanish Armada in 1588, and in 1601 England's forces prevented Spain from meddling in Ireland.

On Elizabeth's death in 1603, the English and Scottish crowns were united on the accession of James I (James VI of Scotland). But the union was more a geographical than a political one. While Spain went into a prolonged period of decline under Philip III and Philip IV, Britain's Stuart monarchs contin-

ued to consolidate the strength of the government. Yet unrest in Ireland and Scotland and then in England itself flared up, culminating in the Civil War in the 1640s and the execution of Charles I in Whitehall in 1649. Oliver Cromwell established the Commonwealth in 1649, and tried to bring Scotland and Ireland into the union by giving them parliamentary seats and social reform. At the same time, Britain's overseas trade and interests were given a powerful boost by Cromwell's Commonwealth. Although Parliamentary union with Scotland was not to come until 1707, and with Ireland not until 1801, the power of the Crown continued to be centralised in London. When the monarchy was restored in 1660, the British state was in a strong position to assert its power internationally, and to build up an overseas empire.

Modern European diplomacy began to emerge during the fifteenth and sixteenth centuries. In France, England and Spain, royal secretaries were appointed, whose responsibilities included the management of foreign affairs. The Renaissance

BELOW *The sun never set on the British Empire. A 1930s Imperial Airways Map. The airline name is indicative of the age.*

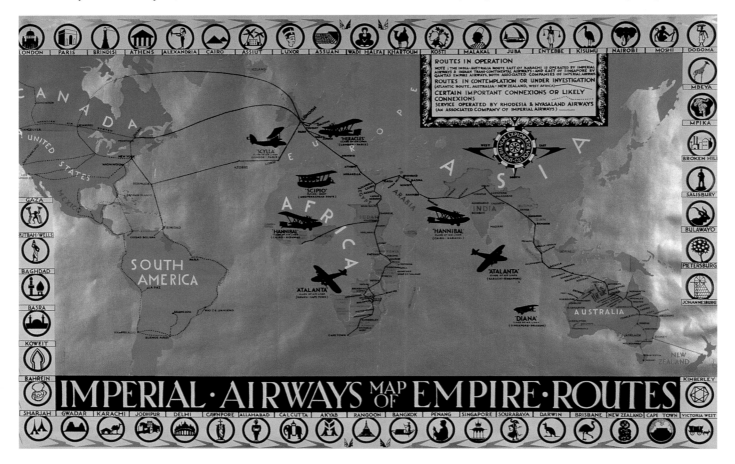

ABOVE *Britain's overseas interests meant an elaborate network of relationships across the globe. This is a view of the engine room of the Foreign Office, in 1941.*

spurred the development of effective systems of administration and record keeping, to ensure that states were kept abreast of the activities of their neighbours. Resident missions equipped with secretaries began to emerge, and these can be seen as the forerunners of the modern embassies. France was the first European state to establish a modern foreign ministry, in 1626. Russia followed in 1720, when Peter the Great created the College of Foreign Affairs, and Prussia too acquired its own foreign minister. Britain was to be a late starter.

EAST AND WEST INDIES

The first European sailors to penetrate India and the Far East markets were the Portuguese, in the early sixteenth century. In 1600 their near monopoly was challenged when the London-based East India Company was formed, keen to trade direct with spice suppliers in the East Indies (now Indonesia). The Dutch were also keen to open up new trade routes, and in 1623 they captured and tortured to death eighteen British merchants in the East Indies. The violence helped turn British traders towards India, where they were unopposed.

The Moghul emperors who ruled India allowed the East India Company a string of trading posts along the east and west coasts. Trade with India, and the fortunes of the company, continued to wax until the end of the seventeenth century and beyond.

British sailors and entrepreneurs had also travelled west, to the West Indies or the Spanish Main, since the mid-sixteenth century. John Hawkins, a Plymouth shipowner, had realised profit could be made from selling West African slaves to the Spaniards. In 1568 his fleet was ambushed by the Spanish in the West Indies. Battle was on. Hawkins returned with Francis Drake to harass and plunder Spanish cargoes, a mission given added piquancy by the fact that the pirates saw themselves as engaged in a holy Protestant war against the traders from Catholic Spain. In 1627 Charles I granted a charter to the Barbados Company, which planted its first sugar crop in 1643 and flourished thereafter. Cheap and hardy labour was needed if sugar was to be harvested economically, and by the 1650s a busy trade was shipping slaves from West Africa to Barbados. An average of 30,000 black Africans, taken from what today are the countries of Gambia, Senegal, Ghana and Nigeria, were sold annually in Barbados, having been transported across the Atlantic in appalling conditions. Most were sold for use in Barbados or elsewhere in the West Indies; others were exported to Virginia or Maryland.

THE AMERICAN COLONIES: GAIN AND LOSS

ABOVE *The Surrender of the British Forces at Yorktown, 1781.*
Painted by Louis Nicolas van Blarenberghe (1716–94), the
painting hangs in the Château de Versailles, France.

What has been called 'Britain's first empire' had come and gone before the eighteenth century had ended. The first European power into North America had been the Spanish, who moved north from Mexico and up along the western coast. Peace with Spain in 1604, and the stability that James I's reign brought at home, provided the impetus for English interest in North America to grow. A military settlement was established at Jamestown in 1607, with groups from London and Plymouth leading the way, and tobacco a major spur. The first domestic settlement came with the landing at Cape Cod on 21 November 1620 of the 'Pilgrims' aboard the *Mayflower*. The form of Anglicanism pursued under the Stuart monarchs prompted those unwilling to conform to search for religious freedom, and in the 1630s up to 20,000 sailed the Atlantic to settle in 'New England'. More settlers then followed from England and from Protestant mainland Europe, for reasons which were no longer mainly religious, and by the mid-eighteenth century 13 separate colonies had been established, stretching almost 1,120 miles from north to south, but which rarely penetrated more than 200 miles inland.

The colonies differed: from Massachusetts with its religious intolerance, as seen in the Salem 'witch' trials of the 1690s, to the more relaxed and accepting mores in William Penn's Pennsylvania, or in Virginia still further to the south. But the colonies were drawn together by common roots, by their desire to trade together, and to defend themselves both against the native American Indians angry at the intrusions of the 'settlers', and against the French. The colonists worked with the British forces in a succession of imperial conflicts between 1689 and 1713, and 1739 and 1763, culminating in the defeat of the French in the Seven Years' War.

Harmony between the colonists and London was to be short-lived. George III and his government in London held the American colonies to be subordinate to the British Parliament and should therefore pay tax, not least to finance their defence. Stamp duties imposed in 1765 were soon withdrawn but the colonists were angered when Parliament tried to impose direct taxes. By 1774 Britain found itself at war with the colonies, a war it was almost bound to lose: defeating a well-armed and committed people three thousand miles away across the North Atlantic was always going to be an uphill task. On 4 July 1776 the Americans declared themselves independent, and when, two years later, they were joined in arms by the French, by now convinced that the British would lose, the end was inevitable. In October 1781 Lord Cornwallis surrendered his British forces at Yorktown. This was followed by the resignation in 1782 of Lord North, the British Prime Minister, who was devastated by the news, and in 1783 a peace treaty was signed at Versailles in which Britain recognised the independence of the sovereign 'United States of America'.

In response to the debacle in America, Britain established its Foreign Office as a separate department in 1782. Charles James Fox became Britain's first Foreign Secretary, and Richard Brinsley Sheridan, the playwright, his Under Secretary. To oversee Britain's still vast possessions and its role in the world, Fox and Sheridan were assisted by a staff of twelve. Its structure evolved slowly, but the Slave Trade Department and Librarians' Department soon developed strong separate identities.

THE EIGHTEENTH CENTURY: WAR AND COLONIAL ADVANCES

From the 'Glorious Revolution' of 1688–9, the joint coronation of the Dutch William of Orange as William III and his English wife, Mary, until the loss of America in 1783, Britain had been almost continuously at war. The Nine Years' War (1689–97) was followed by the War of the Spanish Succession (1702–14), the Wars of Jenkins' Ear and the Austrian Succession (1739–48),

the Seven Years' War (1756–63) and finally the American War of Independence (1774–83). Two interlinked struggles were involved: Britain's continuing desire to build up her overseas trade and colonies at the expense of her two main rivals, Spain and France, and her determination to prevent France from dominating Europe.

The standing of Parliament was bolstered by the events of the 'Glorious Revolution' of 1688–9. The Crown had to give weight to the views of Parliamentarians who counted merchants, shippers and financiers among their number. The City of London became more important as a centre of finance and commerce. From both Houses of Parliament came pressure for the Crown to promote Britain's commercial and colonial interests. During the eighteenth century both Whigs and Tories supported the idea that war, paid for by the burgeoning national debt, would be a tonic for Britain's economy and her overseas interests. The British Empire was widely accepted as an invaluable adjunct to mainland Britain: produce from the colonies was shipped into British ports and factories, and the colonies purchased British manufactured goods in large quantities.

Britain suffered two periods of threat: first in the 1740s and then between 1778 and 1783. By 1744 Britain's war against Spain had turned into a general European conflict. Britain found herself fighting alongside the Netherlands and Austria against Spain, France and Prussia. British troops were pinned down on the continent, defending George II's province of Hanover. Then, in 1745, Prince Charles Edward, the Young Pretender, backed by the French, landed in Scotland. An anxious time ensued

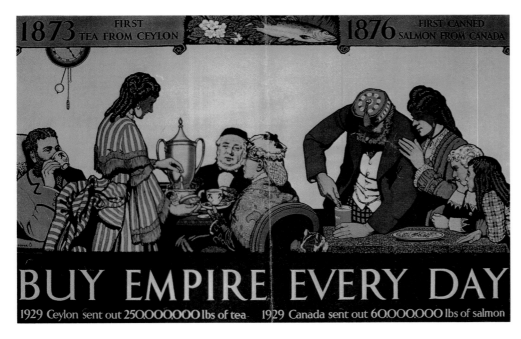

LEFT *The Empire became a major source of imports into Britain. An Empire Marketing Board poster from 1929.*

which was ended when his army was crushed at Culloden in April 1746. Fighting resumed on the continent and in North America, but the Peace of Aix-la-Chapelle in 1748 brought a temporary halt to hostilities. The Treaty of Paris fifteen years later established a longer-lasting peace on the continent, and an extension of Britain's overseas possessions: she retained the slaving ports on the Senegal coast of West Africa; the West Indian islands of Grenada, St Vincent, Dominica and Tobago; Canada, Florida and all the lands to the west of the Mississippi. Within a few years, however, the French were building up their naval power and intelligence sources in 1770 indicated that French and Spanish fleets combined had 121 'ships of the line' compared to Britain's 126. Though the margin of naval supremacy was narrowing, the government believed the British navy was still *sans pareil*. But this was not to last.

The second difficult period arose between 1778 and 1783, and has been compared with Britain's position in 1940, when again she stood alone. By 1778 Britain's navy was outnumbered, and for the following five years she had no allies in Europe.

But within a decade of the humiliating defeat in the American War of Independence, Britain was to reassert her claim to commercial, imperial and naval supremacy worldwide. Britain's first empire might have ended, but a new, and grander, chapter was about to begin.

THE NAPOLEONIC WARS: 1793–1815

Until 1914, the Napoleonic Wars were usually called the 'Great War', on account of their extent across Europe and the Mediterranean, and their duration, continuous from February 1793 until June 1815, apart from an armed truce between 1802 and 1803. For much of the period Britain faced the real prospect of invasion. Fears of radicalism were rife, following the French Revolution of 1789, which unnerved many in Britain's governing classes, and in Napoleon the French had found a leader capable of subjugating European powers and turning them into satellites whose main function was to fuel the French

ABOVE *Napoleon Bonaparte, who for many years before 1815 provided a real threat to Britain.*

war machine. Britain found itself engaged in the most all-encompassing war it had experienced, requiring its largest ever mobilisation of financial and human resources. Over one-tenth of adult males were drafted into the war effort: by 1810, there were over 300,000 regular soldiers and militiamen, 189,000 volunteers, 145,000 sailors and 31,000 marines. The total cost of the war was over £1,000m. Defences were erected along the southern England coastline, which, like the defences against Hitler, remain visible to this day.

British naval power was essential, both to prevent invasion, as it had in 1588, and to keep trade flowing, which was vital to the war effort and its funding. It also largely confined French power to Europe, allowing Britain to occupy the colonies of its enemies. In 1793 the Royal Navy had 115 ships of the line to France's 76, but the balance threatened to tip France's way with the addition of the navies of the Netherlands and of Spain. However, the naval victory by Horatio Nelson at Aboukir Bay in 1798 was followed by that at Trafalgar in October 1805, which ended French hopes of challenging the British navy at sea. The land war continued for a further ten years, until Napoleon's defeat at Waterloo in 1815 at the hands of Wellington's British and Blücher's Prussian forces.

Victory brought the greatest expansion of Britain's overseas territories since the settlements of America and Ireland. Malta, the Ionian Islands, Trinidad, Tobago, St Lucia, the Cape of Good Hope in southern Africa, Mauritius, and a host of naval bases in the Mediterranean and Indian Ocean, were the chief fruits. The foundations of the massive expansion of Britain's global interests in the nineteenth century were thereby laid.

INDIA: THE JEWEL IN THE CROWN

Britain's arrival as a territorial power in Asia originated in the signing by Robert Clive of the Treaty of Allahabad in 1765. His statue now stands guard at the external entrance to the former India Office (now the south-west corner of the Foreign Office building). The treaty brought Bengal, India's richest province in its north-east, under the power of the East India Company.

Twenty million British subjects were added at a stroke. Although Clive came to regret the expansionist intent of the Company, Warren Hastings, who succeeded Clive as Governor-General of Bengal from 1773–85, had no such qualms, and declared that 'the resources of [Bengal] in the hands of a military people . . . are capable of raising them to the dominion of all India'. And so it came to pass. Bengal's capital, Calcutta, was to become the centre of Britain's power in India until 1913, when the capital was moved to its new home of Delhi.

In the late eighteenth century the East India Company expanded its reach beyond Bengal, and the independence of a series of Indian rulers was gradually eroded. The irony of a commercial company coming to rule a growing empire vastly bigger than Britain did not hamper its seemingly ineluctable, if uneven, expansion. Desire by the government in London to gain more control over what was happening, some of which was of doubtful morality, culminated in Pitt's India Act of 1784, which set up the India Board of Control to oversee the Company's Indian administration. Lord Cornwallis, the first Governor-General of Bengal appointed under the new system, introduced a new quality of civil administration, but the changes did not halt the military expansionism of the Company. In 1797 Richard Wellesley became the new Governor-General. With the help of his brother, Arthur Wellesley (later the Duke of Wellington), the Company's influence was extended further to the west and south of India until, in 1805, Richard Wellesley (by then the 2nd Lord Mornington) was recalled in disgrace on account of the expense of his campaigns. His portrait now hangs in the India Office Council Chamber, on the first floor of the former India Office section of the Foreign Office. The pace of expansion continued after his dismissal, and following success in the Maratha War of 1818, the Company's influence was extended over Gujarat and Rajasthan.

Dwindling revenues from Indian exports, dislocation of European trade during the Napoleonic Wars and competition from cheap cotton from the American south all hit the Company. A new breed of reforming Governor-General, notably Lord Bentinck (Governor-General of Bengal 1827–33, and first Governor-General of India 1833–5), sought to try to introduce social reform and westernise Indian society. But he failed to make much mark, and in Lord Dalhousie (1847–56) the Company reverted to a more traditional, military-minded kind of Governor-General, and the Punjab and Nagpur, which included Bombay, were duly absorbed.

Dalhousie's uncompromising rule unsettled Indian opinion, especially in the north, which exploded in 1857 in the so-called Indian Mutiny. In a partial and disjointed series of uprisings, the two great cities of Delhi and Lucknow suffered heavily. Reports reaching London of the slaughter of British wives and children provoked a violent backlash. Delhi was retaken in September, after a series of military encounters. British rule was re-established after a revolt that had never benefited from clear leadership or coordination. The government, unimpressed by the Company's record in India and blaming it for provoking the unrest, passed an Act for the Better Government of India in 1858, establishing a Secretary of State for India and an India Office to direct the administration of India from London on behalf of the British Crown. The Secretary of State was to be advised by a Council of India, and a new Indian Civil Service was created – a white-dominated colonial bureaucracy to administer an enlightened form of British rule. The East India Company's rule in south-east Asia was thereby terminated, and Lord Canning became the first Viceroy of India.

ABOVE *Robert Clive, Governor-General of Bengal until 1773. This statue is on the Clive Steps at the south-west corner of the building.*

ABOVE *'The East offering its riches to Britannia', a painting hanging above the Gurkha staircase in the Foreign Office. The figure representing Britannia is seated on a rock, the embracing children signify the union of the old and new companies. The lion at her feet guards her shield and spear, and the Ganges lies at the foot of the rock. Calcutta is characterised by a basket of pearls and jewels, China by jars of porcelain and chests of tea, Madras and Bombay by a corded bale, Bengal by an elephant, a camel and palm trees, Persia by silks and drugs.*

The creation of the India Office provided an incentive for the establishment of George Gilbert Scott's new Public Offices. His grand building was designed to house not only the new India Office, but also the Foreign Office itself, which had been housed in crowded and unsuitable buildings in Downing Street.

The period up to the outbreak of World War I in 1914 saw British imperial rule consolidated over south-east Asia. India itself became central to Britain's economic and military interests. Building up British influence in north-west India, and in Afghanistan, was seen as vital in creating a bulwark against possi-

LEFT *The India Office Council Chamber, with a life-size painting of Lord Cornwallis, an early Governor-General of Bengal.*

ble Russian expansion south. The first Indian census, in 1871, revealed 235 million Indians either under British rule or in states protected by Britain. The Indian army was much larger than the British army, and the country became the largest purchaser of Britain's exports. India became a major earner of 'invisible' income, while British engineers were deployed helping to build India's vast railway network. From 1853, when the first line was opened, to 1906 when the main network was completed, almost 30,000 miles of track were laid. Aided by another engineering feat, the opening of the Suez Canal in 1869, India became the destination of increasing numbers of genteel Victorian British families.

After the crushing of the 1872 rebellion, in which the Viceroy Lord Mayo was assassinated, armed resistance was contained,

ABOVE *An 1877 celebration in Delhi to honour Queen Victoria on becoming Empress of India the year before.*

ABOVE *Social parties were an integral part of the life of the British living in the Empire. This photograph carries the simple title 'Tennis Party'.*

ABOVE *Lord Curzon (4th from right) in Lucknow. This photograph
was taken when he was Viceroy of India, in 1900.*

∞

RIGHT *The Memorial of Lucknow, which stands in the Residency
Garden, Lucknow. It commemorates the 1857 Mutiny.*

∞

BOTTOM RIGHT *The ruins of Lucknow in the Indian Mutiny,
showing the Gateway opposite the Residency.*

and in 1876 Queen Victoria was declared 'Empress of India'
(though she never was to visit the country).

Unrest may have been driven largely underground, but it
now took other forms. A new Indian middle class, educated in
English in Indian schools, came to demand greater Indian influence in the conduct of public affairs. The Indian National
Congress met for the first time in Bombay in 1885. At first
uncoordinated, and respectful rather than radical, the Congress's
influence spread over the ensuing years, while its thesis that
British rule was a drain rather than a benefit to India began to
reach fresh ears, both in India and in Britain. By contrast, Lord
Curzon, Viceroy at the turn of the century, preached belief in
the noble work of the British Raj in looking after the interests of
the impoverished Indian millions.

At the time of Victoria's death in 1901 there was no reason
to believe that this benign British rule could not continue for
generations, and a great imperial 'durbar' (a traditional court
celebration) was held in Delhi in 1903 to celebrate the accession
of Edward VII. Meticulously planned over six months by Lord
Curzon, the ceremony included the participation of the Indian
Princes, who paid homage to the absent Monarch. Veterans of
all races from the 1857 Indian Mutiny marched in the durbar to
the sounds of 'Auld Lang Syne'. All dissent appeared to be for-
given and forgotten.

AFRICA: THE DARK CONTINENT

Britain's early interest in Africa from the sixteenth century had been based mainly on the slave trade. Following the abolition of British involvement in the slave trade in 1807, London continued to put pressure on the abolition of slavery elsewhere in the empire, until that too was abolished in 1833. Sierra Leone was established as a colony with its capital, Freetown, for blacks to settle in and follow a Christian life, while elsewhere on the 'dark continent' missionaries-cum-explorers penetrated the interior. David Livingstone, the most celebrated of these intrepid figures, spent thirty years probing and preaching until his death in eastern Africa in 1873.

Africa, until late in the nineteenth century, continued to be of only marginal economic and military interest to Britain. She possessed trading posts in West Africa, in the Gambia and on the Gold Coast, but except for those on the river Niger, they did not extend far inland. In the far south, Britain had annexed

BELOW *A painting of the famous meeting between Stanley and David Livingstone, the best known of the African missionaries.*

the Cape of Good Hope in 1806, and rapidly fell foul of the Afrikaner inhabitants – Europeans, mostly of Dutch descent, numbering about 30,000. After a few years during which they resisted British jurisdiction, the Afrikaners took part in the 'great trek' north, between 1836 and 1846, and settled in two republics of their own: Orange Free State and the South African Republic (Transvaal). For the time being, the British and Afrikaners were content to live separately and peacefully.

Britain's limited engagement with Africa was to alter dramatically during two 'scrambles for Africa' in the 1880s and 1890s. Military and economic factors were at play. Since the successful conclusion of the Napoleonic Wars in 1815, Britain had enjoyed a comfortable 50-year period, secure from the fear of foreign invasion, buoyed up by the strength of an economy at the peak of its Industrial Revolution success, and with the Royal Navy's strength uncompromised. No serious contenders challenged her authority. Russia, the significant exception, was defeated by Britain and France in the Crimean War of 1854–56. Palmerston, who ran British foreign policy for much of the golden period from 1830 to 1865, presided over this heyday of free trade, of which Britain was a main beneficiary. A revolution in shipping, with new steamships replacing sail, furthered facilitated the achievements of Britain's merchant navy and Royal Navy.

THE LATER NINETEENTH CENTURY

The Foreign Office staff had expanded in size from 12 on its founding in 1782 to 30 based in the London office and 78 diplomats working abroad by the 1840s. The majority of the diplomats worked in legations. At the time Britain had only two overseas missions classified as full 'embassies' – Paris and Constantinople. But these figures actually under-represent the number of people who were involved in managing Britain's foreign affairs. Relations with states in Africa and India were conducted by the Colonial service and the East India Company respectively. Then there was the 'family embassy', whereby much embassy work was undertaken by honorary attachés.

By the 1860s and 1870s, however, the settled world picture was beginning to change. In the west, the United States, its Civil War over, was beginning to present an economic and military challenge; as was Japan in the east. While Holland, Italy and Spain could be dismissed as minor players, Germany, newly unified in 1871 after a victorious war against France, was powerfully on the move. By the 1870s the growth of the British economy was slowing, and her commercial supremacy began to be challenged.

In Africa, French expansionist plans became evident from 1879, while Germany, under Chancellor Otto von Bismarck, began to look for its 'place in the sun' in 1884–85. This newcomer to African empire building rapidly annexed South West Africa (later Namibia), Tanganyika (Tanzania), Togo and Cameroon. In southern Africa, diamonds were discovered at Kimberley in 1867, and in 1881 the British were routed by the Afrikaners at Majuba Hill. The stakes were raised still further when gold was discovered on Transvaal's Rand in 1886. In the gold rush that followed, non-Afrikaners flooded into the Transvaal, and mining companies, in particular Cecil Rhodes's Consolidated Mines Company, were able to reap huge rewards. With the German annexation of South West Africa, fears grew in London of the Afrikaners (or Boers) breaking away from the British Empire and forming a new alliance. The Jameson Raid of 1895, tacitly supported by the Colonial Secretary, Joseph Chamberlain, in London, failed to overthrow the Boers' President Kruger.

ABOVE *Afrikaners brandishing their rifles during the Boer War of 1899–1902.*

∞

BELOW *Corpses of British soldiers in a trench on the battlefield in Spion Kop during the Boer War.*

ABOVE *General Kitchener saluting as he rides past the defeated Boer leaders, South Africa, 1902. Note the Union flag in the background.*

restraint had been put to one side, and by the end of the century its claims to territories in West Africa (Gold Coast and Nigeria), East and Central Africa, had all been enacted. Following the opening of the Suez Canal in 1869, Britain also decided it had no alternative but to dominate Egypt if it was to secure the route to India. The fear of it falling to another European power was too serious to contemplate. Although it never became a British colony de jure, Egypt became a de facto colony by dint of its administration and economy coming under very careful British oversight from 1882. The Sudan to its south was more difficult to subjugate. The heroic death of General Gordon at Khartoum in 1885 had been a temporary setback: in 1898, the forces of General Kitchener invaded the Sudan from Egypt and routed the Islamic Mahdist regime at the battle of Omdurman. The Sudan henceforward was administered jointly by Egypt and Britain.

THE DOMINIONS

Transvaal and Orange Free State were to be united with Cape Colony and Natal in a self-governing Union of South Africa in 1910. But what of the other countries that formed what were becoming known as the Dominions, and which were to play such an important role in Britain's world wars during the twentieth century?

In 1770 Captain James Cook had sailed up the coast of Australia, making a brief call into Botany Bay. Eighteen years later a British colony was established in the south-east of the country by a group of officials, marines and 736 convicts. The climate and terrain proved hospitable to the British émigrés, and during the ensuing years over 150,000 convicts were shipped out by the perilous route via the Cape of Good Hope. By 1850 colonies had been established in New South Wales, Tasmania (Van Diemen's Land), Queensland and Victoria, and Western Australia had also begun to be settled. The gold rush in the 1850s brought huge numbers of white immigrants to Victoria and New South Wales, and by 1860 the white population had doubled in a decade to over a million.

During the 1830s white settlers began to cross the waters to New Zealand, both to trade with the Maoris and to use the islands as a base for exploration into the Pacific. In 1840 New Zealand was annexed by Britain, and a land settlement with the Maoris was attempted. However, they resisted the invaders, and a series of bloody battles was fought between 1845 and 1872. The outcome was inevitable, as it had been for the Aborigines in Australia, and by 1872 the 50,000 surviving Maoris were outnumbered five times by the white settlers.

War was inevitable and it duly arrived in 1899, its first year seeing the British come under pressure, as in the prolonged siege of the garrison at Mafeking, held by Robert Baden-Powell. Jubilation at the town's relief in May 1900, with wild celebrations on the streets of London and other cities, soon turned sour as the popular mood turned against the war. Liberal opinion was outraged as the British forces resorted to putting the Boer families into 'concentration camps', in which some 20,000 perished from disease. The Boers were eventually defeated in 1902, but the three years it took to subdue the ragged if tenacious Boer fighters led to searching questions being asked about how Britain might fare if it ever did find itself in a war against a major power.

Britain had an easier ride elsewhere in Africa. The Berlin Conference of 1884 had tried to adjudicate on and abate claims by European powers in West and Central Africa. Britain at the time was relatively restrained in its claims, but by the 1890s

ABOVE *Government House, Sydney, Australia, 1870. View from Fort Macquarie.*

RIGHT *French's Buildings, Darlinghurst, Sydney. Note the similarity to typical English Victorian tenement blocks.*

ABOVE *The Metropolitan Intercolonial Exhibition, Sydney, 1870.*

Canada had been the first of the future self-governing Dominions to be settled. When Britain gave up its claims to its American colonies in 1783, only Quebec and Nova Scotia were left to it on the North American continent. While great numbers of English settlers came into Upper Canada (later Ontario), French speakers continued to dominate Quebec, preserving their Catholicism, language and customs. The decade in which Britain's economic fortunes began to turn, the 1870s, saw massive growth in the white populations of Australia, New Zealand and Canada. By 1900, with the pull of its western prairies, Canada had become the most popular destination of all the colonies for settlement. The great transcontinental railway lines helped open up the west all the way to Vancouver, a thriving city by the early twentieth century. Montreal and Toronto, like Sydney and Melbourne in Australia, also became important Victorian cities, and by the outbreak of the First World War in 1914, the combined population of Australia, New Zealand and Canada was over a third that of Great Britain.

Australia, although effectively self-governing from 1850, was the last to see its separate colonies come together as a Commonwealth of States in 1901; New Zealand was self-governing from 1856, becoming a Dominion in 1907, and Canada was established as The Dominion of Canada in 1867. From 1887, their respective Prime Ministers met regularly in London to discuss common interests. The fact that all wanted to remain members of what became Britain's Commonwealth of Nations, as did the Union of South Africa after 1910, and that all were fertile sources of manpower and raw materials, was a source of great satisfaction in London.

THE END OF ISOLATION

The government needed all the solace it could find; the nineteenth century did not end well for Britain. The great imperial jamborees of Victoria's Golden Jubilee in 1887 and Diamond Jubilee in 1897 hid the deep wounds that were opening up. The economy had been in depression, damaged by the agricultural recession of 1873–96. Ireland was impatient for self-rule. France, Germany, Austria-Hungary, Russia, the United States and Japan were all developing modern economies and navies. While Britain had done relatively well in acquiring territories in Africa and the West Indies, its Indian possessions were under threat from Russia. Benjamin Disraeli, Britain's Prime Minister

LEFT 'Victoria Our Queen'. Celebrations to mark the 1887 Golden Jubilee, en route from St Paul's Cathedral to Buckingham Palace.

ABOVE Queen Victoria's Diamond Jubilee outside St Paul's Cathedral, London, 1897.

ABOVE The West Indian Rifles parading at the Diamond Jubilee procession, 22nd June, 1897.

from 1874–80, might have succeeded in checking Russian advance and averting war in the Balkans, but within a few years the settlement seemed to be breaking down.

In the Far East, Britain's interests were being challenged by France, while Russia began building its trans-Siberian railway in 1891, and had designs on Manchuria and northern China. The Boxer Rising in 1900 saw Chinese nationalists joining in protest at overseas intervention, and the British legation was besieged. The questions being asked about Britain's poor performance in the Boer War would not go away, and Britain found itself friendless in an increasingly threatening world. Germany, which looked unpredictable under Wilhelm II, Kaiser since 1890, had formed an alliance with Austria–Hungary and Italy, while Britain's two most feared imperial rivals, France and Russia, signed an alliance in 1894.

Two responses came from London, both associated with leading politicians, neither of whom was Prime Minister. Secretary for the Colonies Joseph Chamberlain wanted to bind the empire together into a closer economic trading and military union. His crusade, launched in 1903, enjoyed only limited success. In October 1900 Lord Salisbury relinquished the Foreign Secretaryship (though not the Premiership, onto which he clung for two more years) to Lord Lansdowne. On five occasions Salisbury had blocked Britain's entry into a formal alliance with Germany.

The new Foreign Secretary, however, saw the need for allies and he entered into an alliance with Japan in January 1902 to help check Russia's ambitions in the Far East. This alliance was followed by an 'entente cordiale' with France, in April 1904, a loose agreement with Britain's traditional rival which soon acquired an importance Lansdowne had not initially envisaged, especially after Russia joined Britain and France in a triple entente in 1907. Europe found itself suddenly in two armed camps, and war was just a flashpoint away.

By the outbreak of the First World War the Foreign Office had grown to support a permanent staff in London of 176 – a ninefold increase since 1782. The increase was due to a number of factors, including the adoption of bureaucratic methods to conduct government business, the revolution in communications technology, the industrialisation and urbanisation of much of

ABOVE *Australian Imperial Forces landing at Suvla, Gallipoli, 1915.*

Western Europe, and the expansion of European commerce. From its earliest history, the Foreign Office had been involved in promoting commerce.

The structure of the Foreign Office and diplomatic service were also changing. A permanent staff emerged slowly in the nineteenth century: John Backhouse was the first Under Secretary (1827–42) to describe his office as permanent. By the 1860s a career structure had emerged with graded posts and a recognisable hierarchy. The 'Hardinge reforms' of 1904–6 enabled young bloods to exercise greater initiative at an early stage in their career, and by 1906 a central registry had been

BELOW *Troops landing at Anzac Cove in the Dardanelles during the Gallipoli campaign of the First World War.*

ABOVE *The 4th Canadian Field Battalion bringing up guns to battle on the Western Front in 1915, during the First World War.*

created, which brought a new level of efficiency and coordination to the Foreign Office's work. The electric telegraph played a key role in transforming the lives of Foreign Office officials, from scribes to advisers. The spread of diplomatic links worldwide in the 30 years after 1878 resulted in the establishment of geographical departments within the Foreign Office, and by the early twentieth century, the structure of the modern Foreign Office, with career officials running foreign affairs at the behest of the Foreign Secretary, had largely emerged.

FROM FIRST TO SECOND WORLD WARS

H H Asquith, the Prime Minister from 1908, and Edward Grey, the Foreign Secretary from 1905, together with most of the Liberal Cabinet, had not foreseen war coming as early as it did in August 1914. None foresaw the epic scale, the horror, or the length of the war. Britain declared war on Germany on 4 August on behalf of the whole empire. Men from the dominions seemed happy to volunteer in large numbers until service was made compulsory throughout Britain, the empire and the Dominions in 1916. The Afrikaners in South Africa and French Canadians were alone in protesting. While British forces bore the brunt of the fighting on the Western Front in Belgium and France, they were joined by empire forces including the Australians at the Third Battle of Ypres, the Canadians at Vimy Ridge, Indian troops at Neuve Chapelle, Newfoundlanders at Beaumont Hamel and South Africans at Delville Wood – these last two on the Somme. Elsewhere, Australian and New Zealand ANZAC troops were prominent in the disastrous Gallipoli campaign in 1915, and, more successfully, in the defeat of the Turks in Palestine and Syria in 1917–18.

The decision of the United States to join in 1917, with its troops arriving in force from 1918, tipped the scales, but although the outcome was eventually victorious, the war had cost Britain 900,000 lives (and 300,000 from the empire),

cont. p 32

THE LOCARNO TREATIES

The crippling cost of the war, and Britain's weakened state, were not immediately apparent in the postwar period. At the Treaty of Versailles, which dismembered the German Empire, and at the great victory parade in London, both in 1919, celebration and national self-confidence were to the fore. The defeat of Germany in 1918 and its immediate aftermath of political instability, with left and right wings attempting coups, and the USA's postwar isolationism removed from the world stage potential challengers to British pre-eminence, as did the Communist Revolution in Russia in 1917.

The new spirit of optimism found its apogee in the Locarno Treaties, signed with great fanfares in the Foreign Office in 1925, which welcomed Germany back into the community of nations and promised to usher in a new era of international harmony. The signing was greeted with ecstatic approval in European capitals. Britain's international standing in the 1920s was

ABOVE *The last meeting of the Locarno Conference in 1925. Seated left to right are Signor Mussolini, Dr Rusca (Mayor of Locarno), Mr Austen Chamberlain (Foreign Secretary) and Mr Hurst.*

ABOVE *The historic signing of the Locarno Treaty in 1925, in the room which is today the Grand Locarno Reception Room.*

further bolstered by territorial acquisitions. In the Middle East, where defence of India (rather than oil), remained its prime concern, Britain acquired mandates over Palestine, Transjordan and Iraq. (These were the gains from the dismembered Ottoman Empire.) Persia, too, moved closer under the British sphere of influence. German colonies were also given as mandated territories to Britain and to the Dominions, including South West Africa to South Africa, and its Pacific possessions to Australia. Britain in the 1920s thus possessed the largest empire in its history, and had more unchallenged influence than in any other decade in the twentieth century. Britain's pride of place in the world in the 1920s, and the meaning of the Locarno spirit, have long been forgotten.

RIGHT *The Grand Locarno Room today.*

ABOVE *The remains of Liberty Hall following the Easter Rising, Dublin, 1916, which deflected Britain's war effort.*

and had damaged both its industrial base and its overseas patterns of trade.

But despite the new optimism generated by the Locarno Treaties, the storm clouds were gathering. Two Irish Home Rule bills had failed to pass through Parliament during the previous thirty years, and the Easter Rising in Dublin in 1916 and post-war unrest led to British troops taking repressive steps that served to heighten nationalistic resentment. The passage of the Government of Ireland Act in 1920 established the partition of Ireland. After further fighting it was agreed that the Irish Free State, or Eire, was to be ruled from Dublin, leaving Ulster, the six Protestant-dominated counties in the north, with their own Assembly, but still in union with Westminster. Eire subsequently distanced herself from the British Commonwealth, was obstructive of London, remained neutral in the Second World War, and in 1949 left the Commonwealth, having declared itself an independent republic.

Britain also saw mounting nationalism challenge its hegemony in India. The tranquil acceptance of Britain's continuing dominance seen at the durbar in Delhi in 1903 proved a chimera. The Hindu Indian National Congress in 1906 committed itself to self-government for India. The same year, the All-India Muslim League was founded to press for Muslim rights in the emerging new India. The nationalists supported the war in 1914, but Indian involvement in the fighting only heightened demands for independence. The Hindu Gandhi emerged as the nationalistic leader that the Indians had lacked in 1857: his campaign of 'non-violent' resistance to the British found wide-spread support. The Government of India Act of 1919, allowing limited self-government, failed to assuage nationalist aspirations. The following year General Dyer ordered the shooting of

ABOVE *Mahatma Gandhi at the Indian Round Table Conference, St James's Palace, London, 1931.*

protesters at Amritsar in the Punjab; in ten minutes of firing into the unarmed crowd, 379 Indians were killed and 1,000 wounded. The same year Gandhi organised a campaign of total non-cooperation with the British Raj. Under pressure from the nationalists, in 1935 London passed a further Act which offered India domestic self-government and the offer of dominion status at some future point; but essential British interests were to remain under the direct authority of the Viceroy. It was as far as the British were prepared to go for the present time, but the Second World War was to hasten Britain's departure, and in 1947 Britain quit India.

Britain's foreign policy between the two world wars centred primarily on the protection of her empire: troops were stationed across the world to protect both the colonies and Britain's trading routes. Britain valued the Dominions, or Commonwealth countries as they became known from 1917, even though it was having to accept reluctantly their ever-growing independence from London, most notably under the Statute of Westminster in 1931. Australia, New Zealand and Canada all suffered economically during the interwar depression, and Australia and Canada's economic ties with Britain weakened as a result. Yet all three countries chose to declare war on Germany in 1939, albeit in their own right.

RIGHT *The British Navy ruled the waves during the period when the British Empire was at its height. This photograph shows the battleship* Prince of Wales.

The 1930s had proved a tougher decade for British foreign policy than the 1920s, with Germany, Italy and Japan showing militaristic ambitions. The policy pursued by the Conservative-dominated national governments under MacDonald (1931–35), Baldwin (1935–37) and Chamberlain (1937–40) was to try to avert war, initially by working with the League of Nations and upholding the ideal of 'collective security', then by trying to appease the dictators, Italy's Benito Mussolini (from 1922) and Germany's Adolf Hitler (from 1933). By the spring of 1939 it had become clear that the policy had failed, and after Hitler's seizure of Czechoslovakia Chamberlain changed tack. There were to be no more annexations. With the German invasion of Poland in September, war became inevitable.

Military planners had long advised the government that it would not be possible to defend the empire in the event of all-out war, but the swift progress of Germany in the Low Countries and France after the 'phoney war' ended in May 1940 surprised even the most jaundiced general. British forces were pushed off continental Europe at Dunkirk, and the empire found itself fighting a series of desperate defensive battles (in contrast to the 1914–18 war, when the empire had been largely on the offensive). Significant inputs were made by forces from India, Australia, New Zealand, South Africa and Canada, notably against the Germans and Italians in North Africa. The entry into the war of Japan in 1941, however, threatened to tip the scales. The Japanese, moving with technologically aided speed similar to that of the Germans, rapidly took Malaya, sank the Royal Navy fleet in the Far East, and took Singapore in 1942, with the surrender of some 130,000 imperial troops. It was one of the worst military defeats in British history, and marked the effective ending of Britain's 300-year status as a global superpower.

THE BUILDING
IN HISTORY

THE FOREIGN AND COMMONWEALTH OFFICE building in Whitehall is one of the finest offices for a foreign secretary anywhere in the world. Its position adjacent to Number 10 Downing Street and close to Parliament, and to Buckingham Palace across St James's Park, its imposing bulk and the grandeur of its state rooms and principal offices all set it apart. Originally designed to accommodate four major government departments, then five from the First World War, it was only built in the nineteenth century, and only survived in the twentieth century after prolonged and bitter political in-fighting.

SHIFTING ORIGINS

The land on which the Foreign and Commonwealth Office stands was once marshy and inhospitable. Fossil remains found in the 19th century reveal that the straight-tusked elephant, the cave lion and the narrow-nosed rhinoceros roamed here before the last Ice Age. In more recent times, development was impeded by daily flooding from the tidal flow of the River Thames, leaving the land often under water. Roman and Saxon remains reveal early attempts at building on what dry land could be found, but it was Edward the Confessor (1042–66) who chose to settle there, at a comfortable distance from the volatile Londoners living downstream in the City. Edward established the collegiate church of St Peter (later to become Westminster Abbey, but known in the early part of its history as 'St Peter's Cathedral') in place of the small Saxon church, and built a new royal palace. Later, to the north of Edward's settle-ment, on the banks of the river Thames, the great royal apart-ments of Whitehall Palace were to be built.

In the 1680s George Downing, a property speculator and one-time spymaster to Oliver Cromwell, erected a cul-de-sac of poorly built houses which came to be known as Downing Street. It appears, together with King Charles Street and King Street, on a map of 1720. Westminster, Whitehall and especially busy King Street, were becoming increasingly congested with traffic. A new, more impressive thoroughfare between Westminster and Charing Cross was proposed, which involved demolishing part of Whitehall Palace (though Inigo Jones's Banqueting House would remain) and other landmarks. The enlarged Parliament Street and Whitehall duly became the first roads in London to have raised pavements and gutters.

In 1732 King George III gave one of the houses on the north side of Downing Street as an official residence for the First Lord of the Treasury (i.e. the Prime Minister). Over the next three

LEFT *The Foreign Office taken from the south in the 1870–80s, before the Treasury had been built. The road in the fore-ground is George Street. Charing Cross is in the distance, to the north.*

∾

RIGHT *A 1947 aerial pho-tograph showing the Treasury building which replaced the series of buildings (left) knocked down in 1896.*

∾

BELOW *An 1884 aerial painting of Westminster, as seen from a balloon.*

years the architect William Kent worked on a series of alterations for the first incumbent, Robert Walpole, joining the Downing Street house to the grander house behind it, to create a more extensive and dignified residence.

The work of government greatly increased during the eighteenth century, as foreign trade expanded. The old Treasury building (now the Cabinet Office) was built by Kent in the 1730s, close to the Whitehall road and backing onto Horse Guards Parade. In the 1820s John Soane added the Board of Trade offices to Kent's work, and then constructed new Privy Council offices to complete the existing facade along Whitehall. Further to the north lay the buildings occupied by the Old War Office and the Admiralty. Here was the heart of British government, whose main concerns on the eve of the

ABOVE AND RIGHT *These two aerial photographs, from 1939 and 1995, show the Foreign Office at the east end of St James's Park. At the opposite end is Buckingham Palace. Lancaster House and 1 Carlton Gardens lie on the north side.*

Great Reform Act of 1832 were defence, finance, law and order, and foreign trade.

The Foreign Office was recognised as a separate department in 1782, when Charles James Fox became Secretary of State for Foreign Affairs (Foreign Secretary) in Rockingham's government. Before 1782 the work had been divided into a Northern Department, where a staff of twelve dealt with relations with the German states, Scandinavia and the Low Countries; and a Southern Department, which handled Irish and American rela-

tions, and affairs with France, Spain, Italy, Portugal, Switzerland and the Barbary States. Fox's new department was initially based in Cleveland Row, next to St James's Palace, but in 1786 the office moved down to the much-altered cockpit of the old Whitehall Palace, and in 1793 transferred to Downing Street. Fox's senior official was the dramatist Richard Brinsley Sheridan, who was his under secretary. The new Foreign Office also employed nine male clerks, two chamber keepers and a housekeeper described as the 'necessary woman'.

Downing Street thus became the focal point for the British government's overseas ventures. The almost constant warfare of the eighteenth century, and the new 'total' commitment of the country to the Revolutionary and Napoleonic Wars of 1793–1815, enormously increased the number of staff required to run such large-scale military operations. After the Napoleonic Wars Britain's empire began to expand, and to administer all this, the Foreign and Colonial Offices spread themselves into the buildings along the north and the west sides of Downing Street.

153.

The old Foreign office. Downing St. October 31st 1861.

By the early nineteenth century, the work of the Foreign Office was becoming more professional. Whereas during Fox's tenure it had been known as Mr Fox's Office, and had the air of a private domain, by the 1820s it was turning into a properly staffed organisation. Lord Castlereagh (1812–22) had been a transitional figure, treating his staff as trusted professionals with wide initiative, though his successor, George Canning, the only foreign secretary to live in Downing Street, reverted to earlier form and 'fell into the way of writing everything himself'.

By the early 1820s the office had extended into five houses, numbers 16, 17 and 18 on the south side of Downing Street, and two houses in the now vanished Fludyer Street, immediately to their south. In 1825 Number 15, in the south-west corner of Downing Street, was also acquired by the government. John Soane gave it a new entrance, and inside, removed internal walls to create two grand rooms overlooking St James's Park. Numbers 17 and 18 were then joined together by knocking down the party wall, and Cabinet meetings would be held in Number 17, which also boasted the new public entrance to the Foreign Office. A good idea of how the old Foreign Office looked can be gained from the above drawing of George Scharf,

ABOVE *The George Scharf drawing of the old Foreign Office in Downing Street, as it was the year it was pulled down in 1861.*

Keeper of the National Portrait Gallery, which was executed shortly before they were pulled down.

Even by the 1820s space in the Foreign and Colonial Offices was deemed inadequate. The number of dispatches emanating from the Foreign Office had increased threefold in 20 years, and there was insufficient room to cram in the staff needed to execute the expanding volume of business. Also, the buildings occupied by the staff suffered from the same poor build quality as Numbers 10 and 11, and from the same balefully inadequate foundations, given that they were erected on marshy ground.

THE SEARCH FOR A NEW BUILDING

In 1826, Parliament passed a bill to purchase the freeholds in Downing Street and Fludyer Street, with a view to building new offices. Grey's appointment of Palmerston as Foreign Secretary in 1830 gave the impetus for the establishment of the new, purpose-built Foreign Office. It was the beginning of a 40-year saga.

For much of the next 35 years, first as Foreign Secretary, then as Prime Minister, Palmerston exercised unrivalled dominance over the conduct of the country's foreign affairs. Within months of his appointment, the dilapidation of the building became apparent. 'Great alarm' was expressed over a bulging wall in one of the large rooms overlooking St James's Park, and Palmerston's concerns about the poor repair of his office, the lack of space, and his wish for rooms suitable for banquets and receptions, all convinced him of the need for action. The architect Decimus Burton was commissioned in 1836 to prepare plans for a new Foreign Office building in Downing Street. That May, Palmerston wrote to the Treasury to request reception rooms capable of taking up to 50 guests for dinner parties and receptions 'occasionally upon the arrival of Foreign Princes in this country'. Burton spent three years working on his designs, and in July 1839 the House of Commons set up a select committee to consider the various plans for the future of Downing Street. The committee rapidly concluded that the private houses which made up the Foreign and Colonial Offices were in such a state of collapse that it would be 'inexpedient to expend any large sum in their substantial repair'.

At this apparently propitious point, the project lost its focus. The Houses of Parliament had been destroyed by fire in October 1834. The cost and distraction of providing a replacement may well have been responsible for the bill advancing Burton's scheme being withdrawn from Parliament on the grounds of financial 'weakness'. But the need did not go away. In March 1845 the Foreign Office wrote to the Treasury to say that the two Foreign Office houses at the most easterly end of the street had 'within the last few days exhibited rents of a formidable nature'. Edward Hertslet, Foreign Office librarian and archivist in the later nineteenth century, recalled the dismal state:

The old Foreign Office consisted of a block of several private houses thrown into one. The larger house contained some very fine rooms, the windows of which overlooked St James's Park; but the smaller ones, the windows of which looked either onto Downing Street or Fludyer Street, were in a very tumble-down condition when I entered the office, so much so that, when the adjoining houses at the King Street end of Downing Street and, later, those of the King Street end of Fludyer Street were taken down, the block forming the east end of the Foreign Office had to be shored up, which for many years gave this important public office a most unsightly, not to say undignified, appearance.

In the 1840s, Palmerston initiated a major organisational reform of the Foreign Office, dividing it into six departments: four for different geographical areas; one consular; and one for the slave trade. The office had grown to a total of 41 staff, as well as house maids and office keepers. From 1847 it also contained its own printing press – an imprudent move considering the weight of the machinery, the reverberation from the press, and the frailty of the flooring on which it was placed. Palmerston was succeeded as Foreign Secretary in 1852 by Lord Malmesbury, who was made painfully aware of the physical state of his new department in the most tangible way when part of the ceiling of his room fell onto his desk.

In 1854 another key figure arrives on the stage. Edmund Hammond, who had first entered the Foreign Office in 1824 from Oxford, succeeded the 'courteous, conservative' Henry Unwin Addington as Permanent Under Secretary. For the next 20 years, a span of unparalleled longevity, the meticulous and tireless Hammond was to oversee the Foreign Office and its work; justly was he described as 'sharp, and a glutton at work'. Hammond became a doughty champion for the erection of the new office. This was also the year of the Northcote-Trevelyan Report which founded the modern Civil Service with its competitive entry, as well as the year in which yet another report was conducted into the condition of the existing office. Undertaken by the Office of Works, it found that subsidence had occurred in the eastern part of the Foreign Office, and that

ABOVE *The old Colonial Office in Downing Street before its demolition. The new Foreign Office is visible on the right, in the background.*

an entirely new building was the only option. William Molesworth, the First Commissioner of Works, re-examined Decimus Burton's plans, but rejected them as implementing the plans would have meant encroaching on St James's Park. Instead, he invited James Pennethorne, architect to the Office of Works, to prepare new designs, and these were submitted to the Prince Consort, Prince Albert, and to the Prime Minister, the Chancellor of the Exchequer and the Cabinet.

The Crimean War of 1854–56 was, however, preoccupying everyone and it was considered imprudent to build new offices during an expensive foreign war. Meanwhile, the building continued to slide. Lord Macaulay kept a regular note in his diary of the daily subsidence of a window in the Cabinet Room. Other pres-

sures pointed to action, too. Speculators were buying up land to the south of Downing Street in the expectation that the government would be building there. The Crimean War had highlighted the drawbacks of having a war directed from so many different buildings in London; rationalisation became a popular cry, with a unified War Office becoming a major justification for a new government building. A desire not to be outdone by Paris, whose impressive public offices had been visited by Queen Victoria, and were lavishly described in the fashionable journals of the day, also played its part in suggesting the need for a grand solution to the problem of government offices. Even *Punch* magazine, in August 1855, stirred by the collapsed ceiling episode, had its say:

BELOW *The Home Office section of the FO c. 1900, taken from Whitehall, looking north. The photograph dates from before the construction of the bridge linking the Foreign Office to the Treasury.*

ABOVE *Lord Palmerston addresses the House of Commons in 1860,*
the year in which he was particularly obstructive to Scott.

First, the old Foreign Office is awfully tottery,
Its bottom a quicksand, its walls all awry:
Its standing or sinking an absolute lottery –
If the fall of the roof should ope that to the sky?
What piles of foul litter from basement to attic!
What dust, meant in John Bull's eyes to be thrown!
What red-taped and docketted lies diplomatic,
Which, but for that smash, never daylight had known!

The final verse (of a somewhat protracted six) was a clarion call to action:

Then to work with you, Palmerston, Clarendon,
Molesworth;
In modelling Downing Street use the recess –
Tis the desperate shows the strenuous soul's worth;
Think how Hercules dealt with the Augean mess.
Then when new Downing Street challenges censure,
Colonial Office, and Foreign, and all –
Grown bold by experience, next year you may venture
On like work in Parliament Street and Whitehall.

History does not record whether this particular piece of doggerel had any noticeable impact on public thinking. In 1855, however, Palmerston did become Prime Minister, aged 71, with Molesworth as Colonial Secretary, and Benjamin Hall First Commissioner of Works. Hall became convinced of the need for a Palace of Government, stretching south from Downing Street all the way to George Street. Instead of using the designs of James Pennethorne, Hall argued the need for '. . . competition for architectural designs, a competition unlimited, open to the whole world, in order that we might at last have some buildings worthy of the metropolis'. Both the Foreign Office and the War Office needed central buildings, he argued. Concerns about the cost of the project began to be heard again in the House of Commons – the purchase cost by the government of the land between Downing Street and George Street was estimated to be some £1.5 million, even before the cost of the building itself was put into the equation. The *Times*, a champion of the cause, responded in a leader on 4 August 1856:

The House of Commons' concern with the cost of the undertaking was misjudged: the fact is that the question of expense is not of so much importance to the public as the doing of the thing itself, and that speedily. A really good building . . . offered a splendid opportunity for an architectural display.

Palmerston was not going to be deflected by financial concerns. Later in August he authorised Hall to invite a number of leading architects to his office to air his plans for the new complex.

THE PUBLIC COMPETITION

It was not a good-tempered meeting. Some architects present in Hall's office protested at the very idea of a public competition, others about throwing it open to foreign architects. Against all the dissent, Hall insisted that Parliament had agreed to the plan, and it would not be changed. The instructions for the competition were read out to the assembled company:

It is proposed to invite architects to offer designs for two new public offices, one for the use of the Secretary of State for Foreign Affairs, the other for the use of the Secretary of State for War. These buildings are intended to be erected onsite between Charles Street and Downing Street. The drawings are to be made to a scale of 16 feet to one inch, and the elevations in line only. Enlarged details to a scale of 4 feet to one inch, and perspective (not bird's eye) views, tinted with light brown Indian ink, may accompany the respective designs. General specifications of the materials proposed to be used in the intended building must accompany each design. Lithographed plans of the site, together with particulars of the accommodation required, and the dimensions of the principal apartments will be furnished to such architect as may apply for them.

The competition provoked unparalleled interest, with enquiries pouring in from Britain, Europe and even India. Hall's beleaguered Office of Works could not cope with the volume of enquiries and it had to apologise for the delays while it lithographed more copies of the plans. Eventually, on 30 September 1856, the competition details and plans were ready, and some 1,628 sets were dispatched by post.

However, many of the architects found the details inadequate, and flooded the Office of Works with letters demanding further information. The influential journal, *The Builder*, inveighed against the government for its shoddy plans for this most important competition in 'the history of British architecture'; in short, the present scheme was, as the newspapers seem to perceive, 'rather indeterminate'; and the terms of the invitation 'vague'.

Most of the detailed questions in the letters reaching the Office of Works appear to have been left unanswered. Nevertheless, by the closing date of the competition in late March/early April 1857, some 218 entries had been submitted, including 30 from foreign architects.

The Office of Works had decided to put the entries on public view, and constructed a series of screens 3.6m/12ft in height and 47.5m/158ft in length inside Westminster Hall, the great medieval building which had survived the 1834 fire and which lay just to the west of the Houses of Parliament. Some 8,000 Londoners and others came to the public viewing, which lasted from May 1 to June 6 and featured 1,834 drawings (and just two models!).

While the public exhibition was running, a jury of seven met to deliberate the entries under three headings: the Foreign Office; the War Office; and a general re-planning of the whole Whitehall area. The group contained representatives from both Houses of Parliament (the Duke of Buccleuch and William Stirling MP), the army (Viscount Eversley), an architect (William Burn), an artist (David Roberts RA), an antiquarian (the Earl of Stanhope) and an engineer (Isambard Kingdom Brunel).

One English architect, renowned for his work on churches and cathedrals and a champion of the 'Gothic revival', was particularly interested in the competition: George Gilbert Scott. By good fortune Scott had been able to retire from other public commissions and focus fully on preparing his plans. In his *Recollections* he wrote:

I designed windows suited to all positions, and of all varieties of size, form, and grouping; doorways, cornices, parapets, and imaginary combinations of all these, carefully studying to make them all thoroughly practical, and suited to this class of building. I did not aim at making my style 'Italian Gothic'; my ideas ran much more upon the French, to which for some years I had devoted my chief study.

On June 27 the jury delivered their verdict to Parliament. For the 'Foreign Department' category, Messrs Coe and Hofland came first, Messrs Banks and Barry second, and the Gothic design of Mr George Gilbert Scott of 20 Spring Gardens came third. Scott's designs fared no better for the other two categories in the competition. He did not, unsurprisingly, form a high opinion of the judges:

When my designs for the public offices were exhibited, they excited much attention; indeed, they were, by those who favoured Gothic, considered generally the best . . . The judges, who knew amazingly little about their subject, were not well-disposed towards our style, and though they awarded premiums to all the best Gothic designs, they took care not to put any of them high enough to have much chance.

George Gilbert Scott was clearly not a man to entertain many doubts about his own abilities.

MORE FALSE STARTS

A bill to purchase the land to the south of Downing Street was immediately put to Parliament. Not for the first time in the protracted story, however, momentum again became lost. Parliament began to have fresh doubts and the voice of critics began to carry new weight. ('I would rather see great men in little offices than little men in great offices,' declared Sir John Trelawney.) Even the *Times* wrote in that August of 1857 (in tones not dissimilar to those in which the press has attacked the Foreign and Diplomatic Service down the years): 'What do we want with the Hôtel de Ville from Paris on the edge of St James's Park in order that a few hundred clerks may execute their daily tasks? . . We do not want palaces . . . but public offices. There is surely a half-way house between a Gothic Cathedral and a Union Workhouse.' The bill to purchase the land was withdrawn from Parliament, which had anyway decided that the winning schemes were too grand, and interest in the competition, which had once been the talk of London, died away.

The Indian Mutiny that year was to be another distraction, but in its wake came a new Tory government, under Lord Derby, in February 1858. Derby injected new life into the office saga, and set up a select committee to look at the way ahead. One problem was that since different architects had been selected for the three different sectors of the competition, the designs did not cohere. Scott's Gothic designs began to find favour with the Tories. No stranger to government, he lobbied hard and enlisted powerful architectural support.

Since Scott's designs had been rated well in all sections of the competition, the select committee decided to nominate him. But the decision over the building of the new War Office was to be delayed, as the army had begun to think of consolidating their various London offices elsewhere under the guid-

BELOW *Gilbert Scott's favoured first Gothic design. St Pancras railway station was once thought to have been modelled on it.*

ance of another architect. In a neat swap, the new India Office would take the place of the War Office in the complex. Scott's design was also liked because it fitted exactly into the space envisaged, and because it could be built in phases, which would allow the Foreign Office to continue for the present in its Downing Street houses.

Scott, delighted at the news about his commission, prepared some revised plans, omitting the adjoining residence for the Foreign Secretary, and submitted the drawings to builders for tendering. The tenders were published in August 1859: Kirk and Parry came in with £259,000; Kelk with just £232,024. All seemed set fair for a speedy resolution, and it looked as if the Gothic had won the argument.

In February 1859 Derby's government approved the designs, and the next month the bill to purchase the land was reintroduced into Parliament. Once again Scott was asked to produce drawings to send out to builders for tender. The quantity surveyors Balam and Nicholls prepared their list of materials needed and a number of builders were invited to discuss with Scott how they might proceed. Scott's final Gothic design had the Foreign and India Offices facing each other across a large internal courtyard, entered through low archways from Downing Street to the north and Charles Street to the south. Towers, capped by high-pitched roofs, rose above both offices.

BELOW *Scott's hybrid second design in the Byzantine style, contemptuously dismissed by Palmerston.*

Yet another hiatus now arose. In June Derby's government fell, and Palmerston once again became Prime Minister. He had been brooding on the long-running saga of the new public offices, and one of his first official acts was to summon Scott to a meeting. The following passage comes from Scott's *Recollections*:

> *Lord Palmerston, however, sent for me, and told me in a jaunty way that he could have nothing to do with this Gothic style, and that though he did not want to disturb my appointment, he must insist on my making a design in the Italian style, which he felt sure I could do quite as well as the other. That he heard I was so tremendously successful in the Gothic style, that if he let me alone I should Gothicize the whole country , &c,. &c., &c.*

On August 8, Palmerston launched a fierce attack in Parliament on Scott's Gothic design, and spoke at length in favour of his preferred Classical style. Members, some with more knowledge than others, spoke passionately: some in favour of the Gothic style (as seen in Charles Barry's recently rebuilt Houses of Parliament) and others in favour of the Classical or Palladian (or Italian) style, as seen in John Nash's terraces in Regent's Park. But it was left to a Mr Osborne to bring members' minds back to the essentials: 'Mr Osborne expressed his opinion that of all their judgements, in matters of taste the House of Commons was the very worst.

Gentlemen talked about different styles, about the horizontal and the perpendicular – when the country was looking to the question – what would the building cost?' After the debate, and with no resolution to the question of styles, Parliament decided to vote £30,000 to establish the building's foundations and to purchase the freeholds to the buildings at the St James's Park end of the site. Many houses had to be bought and then knocked down to make way for the new building.

The following month Scott went away to Scarborough, where he reached the conclusion that if Palmerston remained Prime Minister, he would have to compromise his beloved Gothic:

> I was thoroughly out of health, through the badgering, anxiety, and bitter disappointment which I had gone through, and for the first time since commencing practice, twenty-four years before, I gave myself a quasi-holiday of two months, with sea air and a course of quinine. During this time, however, besides the work sent down to me from time to time, I was busying myself in preparing for the next campaign. I saw that, with Lord Palmerston, Gothic would have no chance, and I had agreed to prepare an Italian design.

Scott resolved not to draw traditional Classical designs, which were alien to him, but to adapt styles he had already deployed on two churches: at Hawkstone Chapel in Shropshire and St Michael's, Cornhill, in the City of London. Here he used what he described as 'a sort of early Basilican style', which struck him as similar to the Byzantine style of the early Renaissance palaces in Venice. Scott spent the latter part of his Scarborough sojourn redrawing his designs in this new Byzantine style, and returned to London in high spirits. Armed with his drawings, he marched in to see the Prime Minister that autumn. The encounter did not, however, go according to plan:

> He kept me waiting two hours and a half in his back room (during a part of which I heard him very deliberately going through his luncheon in the next room), and then sent me away unseen. At length, however, I showed him the design. He was very civil, and I thought he liked it. Indeed, I believe that he did, but thought it hardly consistent with his previous professions to admit it.

Scott was therefore dismayed when he received a letter saying that Lord Palmerston had not liked the Byzantine design, and asking him to modify it and make it 'much more like modern architecture'. Further upset came when Scott heard from a third party that a fellow architect had submitted designs without his knowledge, and that these were now being actively considered in the Office of Works. At this point, in August 1859, John Ruskin, who had remained largely above the controversy, sent a letter to a leader writer of the *Times*: 'What a goose poor Scott (who will get his liver fit for pâté de Strasburg with vexation) must be, not to say at once he'll build anything. If I were he, I'd

BELOW *Scott's successful Italianate design. The unbuilt arch on the north face of the building linked it to Number 12 Downing Street.*

cont. p 51

TWO ARCHITECTS, TWO STYLES

ABOVE *George Gilbert Scott, architect of all but the India Office section of the building.*

∞

BELOW *Scott's Foreign Office quadrangle, looking north towards Number 10. The entrance to the FO is in the centre of the photograph.*

Under the India Act of 1858 the British government took over the government of India from the East India Company, in the wake of the 1857 Mutiny. The Company had run its affairs not just from East India House in Leadenhall Street but from the India Board of Control in Cannon Row, and it was considered essential to consolidate the new India Office, with its Council of India, into one building close to the Foreign and Colonial Offices. The site previously intended for the War Office was judged ideal. But the Company had its own surveyor, Matthew Digby Wyatt, who had worked with Brunel on Paddington station and was secretary to the Commissioners of Crystal Palace during the 1851 Great Exhibition. Digby Wyatt was not prepared to relinquish his position as architect of the India Office building. So in January 1859 it was agreed that he should work with Scott on a collaborative revision of the Foreign Office plans, with Digby

Wyatt to be responsible for the interiors of the proposed India Office. Generally speaking, the two men worked amicably together, but there were tensions. One of the principal clashes came over which office should have pride of place looking out over St James's Park. In classic British style, the architects reached a compromise: the India Office and the Foreign Office would share the view over the park. Scott was to be responsible for all the exterior elevations, but readily acknowledged the influence that Digby Wyatt was to have on the India Office's asymmetrical exterior which protrudes towards St James's Park.

ABOVE *Matthew Digby Wyatt, architect of the India Office portion of the building.*

BELOW *Digby Wyatt's Italianate tower above the curved projection looking towards St James's Park.*

ABOVE *The exterior elevation of Digby Wyatt's original India Office.*

build Lord P[almerston] an office with all the capitals upside down; and tell him it was the Greek style, inverted, to express typically Government by Party: Up today, down tomorrow.' The letter precipitated a complete breach between these two great doyens of Victorian art.

Scott was anyway becoming disillusioned with his hybrid plans: 'My first idea had been toned down, step by step, till no real stuff was left in it. It was a mere *caput mortuum*, as is invariably the case where a design is trimmed and trimmed again to meet the views of different critics.' The House of Commons did not like his latest design, and when the India Office, tired with the prevarication, instructed its architect Digby Wyatt to look for another site in London, it seemed that the whole project was beginning to fall apart. The jaded Scott went to see Palmerston on 8 September 1860, who told him in plain terms that his Byzantine design was 'neither one thing nor t'other – a regular mongrel affair – and he would have nothing to do with it either'. If he did not produce a satisfactory Italian design, he would lose the appointment. Digby Wyatt himself continued to encourage Scott, knowing only too well that responsibility for the whole building would fall on his shoulders were the collaboration to founder.

Scott's ambition not to lose this most prestigious project triumphed over the purity of his architectural instincts. It became almost a matter of his 'existence'; he felt he would be 'irreparably injured if he lost the commission'. So Scott swallowed his pride, and went out shopping for several 'costly books on Italian architecture', travelled to Paris and studied the Louvre and other Classical buildings, and immersed himself in a style which he had studied little since student days. That autumn he worked up his new designs, even inserting fashionable figures and groups into his drawings, though he considered himself to have 'no skill' in figure drawing. Scott's new Italian designs were completed by March 1861 and were again put on display in the tea rooms of the House of Commons. The designs were discussed in July, and in August they were approved. Though Scott's troubles were far from at an end, the 'battle of the styles' had been won, or at least resolved.

'The old Foreign Office in Downing Street was a dingy building enough, with a sort of crusted charwomanly look about it, suggestive of anything but Secretaries of State, Ambassadors and suchlike sublimities.'

BERTIE MITFORD
JUNIOR DIPLOMAT IN JAPAN, 1866

LEFT The building from the west, with the India Office section on the right and the Foreign Office section on the left. The lamp on the left may well have been the one Grey looked out on in August 1914.

THE CONSTRUCTION OF THE INDIA OFFICE AND THE FOREIGN OFFICE

At last the pace began to speed up. In July 1861 the Foreign Office moved into the office vacated by the War Office – Pembroke House in Whitehall Gardens; in September the India Office moved temporarily into the Westminster Hotel; and East India House was demolished, though a number of items, including fireplaces, were put in storage for the new building. In November the Foreign Office houses in Downing Street, together with other houses in the cul-de-sac, were pulled down. There could now be no going back. Messrs Kelk and Co began work on the foundations after their tender of £19,577 was accepted. Employing some 400 workmen, the company dug a 6m/20ft hole in the ground, carting the soil away via a temporary railway to barges on the river Thames. Over 10,000 timber piles which had been used for underpinning the houses on the site were removed. By employing the dubious technique of dropping concrete from a height of 3m/10ft to compact it tightly, a 3.6m/12ft solid concrete raft was laid in the watery hole, suitable for carrying the immense weight of the expected building. Lessons had been learnt from the buildings of Downing Street, including Numbers 10 and 11 and the now pulled-down Foreign Office, which had suffered from constant slippage into the muddy undersoil. By the end of May 1863 the foundations were completed, but only then was Scott ready to hand over his finished drawings for the building tender. 'Too expensive', the Treasury responded, and again Scott had to return to the drawing-board to produce a revised and less grandiose specification.

The tender of Smith and Taylor, at £195,573, was eventually accepted, and work began in September 1863. The contract, and the building, were divided into several sections, with work starting first on the India Office in the south-west corner of the site. By June 1864 the walls were complete up to first-floor level. At the level of the lower basement, which rests on the concrete raft foundation, the walls were 1m/3ft 3in thick (against 52cm/22in for the top storey of the building). Built of brick and covered in Portland stone, the first floor of the building immediately attracted unfavourable comment, and due to the cost of the Portland stone it was already £28,000 above the sum approved by Parliament in the Office of Works' submission. Even closer scrutiny was kept of the building's progress as a

cont. p 54

THE DURBAR COURT

I n July 1867 the India Office, even in its unfinished state, saw its first public function – a grand ball for the Sultan of Turkey, held in the recently completed Sultan's Court (re-named the Durbar Court after Edward VII's coronation celebrations in 1902). Furniture and tableware were borrowed from Buckingham Palace. The Annual Register of 1867 described the event, which cost the princely sum of £11,488.19s.8d:

> *The Secretary of State for India and the Indian Council gave a grand ball at the New India Office, in honour of the Sultan. This new office had not yet been occupied by the department, and, therefore, the whole building was available for the reception of the guests . . . the vast quadrangle in the centre of the structure was covered in and converted for the occasion into a magnificent hall . . . Beneath a canvas roofing was stretched an awning after the fashion of the old Roman velarium, and at the extreme end was erected a daïs and a handsome canopy placed over the chairs of state prepared for the reception of the Sultan, the Prince of Wales, and other members of the royal family. [When the Sultan entered] everyone rose to receive him, but there was no cheering nor any marks of welcome beyond deep reverence.*

ABOVE *A drawing of the lavish ball held in the Durbar Court for the Sultan of Turkey, and attended by members of the royal family, in 1867.*

∽

RIGHT *The Durbar Court, taken from the east, with the India Office Council Chamber straight ahead.*

ABOVE *The first-floor landing, looking towards offices and function rooms.*

BELOW *The sculpture of Lord Teignmouth, on the first-floor landing.*

ABOVE *The Grand Staircase during the FO's first public function in March 1868, to celebrate Disraeli becoming Prime Minister.*

result. The Foreign and India Offices had been due for delayed completion by 1 May 1867, but in June a further application for an extension was submitted by Smith and Taylor on the grounds that inclement Christmas weather had delayed building progress. A curt response observed that, as the commission had anyway been due for completion before Christmas, the weather should not have been an issue.

At the Foreign Office itself – on which work had by this time begun – final details, especially of the State Rooms and the Grand Staircase, were still under discussion. Nevertheless, on 25 March 1868 the latter, too, saw its first public function – to celebrate the appointment of the new Prime Minister, Benjamin Disraeli. Because she found Number 10 so 'decaying and dingy', Mrs Disraeli had asked if the reception could be held in the Foreign Office instead; as the State Rooms were still not completed, the party took place in the Secretary of State's Room. Bishop Wilberforce wrote in his diary: 'Dizzy in his glory, leading about the Princess of Wales, the Prince of Wales [and] Mrs Dizzy'. Within a few weeks, all the rooms were finally completed

and in May a dinner was held to honour Queen Victoria's birthday, to which all diplomats to the Court of St James were invited. By the end of June, under the watchful eye of two superintendents and 30 constables from the Metropolitan Police, the Foreign Office staff had moved from Pembroke House into their new grand offices, accompanied by all their files and furniture.

THE COLONIAL AND HOME OFFICES

Both the Foreign and India Offices were now completed – on the St James's Park side of the plot. Little had happened on the eastern side, except for prolonged discussion and disagreement. Early in 1868, however, Parliament decided to proceed with the building of two further government departments – the Colonial Office and the Home Office – which were to form the second half of the whole building complex. Scott was officially appointed as architect for these two further offices on 24 February 1868, but only when the Foreign Office was completed in June was he able to focus on his new commission. After all the travails and reversals of the previous eleven years, Scott was unable to rest on his laurels; instead, he was instructed to get on and plan the layout of both sets of floor plans. In early 1869 Parliament discussed the bill to purchase the remaining properties between Parliament Street and the Foreign and India Offices.

Scott had originally planned to place the Home Office, the department responsible for law and order, on the north-east corner, adjoining Downing Street, but in March 1869 he was told to reverse his plans, and place the Colonial Office in that position. That June, work began on more mammoth foundations, except in the south-east corner, where properties had still not been purchased. In July, the bill for the funding of the Colonial Office was placed before Parliament, only to be peremptorily withdrawn. Scott, hardened by this time to the caprice of politicians, pressed on with his drawings, with the intention of going out to tender at the beginning of 1870.

Parliament, alarmed at the cost of the whole project, told Scott to revise his design and reduce the building cost to £200,000, or less. There could be no replication of the splendours of the India and Foreign Offices. Once again, the project was delayed. Scott, who had become inured to prevarication, revised his drawing and economised on some of the more expensive features. A new set of tenders was received from builders in

RIGHT *The Grand Staircase as it looks today, after the restoration. The murals by Sigismund Goetze can be seen on the first floor.*

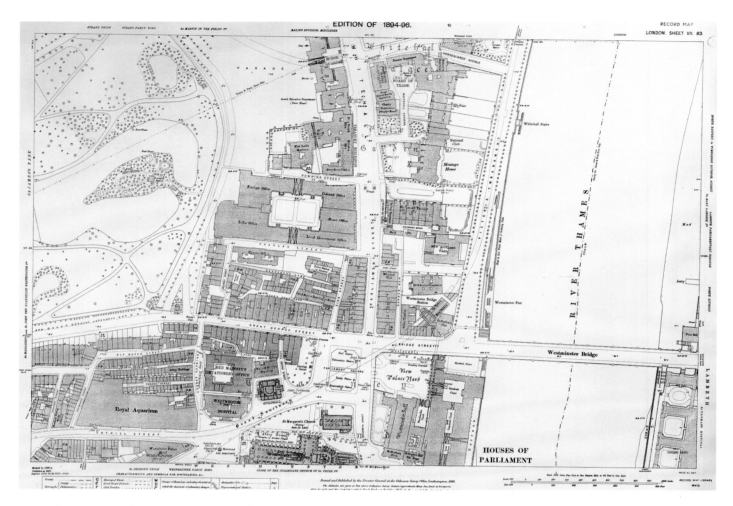

ABOVE A street plan from the 1870s, taken just after the Foreign Office complex was erected, but before the Treasury was built immediately to its south.

September 1870, including one from Thompson at £279,860, and another from Jackson and Shaw at £242,323. Even though the tender from Jackson and Shaw exceeded Parliament's costings it was accepted. Construction began weeks later, and at pace, so much so that the building was completed on 20 June 1874. The Home Office, occupying the south-east section of the building, was the least ornate of the four, as a more restrained style was deemed appropriate by some for the workaday business of the department and the lesser need to impress visitors, especially from overseas, than was the case with the Foreign, India and Colonial Offices.

The question of the road to the immediate east of the building now came to the fore. As the above street map of the period suggests, the block of narrow buildings between Parliament Street and King Street once continued also to Downing Street. The eighteenth-century plans for the uncompleted grand thoroughfare were re-examined. Much had changed. At the north end, Trafalgar Square had been built, surmounted by Nelson's Column, to commemorate the great naval victory of 1805. To

the south were Barry's new Houses of Parliament and the giant clocktower housing Big Ben. A suggestion was put forward to place Cleopatra's Needle outside Parliament to complement Nelson's Column and offer a grand vista, similar to that of the Place de la Concorde in Paris. Although this confident plan came to nothing (the Needle remains on the Thames Embankment), the decision was taken to open up the southern end of Whitehall. Parliament approved the demolition of all the remaining houses on the west side of Parliament Street, thereby creating the wide sweeping road we see today. In the 1920s Edwin Lutyens' permanent Cenotaph was placed there as a memorial to the dead of the First World War. By knocking down these houses, the eastern elevation of the Colonial and Home Offices was exposed to unhindered display in a way that had not been envisaged when the building had been planned.

RIGHT *Blind soldiers marching past the Cenotaph, the Memorial to the Glorious Dead of WWI, temporarily erected in Whitehall for the Peace Celebrations of July 1919. The Home Office is shown on the immediate left.*

∽

BELOW *Volunteers signing up to work during the General Strike of 1926, in the Foreign Office quadrangle.*

THE AFTERMATH

The entire building has a pleasing unity that belies its piecemeal and fraught construction. Scott was not, however, able to enjoy his triumph for long. Six months after completion, in December 1874, a lift killed a Foreign Office employee called Charles Coxhead. The coroner's report singled out Scott for specifying a defective installation. Complaints also flooded in that the many fireplaces smoked and stood out too much into the rooms; that the brickwork was unsound; that the windows let in insufficient light; that everywhere smelled of sewage; and that the entire building was overly grand and expensive. Scott was summoned before a parliamentary select committee and questioned about the apparent failures.

He defended himself as well as he could, as reported in *The Architect* on 1 September 1877:

> *If your question refers to the great quadrangle through which you drive, I was very ambitious to make that a very fine thing. All my earlier instructions on the subject had led to the idea that a very palatial building was required. After I had carried out the first portion which contains the Foreign and India Offices, I was told that we ought not to have done that; but all my first impressions were that that was wanted, and I aimed for it.*

Wearily, Scott argued that, had his preferred Gothic design been accepted, the windows would have admitted far more light. It was a bitter pill, he felt, that he was now being accused of designing a dark building. Scott died, with the argument and recriminations still raging, on 27 March 1878. The rancour no doubt played its part in hastening his end.

THE NEW BUILDING: 1870s–1940s

With Scott's death, some of the criticism of the building ceased. Thirty years later the huge and superficially similar new Treasury building was built to complement the Foreign Office, on the site of a large number of small buildings lying between the Foreign Office and Parliament Square.

The four sections of the new Public Offices functioned almost entirely separately, and ran with only minor alterations until the First World War when the Department of Local Government Board moved in to share the Home Office section, becoming the fifth department to be housed within the building. However, the demands of the war of 1914–18 gave Whitehall a shock from which it never recovered. The volume of government work multiplied enormously, and every spare space adjacent to Whitehall had to be drafted into war service. Behind Number 10, the 'garden suburb', a mass of temporary huts, was erected, while in the Foreign Office huts filled the courtyards. The three State Rooms

RIGHT A fundraising visit in aid of London Hospitals, which toured the Foreign Office in 1929. The visitors were shown round the building by the Librarian Stephen Gaselee. The chairs and stools are protected by dust sheets. The air was notoriously smoky. Here the group is seen in the Grand Locarno Reception Room.

LEFT The Grand Locarno Reception Room as it was in 1930, in its somewhat faded interwar state.

(the Large and Small Conference Rooms and the Cabinet Room), were all crammed full of desks and machinery collected there by the Contraband Department. After peace came in 1918, the rooms became the Registry, and many of the huts were removed.

On 1 December 1925 the Locarno Treaties, the high water mark of international optimism between the wars, were signed in the Large Conference Room, and thereafter the three rooms became known as the Locarno Suite. Never before had these rooms been so much the centre of attention.

After the First World War, the intensity of government activity was not to return to its pre-1914 level, and the interwar years saw greater pressure on space from all the five departments that used the building. Eventually a third floor was built overlooking the larger central quadrangle, but the extra space brought only a temporary respite.

> *'It is, in fact, a terrible building to work in. The rooms for senior members of staff have a certain heavy dignity. But those unfortunate juniors are obliged to work herded together in large, high, cold rooms where five or more telephone conversations and five or more dictating processes make concentration impossible.'*
>
> WILLIAM HAYTER, ON LIFE AS A YOUNG DIPLOMAT IN THE INTERWAR YEARS

By the 1920s fifty years of smoke from coal fires and gas lights had made the Suite very shabby. A reaction had set in against Victorian style, and few raised their voices when the decision was taken in 1926 to brighten the Locarno Rooms with parchment-coloured paint. Decorators set to work with pumice stone and water and removed much of the fine detailing on the walls and ceiling. The repainting was executed on the recommendation of no less a body than the Royal Fine Art Commission.

In the late 1930s, as another war appeared increasingly likely, the government began to take precautionary measures. Heavy aerial bombardment was the nightmare that all feared – as seen in the horror of the bombing of Guernica in Spain and Shanghai in China. Space was created under the Treasury next door to house the Cabinet War Rooms and the work of Number 10, and the lower ground floors of the Foreign Office were reinforced in order to withstand bomb blasts. Openings were cut between the Foreign Office and the India Office to allow staff to reach shelter in the basements more easily.

A brief moment of pre-hostility glamour came in 1939 when the India Office's Durbar Court was used for the entertainment for President Lebrun of France, during which the young John Gielgud and Peggy Ashcroft acted the balcony scene from Romeo and Juliet. When war came, the Locarno Suite was adapted to house the Ciphering Department of the Foreign Office.

THE CRISIS OF SPACE: 1940s–1970s

In 1947 India and Pakistan became independent and the India Office came to an end, its responsibilities being taken over by the Dominions Office, renamed the Commonwealth Relations Office. The Foreign Office moved temporarily into the India Office, while the Commonwealth Relations Office moved into the Colonial Office's space, and the Colonial Office was banished from the building to nearby Church House. It was to have moved into purpose-built offices in Parliament Square, designed by T S Tait, but the building was never erected. In 1966 the Colonial Office was finally absorbed by the Commonwealth Relations Office and was renamed the Commonwealth Office, since the empire had virtually disappeared, and in 1968 the Foreign and Commonwealth Offices merged into a single department: the

ABOVE *The Grand Staircase lined with His Majesty's Lifeguards (blues) on the occasion of the state banquet for the French President Lebrun in March 1939, which was attended by King George VI, Queen Elizabeth and Queen Mary.*

Foreign and Commonwealth Office (FCO). A new floor was added to the Home Office, which had described its space problem as 'really desperate'. When, in 1978, the Home Office moved into its new Basil Spence-designed office in Queen Anne's Gate on the south side of St James's Park, the FCO for the first time had possession of the entire building.

While all these reorganisations were going on, a far bigger drama was being played out, which threatened the very existence of Scott's building. Wartime bomb damage, modernist zeal, new traffic pressures from cars and buses, and a desire to replan the heart of government in a more rational way all played their parts in a series of proposals to redesign the whole area to the north and west of the Houses of Parliament. Scott's

RIGHT *Members of the royal family, including King George VI, Queen Mary and Queen Elizabeth, in the Durbar Court at the party for President Lebrun.*

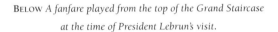

BELOW *A fanfare played from the top of the Grand Staircase at the time of President Lebrun's visit.*

grandson, Giles Gilbert Scott, was also involved. Parliament itself had been heavily bombed in 1941, and the Commons Chamber destroyed. The Tory MP Walter Elliot had been on duty when the fire brigade arrived; when asked which they should save first, the medieval Westminster Hall or the Commons Chamber, he responded, 'Let the pseudo-Gothic go', thus displaying an ambivalence towards Barry's work that many of his fellow MPs were to show towards Giles Gilbert Scott's restored Chamber, completed in 1950.

THREAT OF DESTRUCTION

Now it was George Gilbert Scott's work that came under attack. Did the country need his Victorian pile, known collectively as the Old Public Offices, taking up so much space when the country's needs could be much better served by using the prime position more intensively? Every available bit of space within the

building had, it seemed, already been used. In the early 1950s plans were drafted to move the Foreign Office; one option was to transfer it across St James's Park to a position behind the facade of John Nash's Carlton House Terrace. This plan was aborted, but in 1963 Geoffrey Rippon, Minister of Public Buildings and Works (the successor to the old Office of Works), announced: 'I have decided to demolish the existing building.' As Rab Butler, Foreign Secretary (1963–64) said, 'We can no longer afford to stable a white elephant in Whitehall.' A succession of tower structures was to replace the Foreign Office and the Treasury, similar to those of the appalling Department of the Environment.

Various other ideas were discussed, including the dispersal of central government outside London and the retention of the Foreign and India Office buildings, stripped of their interiors and adapted for a trade and conference centre. The new Labour government in 1964 ratified Rippon's plan, and appointed Sir Leslie Martin to advise on the future of Whitehall 'to ensure

that various Government proposals which are now under consideration for the redevelopment of the Whitehall area are related to each other'. The Foreign Office was just one of several buildings in the firing line. Martin drew up a systematic plan and model for the whole area from the Thames Embankment to St James's Park, showing a continuous, infinitely repeatable grid of ziggurat-sectioned buildings containing private open courtyards and linked by a high-level glazed galleria. Rippon's successor accepted Martin's report in July 1965 as the 'broad framework within which future development should take place'.

A public outcry ensued, led by the newly formed Victorian Society and by the Civic Trust. The architectural climate was changing under the noses of the government; support for conservation was growing, and the taste for modernism and redevelopment in all their concrete soullessness was on the wane. Fevered pressure was simultaneously being put on the government to save the great Victorian railway stations of Euston and St Pancras from the bulldozers (the first case was lost; the second won). A plan to flatten existing buildings to erect a new Home Office on the south side of Whitehall, opposite the Foreign and Commonwealth Office, housing 4,000 staff, at a cost of £15 million, was scrapped. In 1971, the Heath government announced that the Foreign Office was not to be demolished. Finance was stated as a reason for the decision, but without the lobbying, it is unlikely that it would have been

saved. Government and town planners had stirred deep passions. Gavin Stamp, one of the impassioned, attacked those

suffering from post-colonial guilt. They cannot bear the idea of our modern, small, Euro-centric England being represented by pompous and sumptuous Victorian buildings . . . Imagine the alternative to the rooms completed by Scott in 1868: foreign ambassadors being wined and dined in bland low rooms representing the official taste of 1968 in a building like the new British Library or soon-to-be demolished Department of the Environment towers. The French would gloat; the Danes would feel sorry for us; the Indians would be unimpressed; while the Nigerians might feel insulted at so tawdry a welcome.

The outcome of the furore was that in 1970 the building became listed Grade 1, the highest quality of protection that can be placed on a building. The citation speaks of 'Italianate opulence' (at Palmerston's insistence), in the Venetian–Genoese manner evenly distributed in bold relief over the symmetrical Whitehall and King Charles Street elevation but with asymmetry to the Downing Street and picturesquely composed Park front with tower.

Twenty years on death row had meant that little maintenance had been carried out. Electric wiring was tracked along walls, and was in a very poor, even dangerous, condition. The sanitation and plumbing were primitive, as was the catering. Coal was

LEFT *Roof watching on top of the Foreign Office during the Second World War, 1941.*

RIGHT *A photograph of the quadrangle from 1963, when it was announced that the government buildings in Whitehall which housed the Foreign, Home and Commonwealth Relations offices were to be demolished, and new buildings erected in their place.*

still being burned to heat the rooms, only replaced by gas fires in the early 1970s; 40 men had been employed at the end of the war simply to carry coal to the fires. The delicately decorated floors and ceilings were blackened and cracked with the heat. Douglas Hurd, the future Foreign Secretary, who joined the Foreign Office in 1952, recalls the scene:

I was set to work in 1952 in the Locarno Rooms, which was divided up into little cubicles. I could see above my cubicle the great Corinthian cornice. It was all very run down, and hugely uncomfortable. I remember an ageing gentleman who used to come and light and poke the fires. In the November afternoons, London fog would come rolling into the gaunt rooms. I remember walking in St James's Park with a fellow diplomat, and I said what a pity it would be to pull the place down. My friend stopped on the bridge over the lake and said: 'You really meant that? You are not joking!' There was this wide consensus that the building would be, and should be, pulled down.

The *Sunday Times* summed it up in 1967 when it referred to the Foreign Office building as 'the magnificent slum'.

THE GREAT RENOVATION: 1980s–90s

What, then, should happen to the Foreign Office (by now the Foreign & Commonwealth Office – FCO), if it was not to be knocked down? The 1970s was not a propitious time to undertake expensive renovation. In 1976 the Labour government had to go cap in hand to the International Monetary Fund for loans, and inflation and unemployment were high. But it was decided that restoration should be the way ahead for the building, and work began in a piecemeal fashion after the Home Office moved out in 1978, first under the Property Services Agency (which had taken over from the Ministry of Public Buildings and Works), which directed the restoration until the FCO itself took over responsibility in the late 1980s, when David Brown was appointed as Head of Home Estates and Services Department.

One of the first steps had been to create more openings between the four separate buildings. As work began on the Durbar Court, those on the project began to realise the magnificence of the building beneath the grime and the coverings that

LEFT *The close relationship between the Foreign Office and Number 10 Downing Street, which it dwarfs.*

ABOVE *The Grand Locarno Reception Room.*
A view taken from above the false ceiling.

obscured the original work. The Thatcher government concurred that restoration was indeed the way ahead, and invited a private company to direct the conservation and architectural aspects of the work. In August 1982 Cecil Denny Highton (CDH) were commissioned and John Denny, who had just commenced restoration of the Old War Office, was appointed superintending architect. Seventeen years and just over £100 million later, the task was completed. Obtaining the money to keep the project going through its main phases was never straightforward. The mandatory requirement for competitive tendering at each stage resulted in four separate main contractors, each of which needed security clearance, which added greatly to the complexity of the process.

CDH promptly undertook a detailed historical analysis of the building in order to understand the background to the design and construction of the building. The initial research allowed CDH to identify the most historically and architecturally important areas of the building – rooms and spaces of national importance – which must be restored to their original appearance. These 'fine areas' included not just the Locarno Rooms and other grand offices, but also the entrances, the con-

necting corridors and the series of grand staircases. Another key part of CDH's brief was the 'non-fine areas', which constituted the bulk of the building, where its remit was to increase office space to house up to 2,000 staff (up from 200 in the 1870s and 1,300 in the 1970s Foreign Office), and to modernise the dilapidated services. Space was created by reorganising existing usage and relocating plant and other functions into the basements, by using corridor space and backstairs areas, and also by building a new 'mansard' roof at the top of the building, which at one stroke created an extra 2,100sq m/22,604sq ft of office space. Mindful of the aesthetic damage caused by the extra storey visible from the FCO's central quadrangle, the architects ensured that the extra floor was not visible from street level.

The whole restoration was a daunting assignment, especially as the FCO was not going to vacate the building during the renovation. This decision meant that conservation, maintenance and refurbishment work would have to be carried out in a phased programme, to ensure that at least three-quarters of the

ABOVE, LEFT AND RIGHT *Details of the restoration work during the 1990s. Specialist artists and craftsmen were called in to execute this intricate and complex work.*

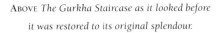

ABOVE *The Gurkha Staircase as it looked before it was restored to its original splendour.*

ABOVE *The FCO Bag Room before restoration, on the ground floor of the former India Office.*

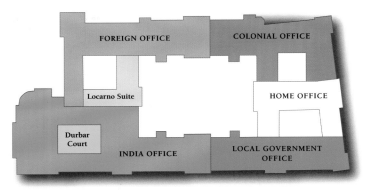

ABOVE *The architects' floorplan, showing the location of the ministries formerly in the building.*

building could remain in use throughout. An early windfall came with the move of the Home Office to its new office in 1978 (the Department of Local Government had left long before). The area the Home Office vacated (20% of the total building) provided space into which staff could be decanted during the phased programme. The linoleum was stripped away and the offices and corridors made reasonably presentable. During the 17 years of the restoration, the FCO had to cope with the Falklands War, the end of the Cold War, the Gulf War and a series of crises in the 1990s in the former Yugoslavia.

Modern scientific advances aided the process of researching Scott and Digby Wyatt's original intentions and designs. After boarding and other coverings had been carefully taken away, paint scrapings from the walls were sent to London University for electron microscope analysis. From this, exact colour matches could then usually be made. There were occasional scares: once, an analysis from a ceiling sample came back as an unlikely bright red; when the laboratory was asked to check, it was discovered that the sample had come from a spot where a Victorian workman had accidentally transferred some of the red paint from his scaffolding onto the roof!

Research was conducted to locate all surviving photographs, drawings and paintings of the interiors, and the Public Record Office was found to have preserved many of the detailed original drawings. CDH also studied Gilbert Scott's Albert Memorial, executed by the FCO's original decorators, Clayton and Bell. The Midland Grand Hotel at St Pancras railway station, mistakenly

LEFT AND ABOVE LEFT *Abseilers cleaning the sculptures and stonework of the Durbar Court after additional work on the roof.*

RIGHT *A nighttime view of the Durbar Court. The courtyard is at its most attractive when lit at night.*

ABOVE *Details of the Locarno Rooms today, restored to their full glory. These three photographs show examples of the fine design and craftsmanship on the walls and ceiling.*

∞

RIGHT *One of the fireplaces in the Grand Locarno Reception Room. It may well have come from the old Foreign Office in Downing Street.*

∞

LEFT *Looking through the massive wooden doors from the Locarno Dining Room into the Locarno Conference Room.*

rumoured to be based on Scott's original Gothic design for the Foreign Office, was also studied for further clues. A most meticulous inventory of furniture has been carried out and has identified some extremely important items. The restoration was a thoroughly professional exercise, executed under the watchful eyes of English Heritage and the Victorian Society. The only serious difference of opinion with English Heritage came over the grand Locarno Rooms, where English Heritage argued in favour of retaining the 1920s parchment colour. The restoration team wanted to restore the room to Scott's original colouring, and their task was made easier when some original paintwork was found unerased in the fifth bay; from that piece of serendipity, perhaps due to the laziness of a 1920s workman, the original colourings could be restored.

The whole project was divided into six sectors, each identified by a separate colour. The Home Office was the white sector, handed over in 1982, and restoration work began on the red sector, which covered much of the old India Office, in 1984. Some of the glass in the roof of the Durbar Court had gone; the floor was covered in dirt and full of portakabins; and pigeon droppings were ubiquitous (many tonnes had to be removed from the building). No one was aware that the floor was marble until they started to polish one corner of it. A fire in late 1985 damaged part of the Durbar Court roof, which had its glass replaced and its cast iron strengthened. The India Office building was finally handed back in January 1987.

Attention then shifted to the original Foreign Office, which together with the north part of the India Office became the blue sector. Before work could begin, alternative and secure accommodation had to be found for the staff who had to move out. The first floor of the old Home Office, including the former Home Secretary's and the Permanent Under Secretary's rooms, were duly prepared. Work on the blue sector began in September 1987, while Geoffrey Howe was Foreign Secretary, lasted throughout John Major's three months in 1989, and ran until the end of 1990 when Douglas Hurd was Foreign Secretary.

While work on this sector was in progress, renovation began on the yellow sector, which included many of the remaining

ABOVE *Prince Charles came to the Foreign Office after the restoration was complete. This plaque is to be found on the Grand Staircase.*

rooms of the FCO, among them the Locarno Suite. In the 'fine areas' the policy was wherever possible to return to the original, and to preserve records of subsequent changes. Materials – stone, marble, granite, mosaic, ceramic tiles and glazed majolica work – were cleaned in turn, and where necessary were repaired in matching materials. Simultaneously, restoration began on the sector containing the remaining part of the original Foreign Office surrounding the open archway to Downing Street. These sectors were completed in April 1992, in time for the general election.

The brown sector, covering the old Colonial Office, and the green sector, the remainder of the old India Office, were completed in January 1995 and January 1997 respectively. The final act of restoration, in the India Office, was the refurbishment of the statue of a Gurkha soldier and its subsequent relocation to the entrance.

Few complained of the cost of this extraordinary restoration, not least because of the widespread and favourable reviews that it received. Openly giving information on the cost and benefits of a more efficient building to the media and informed opinion also helped. Fifteen thousand visitors walked round the building on the London Open House weekend when it was available for public viewing in September 1997. Power, computer and telephone cables had been installed and discreetly positioned. Several new lifts had replaced redundant staircases. On the outside of the building, the stone facades, the statues and chimney stacks had been surveyed, cleaned and, where necessary, repaired. A new staff restaurant was installed to cater for 160 people, and a kitchen and serving area created which could serve up to 80 guests in the Locarno Suite. Important meetings could now be serviced entirely within the FCO, uninterrupted by the need to transport delegates to other government buildings – a saving in both time and security.

It seems a miracle that this marvellous building, which came so close to being destroyed and replaced by concrete anonymity, should have been restored in this way to its former glory and, at the same time, have been converted into a high-tech and elegant office, with a quarter more usable space.

THE BUILDING
TODAY

SCOTT'S BUILDING REMAINS one of the country's most impressive public buildings, with a pleasing unity that belies its piecemeal and fraught construction. What became known as the Old Public Offices contains hundreds of separate rooms (no one knows exactly how many) and some of the most elegant spaces and offices, facades and courtyards to be found anywhere. But what is the building like behind that imposing facade, seen most strikingly from St James's Park or from Whitehall, lying so solidly between Downing Street and the Treasury? The aim of this chapter is to reveal that building, in words and pictures.

EXTERIORS, ELEVATIONS AND COURTYARDS

ABOVE AND RIGHT The Foreign Office from the quadrangle, and the facade of the building viewed from Whitehall.

The building can be entered either from Downing Street or King Charles Street through three-arched and pedimented porches. Surprisingly perhaps, these entrances are neither on the park nor on Whitehall, but off side streets. Somerset House on the river Thames, one of London's first purpose-built government offices (1776–96), apparently provided the inspiration for this little conceit. Within Scott's Foreign Office lies a great 1.6 ha/4-acre quadrangle; the total area of the site is 2.4 ha/6 acres – much the same as Horse Guards Parade. To let light into the rooms, Scott designed four smaller courtyards for each original department, close to the four corners of the building. None of this open space within is apparent to the pedestrian surveying the FCO from the street.

The view from King Charles Street is of a three-storied Renaissance-style building. On three sides, the external elevations are of a conventional Classical style, with the ground floor clad in rusticated masonry, a protruding pavilion at the end of each elevation, and in the middle of each facade a central fea-

ture. Cornices emphasise the three separate levels and columns are placed on primary facades. However, the elevation facing the park is asymmetrical. Although the exteriors are all attributed to Scott, the influence of Matthew Digby Wyatt on that fourth, west-facing side, can be clearly seen. The park elevation boasts two towers, a larger one over the India Office and a squat one over the north-west corner of the Foreign Office. Towers over the Home Office and the Colonial Office were cut out from Scott's designs because of cost. The India Office elevation on the south-west side facing the park extends some 15m/50ft towards the park and boasts a quarter-circular bow facing north-west, then roofs to the south rising by two levels back to the height of the rest of the building. The explanation of the India Office protrusion was that it was decided late on to knock down the State Paper Office which occupied that site. This was a late Soane building and architecturally the most important edifice to be knocked down to make way for the building.

ABOVE, LEFT AND RIGHT *The arch bridge between the Foreign Office and the Treasury. There are three arched openings, and the spandrels with sculpture detail are by W S Frith (LEFT). Symbolic figures, like these representing Education, Australasia and Agriculture, are on the Whitehall facade of the building.*

Scott and Digby Wyatt's original building consisted only of two offices, the India Office and the Foreign Office, both on the west side of the site. Scott deserves praise for resisting government parsimony and refusing to economise on the styling for the elevations of the later Home and Colonial Offices. The internal courtyards of both these new offices were designed with their east side at an angle, to allow Scott to align the front of the building with the orientation of Whitehall and Parliament Street. Today, Scott's Foreign Office, Inigo Jones' Banqueting House and Charles Barry's refronting of the old Treasury give the south end of Whitehall a sense of a series of renaissance palaces, contrasting with the Gothic splendour of Barry's Palace of Westminster immediately to the south.

Both exterior and interior elevations of the Foreign Office building are enlivened with a wealth of statues and bas-reliefs – although many of these are difficult to appreciate without binoculars. Due to economies, some statues, including those seen on Scott's drawings of the Foreign Office tower, were never erected, and some bas-reliefs were left incomplete. Nevertheless, there is still, as Christopher Hussey wrote, 'an enormous amount of sculpture' . . . 'as good as any of its age in England', which Nicholas Pevsner describes as 'an opulent decoration without being showy'.

The Whitehall facade of the former Colonial and Home Offices has portrait medallions and symbolic figures by H H Armstead in the spandrels: Africa is represented by a Hottentot figure with a hippopotamus; Asia by a seated figure with an elephant in the background; and Education, fittingly, by a partially clad youth reading a book. At the top, figures on the balustrades stand out confidently against the London sky. The India Office's statues are especially opulent, perhaps because they were erected before the need for economy. On the facade facing the park, governor-generals are deployed instead of gargoyles, and symbolic figures represent the rivers and states of India.

The external facing walls of the Foreign Office itself have no statues or bas-reliefs. The long Downing Street facade is bare of ornament, apart from a plaque, unveiled by Stanley Baldwin in 1937, to Lord Grey of Fallodon (formerly Edward Grey), designed by Edwin Lutyens and executed by William Reid Dick. It bears the inscription: 'Secretary of State for Foreign Affairs

ABOVE *Two of the statues in the quadrangle. The one on the left represents Liverpool, the one on the right Birmingham.*

∞

LEFT *Lord Halifax, photographed in 1940, walks past the famous inscription about Edward Grey.*

1905–16', and below it 'By uprightness of character, wisdom in council and firmness in action he won the confidence of his countrymen and helped to carry them through many dangers.' On the same wall the beginning of an arch can also be seen. When I was writing *10 Downing Street: The Illustrated History* no one was quite certain why this unfinished arch was there, but sight of Scott's final drawings (see page 47) on the front to the park revealed that he had intended to have a triumphal archway guarding the western entrance into Downing Street similar to the later archway linking Foreign Office to Treasury.

The main internal quadrangle of Scott's building also gives an impression of consistency of design, even though the two new offices built in the 1870s meant that the space was no longer to be open to the east, as the architect had intended. In the courtyard, entrances to the four original departments have two-storey porches and there are other pillared and pedimented protrusions on the internal facades. Scott was meticulous about the height of the courses: the first floor is the loftiest, with ceiling heights of 6.3m/21ft; the ground floor is 5.25m/17ft 6in high; and the basement and second floors are each 3.9m/13ft high.

On the cornice above the first-floor window arches, with their hint of Scott's rejected Byzantine middle design, perch 66 statues. The richest and most plentiful are the statues over the India Office; relief portraits of distinguished British orientalists; eight figures representing what were believed to be the leading races of the Indian Empire; and eight statues of Indian rulers who were allies during the Mutiny. The India Office Library and Records holds Digby Wyatt's notes listing the candidates for the statues, and complaints about the difficulties of establishing likenesses.

The other three Offices are also adorned with appropriate statues and sculptures on their quadrangle facades. The Home Office has sculpture representing British cities; the Foreign Office has statues representing overseas powers.

The roadway running around the edge of the inner quadrangle was originally finished in wooden blocks in an attempt to dampen the noise of horse-drawn carriages and delivery vehicles, but with the advent of motorcars in the last century, asphalt was laid to replace the wood. Regrettably, the cars (though necessary, given the unsocial hours worked by many FCO staff) as much as the extra storey serve to mar the purity of the architecture.

THE INDIA OFFICE

No other country in the British Empire had a department in Whitehall dedicated to it alone, as India had from 1858–1947. But in no other country lived 20 per cent of the world's population, as was the case in India by the early twentieth century. At a time, following the Mutiny, of uncertainty and nervousness, the Council of India wanted their new building to make a strong statement about British rule in India. They were not going to be satisfied with half measures, and they oversaw the building of the most dramatic and striking of all the four offices. The Council's mission, and Digby Wyatt's design, were aided by there being more ready money at their disposal than for other parts of the building.

If one enters the Foreign Office, as all but the most exalted do, by the arched entrance from King Charles Street, the India Office porch is on the left. Climb the steps and enter the door, and one is immediately aware of a distinctive style. Digby Wyatt

ABOVE *The Foreign and Commonwealth Office, Whitehall facade, as it looks today. Notice the statues standing out against the sky and the way in which the third-floor roof extension is obscured from street level.*

∞

BELOW *A floor plan showing the location of the India Office and of the Durbar Court within it.*

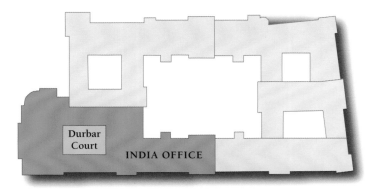

ABOVE AND LEFT *The majestic Muses' staircase. You can clearly see the enchanting goddesses of plenty at the top of the domed ceiling, supported by the pairs of cherubs representing Roman virtues. Below are the portraits of Napoleon III and Empress Eugénie.*

had been official architect to the East India Company in 1855 and was given responsibility for all the new India Office interiors in 1859. His tastes and experience were different to those of Scott. Digby Wyatt had been secretary to the royal commissioners for the Great Exhibition of 1851, had advised Henry Cole over the South Kensington Museum, and collaborated with I K Brunel on Paddington Station. Digby Wyatt and his circle preached the high Renaissance of Italy as enthusiastically as Gilbert Scott and his circle did the medievalism of the Gothic. Both rose to the top of their professions, Scott as professor of architecture at the Royal Academy, Digby Wyatt as the first Slade professor of fine arts at Cambridge University. Whereas Digby Wyatt was outstanding at the decoration of interiors Scott was undoubtedly the finer architect.

Once inside the India Office, one climbs a short staircase to the Entrance Hall, which boasts two fireplaces. That on the left, hidden until the 1980s behind office partitioning, is supported by seventeenth-century stone statues, probably brought over in the 1860s from East India House; the one on the right is a replica, placed there when the India Office was constructed.

From here a grand corridor (the length no doubt purposely being designed to impress visitors) passes the main Gurkha stairs, named after Richard Goulden's statue of a Gurkha (1929–30), which was eventually moved to allow greater prominence and security to the main India Office entrance. Halfway up these

INDIA OFFICE

stairs, on the northern wall, are full-length marble statues of commanders-in-chief or governor-generals in India: Eyre Coote (1788), Lord Cornwallis (1793), Richard Wellesley (1845), and of Wellesley's brother the Duke of Wellington who also fought in India (1853).

Crossing the south side of the Durbar Court, one gets a first view of this focal point and greatest splendour of the India Office through glazed screens placed between the inner and outer columns; runners that allow the panes to be opened make a sound like a steam train travelling on rails. Better views of the court are to be gained from the windows of the India Office Council Chamber. Leaving the Durbar Court behind, one arrives at the south-west corner of the building and at another staircase, opposite the entrance to the building from the Clive Steps leading up from St James's Park. Turning the corner and moving north brings one to the Muses' or Naiad stairs, close to the northern extremity of the India Office where it 'bulges' out towards the park. This is the most arresting staircase of all those in the India Office. Its roof shows goddesses of plenty and cherubs, with curved plaques bearing the names of the great virtues, ornamenting the glass lantern of the dome.

ABOVE *Richard Goulden's statue of a Gurkha (1929–30), which stands at the main India Office entrance.*

elaborately decorated rooms in the India Office, and was designed to display furniture from the directors' Court Room in Leadenhall Street. The chairman's seat, from about 1730, the boardroom tables and the early eighteenth-century chairs had all been used by those who were in charge of directing Indian affairs through the East India Company up to the Mutiny of 1857.

When the room was restored in the 1980s, with pale green walls and lavish gilding, some of the furniture was relocated, though the chairman's seat, bearing the East India Company's crest of a rampant lion within a medallion, was retained. So, too, was the great Michael Rysbrack overmantel relief on the chimneypiece in several colours of marble, which had also been brought across from East India House. The Flemish sculptor was paid £100 for this work in 1730.

The carved overmantel above the fireplace depicts Britannia receiving the riches of the East Indies. Behind her stand two female figures which symbolise Asia and Africa (the former leading a camel; the latter a lion), and on the right is a river god which represents the river Thames. In the background ships are setting off to sea. The cast-iron fire basket, surround and fender are also original.

At the great reception for the Sultan of Turkey in 1867, the Council Chamber was transformed into a dining room for the principal guests. It is reported that every item on the table, bar the food and drink, was made of gold. After the India Office moved out in 1947, the German department of the Foreign Office moved in. After 1948, preliminary discussions relating to the first meeting of the NATO deputies were held in the room. Now it is used for meetings and a wide range of other functions. One can still feel the splendour and confidence of the room in which the Council of India deliberated Indian affairs during its ninety-year existence.

THE INDIA OFFICE COUNCIL CHAMBER

The India Office Council Chamber leads off the west corridor. It has very tall eighteenth-century doors from the East India Company's office in Leadenhall Street. This is one of the most

LEFT *The chairman's seat is carved with the East India Company's crest within a medallion.*

∞

RIGHT *The India Office Council Chamber, showing the wonderful carved overmantel. The chairman's seat can be seen located in the corner of the room. Through the window can be glimpsed the Durbar Court.*

INDIA OFFICE

THE DURBAR COURT

The windows of the India Office Council Chamber afford perhaps the best vantage point from which to admire the Durbar Court, one of Britain's most splendid and dramatic courtyards and the great visual achievement of Digby Wyatt's career. This courtyard, inspired, it has been suggested, by Bramante's *cortile* in the Palazzo della Cancelleria in Rome, and originally conceived as being open to the skies, was described in the following terms in *The Builder* on 12 September 1868, which highlighted

The remarkable variety of materials employed in the building for decorative purposes, a variety unknown in practice comparatively few years ago. The floor of the court is of tiles, laid to a pattern, and has parapets of Portland stone.

The main portion of the walling, plain and decorative, is of Portland stone. The Doric columns which face the piers dividing the bays of the ground storey and first storey are of Peterhead red granite, with red Mansfield capitals. The dividing columns of the second floor are of dark grey Aberdeen granite (now, we believe, worked out), with dark grey Dean Forest stone capitals. In addition to these materials there are majolica and mosaic friezes and pateras, and tesselated floors and ceilings in the loggias.

The courtyard, measuring 34.5m x 18m/115ft x 60ft, and 25m/80ft high, was covered by a canopy for the Sultan's grand reception in July 1867. By the following year, the case for covering the area permanently, in view of the inclement weather, became inescapable. Digby Wyatt was worried that it might make the interior and the rooms that led onto it too dark, thus compromising his whole conception. *The Builder* described how he circumvented this problem, perhaps drawing on his experience of the canopy over the platforms at Paddington Station:

The whole of the daylight to be obtained had to be received from the sky-opening, which is 80 feet above the floor of the yard; it was therefore essential that the minimum of opaque surface should be presented, and to this end iron as the bearing agent, and glass as the medium for light, were the only materials that commended themselves for use. The covering of an area 115 feet long, with a span of 60 feet, would have necessitated the use, had the roof been constructed of timber, of a large aggregate of light-obscuring surface, and diverse broad stripes of shadow, which the use of iron obviates.

The roof did not prove as durable as Digby Wyatt envisaged. At some stage the gable end glass was removed, allowing pigeons to come in. By the time of the 1980s restoration, the roof consisted of two panes of protective glass with a wire mesh in between, which not only let in little light but also conducted heat into the courtyard, making the top office floor almost unbearably hot. So the glass was completely replaced by a Pilkington glass which reflected most of the heat back, while still letting all the light through, and thus rendering the upper floor usable again.

The floor of the Durbar Court was originally on two levels: a floor of tiles above the basement and a 'terrace-walk' crossing the centre of the courtyard from north to south and east to west. There may have been water in the lower level. However, by 1906, when the India Office's works of art were catalogued, the floor had levelled, and had panels of green cipollino marble from Greece surrounding white arabesque marble from Sicily, and border lines of black marble from Belgium.

Digby Wyatt's decorative work in the Durbar Court becomes richer the higher one looks. The frieze between ground level and the first storey is of Minton's Della Robbia ware: highly glazed, creamy-white relief on a pale green background. Minton was an old friend and collaborator of Digby Wyatt. The upper frieze is of Maw's tiles, decorated in grisaille on a light blue ground, with elements of yellow and red. The columns and stonework, described above, are rounded off by sculpture and carving in celebration of Anglo-Indian history, with full-size figures of British heroes, reliefs of treaty signings, names of Indian cities, rivers and states, and at the top tablets inscribed with the names of battles. Outstanding are four reliefs by the Belgian Theodore Phyffers who had worked for Barry on the Houses of Parliament, representing important events such as 'The Grant of the Diwanni to Lord Clive' (*Diwanni* was the Moghul word for tax revenues).

Matthew Digby Wyatt was not lacking a sense of his own importance and not averse to self promotion. Carved in the stone of the brackets supporting the balustrade is THIS COURT WAS BUILT AD 1866 M D WYATT ARCHITECT. His monogram appears on the panels of carved stone at the doorways into the loggias; and in one place he has inscribed his own monogram above that of Queen Victoria. Her Majesty, it seems, never learned of this piece of immodesty.

LEFT *The statue of Lord Teignmouth on the balcony which overlooks the Durbar Court. A reflection of the Court is visible in the window.*

LEFT *The ornate chandelier in the
Secretary of State for India's Office.*

RIGHT *One of the paired double doors
that lead into the Office. Apparently
designed so that dignitaries could
enter the room at the same time, and
thus be afforded equal respect.*

BELOW *The carved wooden
overmantel adorned by the cherub
bearing the name of India.*

THE SECRETARY OF STATE FOR INDIA'S OFFICE

Leaving the Durbar Court and climbing the Muses' Staircase brings one to the Secretary of State for India's Office – the room in which the minister responsible for all the territory which is now India, Pakistan, Bangladesh, Burma and Sri Lanka worked. Yet what initially surprises one is how relatively small it is, and how much more like a drawing room it is than an office.

The room is oval and dominated by two matching fireplaces surmounted by mirrors with heavy wooden surrounds. Three rectangular windows look out over St James's Park and let in ample evening light, for the room looks not east towards India but west. John Cornforth thinks Digby Wyatt may have been influenced in this room by the interiors of Adam: 'It is as if [he] re-interpreted them to create a room of deliberately unexpected richness and complexity to surprise and delight visitors, who would notice that the gilded cherubs in the pediments of the over-mantel glasses hold labels spelling out India.'

Although not everyone may respond to the room in the same way as Cornforth, the domed and gilded ceiling certainly imparts an oriental atmosphere, and

there is an unusual pair of double doors leading into the room, which were apparently designed so that if two Indian princes or other notables were paying a visit to the Secretary of State, neither would have to play second fiddle to the other. Quite how the Secretary of State managed the protocol of which to greet first is not recorded. Ancillary wooden doors lie on either side of the fireplaces. On one occasion an ambassador decided to make a protest by banging the door behind him as he left. Unfortunately he chose the wrong door and found himself face to face with the Secretary of State's drinks cupboard! The story is verifiable, but not, regrettably, the identity of the hot-headed visitor.

THE FOREIGN OFFICE

The Foreign Office interiors are undoubtedly the finest and most opulent of Scott's work. Alexander Beresford Hope, MP, the chairman of the select committee on the construction of the new Foreign Office and a supporter of Scott, wrote that the

RIGHT *The desk once occupied by the
Secretary of State for India. Note the
absence of straight lines in this room.*

cont. p 90

ABOVE *The smooth marble balustrade, designed to impress visitors on their way to the State Rooms.*

ABOVE *The incredible detail on the walls, which adds rich colour and depth to this area.*

ABOVE *The royal insignia, with the initials of Queen Victoria, is part of the mosaic pattern on the floor.*

THE GRAND STAIRCASE

The Grand Staircase was described by Hussey as 'the most grandiose of its kind in London after that of Lancaster House' (Lancaster House being the government building on the other side of the park and the venue for many international conferences). Three stories high, and in scale the one feature of the Foreign Office to rival the Durbar Court, it was designed expressly to impress visiting ambassadors and other overseas dignitaries. Decorated in marble, red paint and gilding, and magnificently restored, it still inspires and stuns. One imagines oneself to be in the richest of palaces, somewhere between Italy, the Orient and Transylvania. The red-carpeted stairs soon divide, and then return at right angles towards a pillared three-sided arcade. They are lit from the inner courtyard to the south. Above are barrel vaults and a mighty dome in the centre, decorated with four groups of five female figures representing the most important countries of the continents of Asia, Africa, America and Europe which had diplomatic relations with Britain in the 1860s. The two central and several smaller ormolu and bronze gasoliers, now with electric bulbs, were made by Skidmore's Art Manufacturers Company of Coventry;

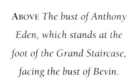

ABOVE *The bust of Anthony Eden, which stands at the foot of the Grand Staircase, facing the bust of Bevin.*

the floor tiles are by Minton-Hollins, all to designs by Scott; and the stencilled decoration is the work of Clayton and Bell, notable church decorators, who also worked with Scott on the Albert Memorial. Around the feet of the 20 painted figures in the central dome is a quotation from Psalm 67: LET THE PEOPLE PRAISE THEE O LORD YEA LET ALL THE PEOPLE PRAISE THEE O LET THE NATIONS REJOICE AND BE GLAD FOR THOU SHALT JUDGE THE FOLK RIGHTEOUSLY AND GOVERN THE NATIONS UPON THE EARTH. It was an appropriate and uplifting motto to crown this opulent central thoroughfare of the nation's Foreign Office – a contrast to Digby Wyatt's choice of inscription in his Durbar Court. Five pieces of sculpture stand out on the Grand Stair: marble statues of George Villiers, Earl of Clarendon and Lord Salisbury; a bust of Ernest Bevin (Foreign Secretary 1945–51); another of Anthony Eden (Foreign Secretary 1935–38, 40–45, 51–55), unveiled by his widow; and one of Edmund Hammond, Permanent Under Secretary, who famously, towards the end of his career in early July 1870, told the Foreign Secretary that he had never known such a lull in European affairs. Three weeks later, the Franco-Prussian War of 1870–71 broke out.

ABOVE *One of the murals by Sigismund Goetze that grace the walls on the first floor of the Grand Staircase.*

ABOVE *A floor plan showing the location of the Foreign Office section of the building, and of the Locarno Suite within it.*

State Rooms were intended to be 'a kind of national palace or drawing room for the nation'. Christopher Hussey wrote in his campaigning article to preserve the building (1964):

> *Its grandiose scale was still appropriate for a building devoted to relations with the monarchical régimes in Paris and Turin, Berlin and Madrid, when the Foreign Secretary alone conducted all important negotiations with great powers' ambassadors in a climate, we may feel, more suggestive of the Almanach de Gotha than of Hansard.*

Scott might have relinquished the India Office interiors to Digby Wyatt, but he was not going to allow unfavourable comparisons to be made with his plum and long sought-after commission.

Entrance to Scott's Renaissance palace is through the internal porched lobby on the north-facing wall of the quadrangle. Walk via a flight of stairs and one imagines one is in a London club, unconsciously waiting for a porter to appear, slide open a glass panel and ask: 'Which member are you waiting for, sir/madam?' Instead, one is left alone in the Entrance Hall with its patterned tile floor, pillars and round arches, and its stencilled and inlaid ceilings with their original strong reds and blues behind the gilding of the cornice which was reinstated during the restoration. Above one of the building's countless fireplaces hangs a portrait of George Gilbert Scott, casting a cold eye on all who enter his creation.

A large open waiting room overlooks Downing Street, with newspapers and magazines strewn over the tables, and with a display of Queen's Messenger badges; this, too, has the atmosphere and appearance of an Italianate Pall Mall Club. To the

RIGHT *The Grand Staircase looking west. In the distance is one of Goetze's murals, bearing the title 'Britannia Sponsa'.*

right are rooms used by Britain's overseas ambassadors when on visits to London, but this is private territory and our tour takes us west from the Entrance Hall, along a wide corridor and through fire doors introduced during the restoration in Scott mould, so as not to sully the integrity of the building.

THE MURALS

The first floor is now embellished by murals, painted by Sigismund Goetze between 1914 and 1919. A wealthy man with an established reputation, Goetze lived at Grove House in Regent's Park – a house designed, ironically, by Decimus Burton, a former candidate for the Foreign Office commission. The murals provide a diverting story, not least because Goetze received similarly rough treatment to the main architect of the building. A traditionalist, he was in tune with the taste of older Royal Academicians rather than with the swelling band of modernists, to whom his subject matter and style were anathema. In March 1912, Randall Davidson, Archbishop of

Canterbury, delivered a widely publicised speech at a Royal Academy banquet, in which he drew attention to the drab offices in which government officials worked, in contrast to the public buildings of the Renaissance. Indeed, the Uffizi in Florence (built in the sixteenth century to contain all the public 'offices' and now the art gallery) is still thought to be the world's first office building. Goetze, who was abroad at the time, read a report of the speech in the *Times* and hurried back to London to write to Archbishop Davidson to say he was 'compelled to offer my services to help to remove the reproach that Art has no place in the surroundings of those who are governing this country'. He offered to decorate, with scenes depicting the story of Great Britain, and for no remuneration, some of the government's walls.

ABOVE AND BELOW *Sigismund Goetze, whose generosity in painting the murals was rebuffed by an ungrateful Lord Curzon. Here we see him in his studio, preparing 'Britannia Pacificatrix'.*

His generous offer was accepted, and after a tour of government departments it was decided he should prepare designs for the corridors at the head of the Grand Staircase in the Foreign Office. After touring Europe to inspect murals, he decided the right course would be to evolve 'a sober, dignified scheme . . . hinting at rather than realising the greatness of this Island Empire, without bombast, without offence to other people through their Ambassadors'. For its day, it seemed an eminently 'politically correct' approach.

Early in 1914 his sketches for the murals were shown to Edward Grey, the Foreign Secretary and to H H Asquith, Prime Minister (1908–16). On May 14, Lord Beauchamp was instructed to write to Goetze: 'They commission me to accept your generous (and anonymous) offer.' Goetze decided on five large panels in 'spirit-fresco', a method perfected in France in which the paintings are applied to a specially prepared cloth which is then fixed to the wall. His palette, he decided, would be

restricted to just three pigments – yellow ochre, Venetian red and cobalt – to avoid being too vivid and intrusive on Scott's designs.

The five subjects of the panels were: 'Britannia Sponsa. The Sea-farers claim Britain as their bride'; 'Britannia Nutrix, She teaches her children the arts of peace'; 'Britannia Bellatrix, She teaches her sons the arts of war'; 'Britannia Colonorum Mater, Mistress of the Seas she send her sons into distant lands'; and finally, 'Britannia Pacificatrix . . . To the motherland they offer aid and counsel. Friends acclaim the righteous peace'. Only the last was to be radically altered, as a result of the outbreak of war in 1914: Goetze changed the sketch where he had originally depicted England and France shaking hands with Germany. India, its support for the allied war effort recognised, was duly painted into the picture as a dignified standing figure, rather than a kneeling figure, and Germany was removed.

Dogged by illness throughout the war, Goetze managed to complete all but one of the murals – 'Britannia Pacificatrix' – by November 1918. By then, objections to the murals began to be heard, emanating especially from Lord Curzon, Foreign Secretary 1919–24 and, earlier, Acting Foreign Secretary while Arthur Balfour attended the Paris Peace Conference following

BELOW *Britannia Pacificatrix 'To the motherland they offer aid and counsel. Friends acclaim the righteous peace'. Goetze had to paint Germany out of the picture after the outbreak of war.*

FOREIGN OFFICE

the armistice. Curzon hated Goetze's work, but he also seemed to dislike Goetze personally, in an anti-Semitic and xenophobic fashion, although Goetze was neither a Jew nor a foreigner.

Curzon invited art critics to inspect one panel of Goetze's work and they were duly unimpressed, finding it 'theatrical'. Curzon suggested sending the murals instead to the newly built County Hall on the south bank of the Thames. Goetze refused, and the Office of Works was asked to mediate. As Lionel Earle from the Office of Works put it: 'The Foreign Office I understand are dead against these panels going up. Personally, I do not much admire the art, but at the same time I think that Mr Goetze would be very badly treated if they are ruthlessly turned down at this stage after he has spent about six years labour on them . . . The Foreign Office are evidently nervous of the German origin and connection and feel that they are liable to a good deal of abuse and attack by the wild men that are about everywhere.' One such wild man wrote an article that appeared in a journal, *Plain English*, edited by Lord Alfred Douglas, Oscar Wilde's lover. The article criticised the commissioning of the work by Alfred Mond 'who is a fellow-tribesman and a brother-in-law of the artist. Both parties concerned are aliens in common law and perpetual enemies of this Christian empire. Where were our British artists?' (Alfred Mond, Goetze's brother-in-law, was Jewish. He was also an ICI industrialist and Lloyd George's First Commissioner of Works.)

The murals were probably saved by the appointment in 1921 of the Earl of Crawford and Balcarres as First Commissioner, and by the support of Lloyd George himself. At a cabinet meeting to decide the issue in November, held in the Foreign Office, only Curzon voted against hanging the murals. Lloyd George later said: 'Well, gentlemen, whenever I have entered this building, I always thought I was entering a tomb, now I begin to see light.'

The murals have continued to arouse passions. Welsh Nationalists have taken offence at the reference to 'an earlier and ruder race [i.e. the Celts]', and the 'little Swahili boy' in 'Britannia Pacificatrix', who 'reminds us of our obligations and responsibilities in the dark continent', can upset almost anyone so disposed today. But as art historian Caroline Dakers rightly says: 'Though no one could suggest Goetze was ever a first-rate artist, his murals can now be seen as an evocation of a past age,

'. . . the Private Office . . . is the place where politics and diplomacy come together, Minister and the machine interlock, home and abroad meet; a clearing-house for papers, a crossroads, a meeting-point, a bedlam. It is the most exciting room in the whole Foreign Office. There is always something going on there and enough static in the air to produce shock at any time.'

NICHOLAS HENDERSON, BRITISH
AMBASSADOR IN WASHINGTON 1979–82

of a particular moment in the history of the British Empire.' Indeed, the battle seems now to have been won. When, towards the end of his first year in office as Foreign Secretary, Robin Cook announced one morning 'Those murals will have to go' his office was flooded by messages pleading a stay of execution. Thus quickly does the Whitehall bush telegraph work. A red-faced official went in to tell him about the mounting chorus of opposition. 'April Fool,' the beaming Foreign Secretary retorted.

THE FOREIGN SECRETARY'S ROOM

The Foreign Secretary's Room at the top of the Grand Staircase was designed to impress, and it still does today, with its combination of height, resplendent gilding and historical echoes. All foreign secretaries have used the room, with the exception of Lord Salisbury, who often preferred to work from the Cabinet Room of the Locarno Suite during his four tenures of office. (It was he who likened the foreign policy of the first occupant of the room, Lord Stanley [1866–68] to floating 'down a stream occasionally putting out a diplomatic boat-hook to avoid collisions'.) Most of the incumbents have shown their appreciation of the room, few more so than Lord Carrington (1979–82), who exclaimed, 'Lovely, lovely', upon first entering it. At the opposite extreme we find Curzon who, when appointed Acting Foreign Secretary in 1919, exclaimed, 'How ghastly. How positively ghastly!'.

It is difficult to understand Curzon's contempt for the room, because it is spacious, naturally lit, and attractively decorated. It is not only the largest office of any cabinet minister (far bigger than the Prime Minister's), but it also enjoys the best view: over Horse Guards Parade to the north and St James's Park to the west. The room received its baptism in March 1868 when it was used for the party to celebrate the appointment of Benjamin Disraeli as Prime Minister. The *Illustrated London News* made much of the grand occasion, and depicted it in an engraving (see page 54).

RIGHT *The Secretary of State's desk in the Foreign Secretary's Room. On the desk can be seen his daily programme stand: the appointments for 17 February 2000 are shown on page 131.*

ABOVE *The cabinet in the Foreign Secretary's Room, showcasing the best of British design – a Robin Cook innovation.*

ABOVE *Photos of Queen Elizabeth and the Duke of Edinburgh on the cabinet in the Foreign Secretary's Room, behind his desk.*

Most famously, this was the room where Lord Grey, as he later recalled in his memoirs, *Twenty Five Years:1892–1916*, stood by the window on the eve of the First World War, full of fear for what the future might bring:

> *a friend came to see me on one of the evenings of the last week – he thinks it was on Monday, August 3. We were standing at a window of my room in the Foreign Office. It was getting dusk, and the lamps were being lit in the space below on which we were looking. My friend recalls that I remarked on this with the words: 'The lamps are going out all over Europe; we shall not see them lit again in our lifetime'.*

Grey does not record, and neither has anyone else, which window he was looking through. Two distinguished Foreign Secretaries on the same day swore to me that they knew: each had Grey looking out in a different direction!

The floor on which Grey stood is still of carefully selected English oak, as are the dadoes. The window cases contain marquetry panels of mahogany, walnut, lime and cedar. The ceiling is divided into three panels by two iron beams (Scott used metal extensively within the building, as well as concrete for floors, partly because it was more fire resistant than wood). The beams are supported on massive curved brackets, the undersides of which are stencilled in gold with rivet heads and gilded pendants, and the sides of the beams are clad in moulded majolica panels with floral decorations. The walls are painted in a light green colour with stencilled star motifs in black and gold (one senior official complained the decoration scheme made the room 'into a sort of Star Chamber'). The marble fireplace may have been transferred from the old Foreign Office in Downing Street; at one time a portrait of George III hung above it, and until recently a painting of a Nepalese prince renowned for his Anglophile inclinations. However, Robin Cook found his glowering presence with curved sword in hand too oppressive, and the painting has now been transferred and hangs in the India Reading Room at the British Library. Unable to find a suitable picture to replace it, Cook left the space empty for his first three years in office, before filling it with a painting by John Bratby.

Another Cook innovation was to remove the Hansard parliamentary reports from the bookcase on the south wall and to replace them with examples of British invention and design, which highlight how much of the FCO's work is still connected with the promotion of Britain's commercial interests. The room has otherwise remained unchanged, and has three principal areas: the desk, at which the Foreign Secretary works through his red boxes; a long table at the north end for formal meetings of up to 12; and a comfortable seating area with a red leather settee and matching armchairs for less formal meetings. On the Foreign Secretary's desk stands his daily appointments card, which allows him to see at a glance what is next on his busy agenda.

Frequent changes of clothes are the lot of all foreign secretaries, and through the east-facing door is a private bathroom and also room for the ever-present detective. Douglas Hurd recalled how, 'one was constantly having to change in a hurry into a white tie or a black tie. There was one of those rather flimsy showers. I would rather have liked a bath, but I wouldn't have dared put one in. There was a thin towel rail, and I feared if I bumped into the shower it would have fallen down.'

Helping to prevent the Foreign Secretary from bumping into anything and to steer him effortlessly on his way, is his Private Office, which is situated adjacent to the Foreign Secretary's Room. The office is presided over by the Principal Private Secretary, often a formidable individual who will rise to the top of the service or to one of the top ambassadorial posts overseas. The room is decorated with portraits of previous foreign secretaries, and has desks for three other private secretaries who make up the Private Office team.

Near the Foreign Secretary's Room, and with a good view over Horse Guards Parade, is the Ambassador's Waiting Room, where the visitors to the Foreign Secretary wait for meetings.

ABOVE *Charles Hardinge of Penshurst, the Permanent Under Secretary, who clashed with Lord Curzon.*

Important visitors traditionally enter the building via the St James's Park entrance, to the west of Downing Street. As part of the restoration, a new lift, panelled in wood for the benefit of the VIPs who would be using it, was inserted to take the place of its exceedingly slow predecessor.

Immediately below the Foreign Secretary's Room is that of the Permanent Under Secretary, the man (it has always been a man) who is the official head of the Diplomatic Service. The PUS's Room is about three-quarters the size of the Foreign Secretary's Room, but is in many respects similar. The ceiling has an iron girder, similar to those in the room above, and the walls had their stencilled decoration restored in the 1980s. It was once connected to the room above by a speaking tube, of the kind used in steamships and old motor cars. In 1918, Curzon would breathe down the tube to attract the attention of his PUS Charles Hardinge, who would respond, 'Yes, George', barely concealing his contempt for his by then superior – both men were former Viceroys of India. The room is dominated by a large table, around which, each morning at 10.30 am, the 24 or 30 most senior officials meet. John Coles (PUS 1994–98) wrote: 'I found it invaluable, the key moment in the day when I and everyone else could get a feel for what was going on in foreign affairs.'

BELOW *Taking tea in the pivotal Private Secretary's Room. From left to right are Rab Butler, Alexander Cadogan and Horace Seymour.*

BELOW *Robert Vansittart with Mr Dunlop, Head of the King's Messengers and Communications Department, 1941.*

FOREIGN OFFICE

While many pre-1980s PUSs, such as Charles Hardinge (1906–10, 1916–20), Robert Vansittart (1930–38), Alexander Cadogan (1938–46) and Michael Palliser (1975–82), had considerable influence on policy, most recent PUSs have had to concentrate largely on the practicalities of administration and management, especially as they are the department's accounting office. Patrick Wright (PUS 1986–91) said, 'I worried, especially after I read Alex Cadogan's diaries, that I was thinking far more about running the service than about high policy, as he had done. I would not have had the time to write minutes on the direction of foreign policy.' Hurd was concerned that he had offended David Gillmore (PUS 1991–94) when, discussing Gillmore's appointment, he described the job of PUS as running the service and keeping it contented; policy was for others. John Coles found he was having to spend over half his time on governing, and has written that he thinks the balance has tipped too far away from policy.

John Kerr, the present PUS, has built a reputation as a key policy adviser to successive foreign secretaries and prime ministers, and is certainly not content with a merely administrative role. Hurd himself was something of a connoisseur of PUSs, and had been Private Secretary to Harold Caccia who had liked to be a policy man but protested if anyone put anything in his 'in tray', as he hated to think he had unfinished work.

In the 1960s, the PUS's room housed a safe, containing, among other secrets, information on the sexual habits of consuls in China and correspondence about an Ottoman prince who claimed to have rescued the British community in Constantinople after 1914, and who had subsequently taken refuge on a British warship at the end of the First World War. A mixture of the sublime and the ridiculous has always lain at the heart of the Foreign Office's work.

THE LOCARNO SUITE

Returning to the sublime brings one back to the last 'fine area' of the FCO, the Locarno Suite. These three rooms are reached by

BELOW *The Grand Locarno Room laid out for a banquet for the President of France. This 1939 photograph is taken from what was the Band or Cabinet Room, and shows the Royal coat of arms.*

ABOVE *The furnishing scheme for the restored rooms was created by Pat Foley, who worked closely with the architects.*

the first-floor corridor leading from the Grand Staircase. The corridor is itself highly decorated, with patterned tile floor, deep pink walls stencilled in gold, and a sky blue vaulted ceiling with gold stencilled stars. The names of the countries on the corridor arches were members of the League of Nations.

The Locarno Suite was named after the Locarno Treaties, which were signed and sealed here on 1 December 1925, among much ceremonious trumpeting, by delegates from Germany, France, Belgium, Italy, Poland and Czechoslovakia. The treaties had already been initialled the previous October in the town where the discussions had taken place, Locarno in Switzerland, but a formal signing ceremony in London was considered a useful propaganda and morale-boosting exercise, as it finalised reparations paid by Germany after World War I. According to the *Times*, journalists from half the world 'wedged in tiers' behind a barrier half-way down the room and 'photographers and cinematographers . . . perched high up in nooks above the windows'. Austen Chamberlain, the Foreign Secretary at the time, declined to let the newly formed British Broadcasting Corporation attend, lest he should say 'd—' if his pen slipped.

The three rooms making up the Suite had, in fact, been designed for entertaining; the parliamentary committee on the reconstruction of the Foreign Office had suggested that in any new building it was 'essential that the Secretary of State for Foreign Affairs should have the means of giving large dinners and that he should have reception rooms capable of holding 1,200 or 1,500 people'. Scott more than met the committee's wishes. From 1868 until the beginning of the First World War, the annual royal birthday reception was held here, normally attended by some 1,500 to 2,000 people (which must, even with the three rooms, have been a squash). However, so run down had the rooms become by 1925 that they had to be hung with large royal portraits during the Locarno signing to hide the shabbiness of the decoration. Nevertheless, in spite of the removal of Scott's decorations in 1926, and with a simpler decoration scheme, the custom of holding a dinner to celebrate the King's birthday was resumed, as were dinners for foreign dignitaries: the King of Afghanistan was entertained to dinner here on 14 March 1928, and the most celebrated dinner was for President Lebrun of France on 23 March 1939, in the presence of King George VI, Queen Elizabeth and Queen Mary, followed by entertainment in the Durbar Court.

The three Locarno rooms form a right angle around two sides of the internal courtyard, and the largest, measuring some 20m/70ft x 10.5m/35ft, and 12m/40ft high, also overlooks the main quadrangle. This room is now named the Grand Locarno Reception Room, but has been described as the Large Conference Room. It may have been used for cabinet meetings under Lord Salisbury's Premiership (1885–92, 1895–1902). Salisbury disliked Number 10, and the Foreign Office room is certainly far grander and less claustrophobic than the Cabinet Room at the north-east end of Number 10. But what Prime Minister (unless he was, like Salisbury, also Foreign Secretary) would willingly transfer cabinet meetings from his own patch onto that of one of his most powerful rivals?

Palmerston, celebrated for much, but not for his judgement in matters artistic, nor for the moderation of his language, complained that Scott's Gothic designs reminded him of the 'barbarism of the dark ages'. The word 'barbarism' can be more justly applied to the state into which the rooms had been allowed to deteriorate, especially the Cabinet Room. After the pumice-stoning of 1926, it was believed that the original decoration had been totally destroyed. An engraving from 1878, and more recent photographs, showed the elaborate stencilled patterns on the great barrel-vaulted ceiling, pilasters and walls, but these pictures provided no clue to the colouring. Then came the discovery, in the fifth bay, nearest the Grand Staircase, that original paintwork remained under the parchment paint; the exact colourings could now be established. Large roundels on the vaulting contained the sun, moon and the six planets known at the time. Further detailed research established that 12 of the 16 small roundels had been occupied by signs of the zodiac, though the remaining four were still a mystery. However, oblique lighting revealed the shape of boats. The National Maritime Museum was contacted and provided the answer: the roundels contained the four constellations mentioned in the ancient story of Jason and the Golden Fleece.

Another casualty of the 1926 redecoration were the light fittings in the three rooms. Fortunately, it was discovered that a single chandelier, sent first to the British Embassy in Montevideo, had been shipped back to the Wallace Collection in London. From this survival, and from the pictorial evidence of

ABOVE *An engraving of a ball which was celebrated in the Grand Locarno Reception Room in 1878.*

ABOVE *Detail of the chandeliers in the Grand Locarno Reception Room. One of the original chandeliers found its way to the Wallace Collection, and was used as a model during the renovation.*

LEFT *The splendour of the Grand Locarno Reception Room, the largest of the three rooms of the Locarno Suite.*

FOREIGN OFFICE

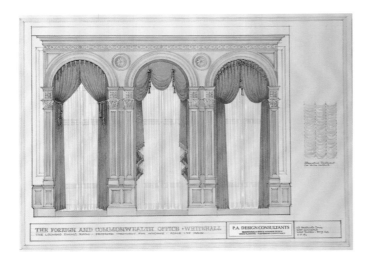

ABOVE *A watercolour of the design by Pat Foley showing the
treatment of the arched windows in the Locarno Dining Room.*

ABOVE *The stately Locarno Dining Room, with its rich red
curtains and chairs, and octagon-encrusted ceiling.*

the pre-1926 rooms, new electric fittings were copied. Two new chandeliers in the Grand Locarno Reception Room can be lowered for maintenance by remote-control winches, and discreet fibre-optic lights on the high-level cornice now illuminate the barrel vault. The marquetry inlay 'over-doors' had also been taken away in 1926, and these had to be copied and reconstructed, mostly with new materials. The only change of consequence was the replacement of the original floor grilles for heating by a sophisticated underfloor system; this took thousands of man hours to achieve, as the wooden floorboards had been pegged together and each one had to be individually prised apart. No unsightly radiators now compromise the harmony of the room; the heat merely wafts up from underneath the carpet.

THE LOCARNO DINING ROOM

The second room, looking out over the main quadrangle, forms the hinge between the two larger rooms. Originally designated the Cabinet Room, it has had several names over the years, and in the postwar period it became a furniture store. Of the three rooms, this one received the least 'barbaric' treatment in 1926 when the walls had been covered with red silk damask fixed on battens over the original decoration. The earlier stencilling, line work and colours in olive and gold, with red and gold borders, were still in evidence behind, though in poor condition. Rather than stripping down what remained of the original, it was decided to plaster over it so that the 1860s work could remain for analysis by future generations. The ceiling, however, has deeply recessed octagons, which were stripped and repainted to

the original scheme. The finest feature of the room is the joinery: three bays of arched timber screens surround the windows at the east end of the room, and the windows themselves are separated by ornate carved wooden columns with veneered marquetry inlay, terminating in a cornice. The best time to view the room is at night when it is lit by the central chandelier; daylight makes it difficult to see the screen.

Two doorways made of oak, finely gilded, and matching Scott's originals were cut through the south wall, to give direct access to the former India Office and to the kitchen area. The room is now named the Locarno Dining Room and has a long antique wooden table in the centre, with red upholstered chairs to match the curtaining. The marble fireplace on the south wall, like the other fireplaces in the Suite, date from the eighteenth century and may have been transferred from the old Foreign Office. The two doorways on the north wall lead into the Grand Locarno Reception Room, while the double doors in the west wall take one into the final room in the Suite.

THE CONFERENCE ROOM

The Conference Room, as it is now called, is the second largest in the Suite, and was the first to be restored; the work was completed in the summer of 1990. The original intention had been to convert the room from its plasterboard cubicled state into an open-plan office with desks serviced by underfloor cables. But when Douglas Hurd saw the work in progress soon after his appointment in 1989, he insisted that the room should be seen in all its glory and be kept as a large meeting room. He also

ABOVE *The Conference Room, viewed
from the Locarno Dining Room.
Notice the circular plaques bearing
the national emblems of different
countries in the curved roof supports.*

∽

RIGHT *The ceiling of the Locarno
Conference Room, showing two of
the national coats of arms.*

∽

LEFT *An example of the fine stencil
work on the Conference Room walls.*

ABOVE *The Entrance Hall to the Colonial Office. Note the more understated finish compared to that of the Foreign Office.*

ABOVE *The octagonal staircase of the Colonial Office, known as the Royal Stair, showing the glass lantern.*

urged that work on the other two rooms should be advanced in anticipation of their use for other official functions.

Before the work on the Conference Room began, a panel in the false ceiling was removed, and by darting torchlight, as if peering into the wonders of Tutenkhamen's tomb, the original splendours were revealed: the gold leaf and multicolouring of an ornate coffered ceiling. Further investigation revealed that the huge oak doors to the central room had been walled up with plasterboard.

The Conference Room ceiling, with its recessed octagons, is one of the finest in the entire building. Divided into bays by the same iron beam technology Scott employed elsewhere in the building, it is supported by cast-iron quadrants in which circular majolica plaques bear the national coats of arms of 20 countries, including those of the United States and Austria but not that of Germany, since the room was completed before its unification in 1871. These coats of arms are an odd construction and as yet no one has been able to explain how they are linked to each other.

The colours and detailing on the walls proved a problem. However, a black and white photograph shot in 1896 was dis-covered, which provided evidence of the wall and plaster deco-ration, and from this stencilling and line work the decoration could be reproduced. The pilaster decoration proved harder to ascertain because of the oblique angle of the photograph, but after trial and error, and reference to colours in adjoining rooms, the decision was taken to employ the pleasing pink and gold patterning seen in the photographs of the room today. The room is lit naturally by north-facing windows looking over the inner courtyard, and artificially by two chandeliers centrally placed over a long wooden table, made around 1842 and acquired during the restoration from a Midlands furniture dealer; it can seat up to 30 on chairs upholstered in green.

The rooms were finally completed in June 1992, and judged to be admirably close to the original decorative scheme of Scott's interiors. Praise and awards were heaped on the building. A plaque recording the award of the Europa Nostra medal of honour has been placed on the wall of the Grand Staircase. Following extensive use during Britain's Presidency of the European Community in 1992, the Suite has been in continu-ous employ for a wide range of official and other functions, including important Anglo-French and Anglo-German summit meetings in the 1990s. A meeting with a Chinese delegation in the early 1990s even had to be delayed for 15 minutes while the visitors studied the surroundings in 'rapt silence'.

THE COLONIAL OFFICE AND HOME OFFICE

These two offices are undoubtedly duller than the India Office or the Foreign Office, as a result of Scott's instructions in the 1870s to save money on their construction. How later generations rue the parsimony of earlier generations! Yet each office contains treasures. The Entrance Hall to the former Colonial Office is not noticeably inferior to that of the Foreign Office, and boasts similar mosaic tiles, marble columns and a gilded recessed ceiling. From the steps leading up to the Entrance Hall, Colonial Secretary Joseph Chamberlain reviewed the colonial troops who had come over to take part in the military review at Edward VII's coronation in 1902. The octagonal staircase, known as the the Royal Stair on account of the portraits of kings and queens that used to hang there, has been carefully restored and its walls painted the plain rich green of the original. At its apex is a pointed lantern made of stone corbels and glass.

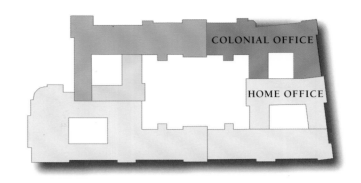

ABOVE *A floor plan showing the location of the Colonial Office and the Home Office.*

The office of the Secretary of State for the Colonies (or Commonwealth Secretary in the postwar period) overlooks the main quadrangle. In here were taken many of the key decisions affecting the growth, and the rapid contraction of the British Empire. It takes its current name, the Map Room, from the large burr-walnut map case bearing the names in gold lettering of 22 parts of the globe. The maps could be pulled down so that the figures meeting at the grand central table could see in detail the part of the empire under discussion. How much more elegant and more romantic than the wide computer screens that grace modern crisis rooms! At the other end of the room is another eighteenth-century marble chimneypiece brought over from the old Downing Street offices before they were demolished. It was in front of this fire, the story goes, that Wellington and Nelson met for their first and only time – probably on 12 September 1805, the day before Nelson left London to join *HMS Victory* at Portsmouth, and thence on to his death at Trafalgar. The

ABOVE *The unique cabinet in which the maps are stored.*

encounter got off to a frosty start, but thawed considerably when the conversation turned to war and politics, and Wellington was to declare that he had never had a conversation that had stimulated him more. Knight painted the meeting in about 1840, and places the fireplace in the background. Portraits of Nelson and Wellington now hang on either side of it. The room is lit by a chandelier of many foliated brass candelabra brackets, decorated with three female figures. The walls and ceiling were painted in the original green and off-white colours discovered after investigation. During the restoration of the building, discussions took place on whether to build Scott's uncompleted towers at either end of the Whitehall facade; Scott had envisaged a great cupola surmounting each tower in seven stages. But government caution, and a wish to retain the space for other purposes, once again prevented their erection, though Scott's unfinished balustrade was completed when the mansard extra floor was added.

The corridors in the Home and Colonial Offices are plain in design, with long barrel-vaulted ceilings instead of the groined arches of the Foreign Office. The focal point at the Whitehall frontage of the building was the entrance onto the street. When the Home Office moved to its new Queen Anne's Gate office in 1978, this entrance was only used for Remembrance Sunday ceremonies at the Cenotaph. Now it is the entrance to the FCO Information Centre. During the mid-1990s, the original fireplaces and tiling were reinstated, and the walls redecorated in original colours.

THE LIBRARY

The other fine room in the old Colonial Office is its library, now the Foreign and Commonwealth Office Library. Floors were extended into part of the Colonial Office courtyard to create extra accommodation and a reading room. The Library retains its Victorian pillars and its gallery, which is not for those with vertigo! The ceiling is supported by five cast-iron columns, painted white, with copper enrichments on the capitals and a ring of lions' masks halfway down each one. At the north end of the Library, hanging just below the balcony, is a stuffed anaconda which recently celebrated its hundredth birthday in its dignified final resting place. The gift, it is said, of a bishop in what is now Guyana, it was presented to a colonial secretary at the end of the nineteenth century. History has not recorded how he received his unusual gift, which had to be removed from the building during the early 1990s, itself requiring restoration.

ABOVE *Stephen Gaselee, the trusted Foreign Office Librarian and Keeper of the Papers.*

LEFT *The original library as it appeared in 1896.*

ABOVE *A view of the Map Room, with the portraits of Nelson and Wellington by the fireplace where they were rumoured to have met.*

RIGHT *The library as it appears today.*

The building has been bombed, or nearly bombed, twice. In March 1991, when the IRA fired mortars at Number 10 one overshot and damaged windows on the north side of the FCO. Less well known was the explosion in the Local Government section of the Home Office on 15 March 1883. According to the *Illustrated London News*, Irish nationalists were responsible: 'The terrible explosion which caused so much havoc in the office of the Local Government Board in Downing Street on the night of Thursday, the 15th (luckily without loss of life), and startled the House of Commons then in session, is reasonably attributed to Fenian conspirators. That the destruction was caused by a large charge of dynamite is the unanimous conclusion of experts.' No trace remains today of the damage, but the Home Office, the department responsible for law and order, has always been associated with violent deeds. Apart from dealing with murders, bombings and other terrible crimes, it also works with MI5 to protect the country from overseas intelligence services and 'enemies within'. The Home Secretary's Room, in which Churchill pondered how to react to the Sidney Street crisis in 1911, Joynson-Hicks to the General Strike in 1926, and where successive secretaries of state have agonised over whether to sign death warrants for murderers, is now a humdrum office, barely recognisable along a faceless corridor.

History teaches us that today's settled matters will become tomorrow's open questions. The Foreign and Commonwealth Office has served the country for over 130 years, and has been adapted to the demands of a high-tech era without sacrificing the elegance and style of its building. It is to be hoped that the equivalents of Leslie Martin and Geoffrey Rippon in the twenty-first century will think long and hard before deciding to pull down this marvellous monument to Britain's past and future.

A sense of continuity and of history is important to the making of foreign policy, and the building conveys it. Foreign policy is also about portraying a sense of Britain both abroad and to Britain's overseas visitors and ambassadors. Again, the building conveys that sense – today, in the early twenty-first century, just as it did in the 1860s. One can only imagine what impression visitors would have received from the cement and glass towerblock that had been planned in the 1960s.

THE GREAT &
THE GOOD

WITH ITS MASSIVE ROOMS AND HIGH CEILINGS, it was as if Scott had designed a building for giants. Some of the incumbents have certainly regarded themselves as such. But the Foreign and Commonwealth Office is staffed by mere mortals: ministers, headed by the Foreign Secretary (or to give him his official name, the Secretary of State for Foreign and Commonwealth Affairs); diplomats (or officials), headed by the Permanent Under Secretary (PUS); and by an army of porters, secretaries, messengers and others. But the key figure is the Foreign Secretary. This chapter offers a selection of some of the more successful, colourful or downright eccentric incumbents.

THE GREAT, THE GOOD AND THE ANONYMOUS

Strange as it may seem, of the many foreign secretaries who have graced the room since 1868, few have left much noticeable mark on the conduct of foreign affairs. Those who have influenced the nation's foreign policy are men who knew a great deal about international affairs (many did not), had an ability to read and digest vast quantities of material, were decisive (many were not), enjoyed time in office of at least three years (over two-thirds have served for less), and usually served during a time of crisis. A command of overseas languages and a liking for foreigners scarcely count.

The relationship between the FCO and Number 10 is critical. The longer a prime minister is in office, the more he or she will want to run foreign affairs (Lloyd George or Mrs Thatcher are examples). Former foreign secretaries who become prime ministers are often unwilling to relinquish responsibility for foreign policy (Lord Salisbury and Harold Macmillan are conspicuous). It has been the Foreign Secretary's misfortune that as Britain's authority in the world has declined in the twentieth century, the Prime Minister's involvement in foreign affairs has increased. Wars, major or minor, have always pushed the Prime Minister onto centre stage. Who knows, for example, who succeeded Edward Grey as Lloyd George's Foreign Secretary in 1916? Answer: A J Balfour. It is prime ministers, not foreign secretaries, who tend to take the stage on major tours abroad or when a foreign leader passes through London. The more important the foreign leader, the more the Prime Minister will wish to come to the fore.

The proliferation of multinational bodies since the League of Nations has further acted to bring the Prime Minister into the limelight. Britain's entry into the European Economic Community in 1973, and her attendance at the European Council from 1975, has also helped to raise the profile of the Prime Minister as against that of the Foreign Secretary. Membership of the UN, NATO, the Commonwealth Heads of Government and the 'Group of Five' (which became G7 and is now G8) have had a similar effect. As more countries entered into diplomatic relations with Britain after

ABOVE *The bust of Ernest Bevin on the Grand Staircase. The only time Bevin could sit for the bust was on Saturday mornings.*

1945, it was to Number 10 rather than to the Foreign Office that they often looked. Membership of the European Community has reduced the importance of the FCO in other ways: increasingly from the 1980s the growth in influence of Brussels has meant that other Whitehall departments – such as the Treasury, the Ministry of Agriculture and trade departments – now conduct foreign relations independently with their European partners. The European secretariat of the Cabinet Office provides another coordinating funnel for European relations with Whitehall.

At certain times the Principal Private Secretary (PPS) to the Prime Minister has been a key foreign policy adviser: notably Jock Colville (1951–55), Freddie Bishop (1956–59) and Robert Armstrong (1970–75). The Private Secretary for Overseas Affairs in Number 10, the second most important official in Downing Street, has also become a key player since 1945. Under Harold Macmillan, Philip de Zulueta (1957–63) eclipsed most Foreign Office diplomats in influence, while Charles Powell's (1984–91) role became akin to that of the National Security Advisor in the White House. It was Powell who would accompany the Prime Minister rather than the Foreign Secretary or FCO officials when high-level meetings took place. The ultra-secure hotline to the White House was to be found not in the FCO or Ministry of Defence but on Powell's desk, and many important communications between President and Prime Minister, or with other foreign leaders, would bypass the FCO. As John Major said about his Premiership (1990–97): 'All I had to do was pick up the phone and within seconds I would be talking on first name terms to any one of a number of overseas leaders.' The telephone in recent times has often played a more important part than have foreign secretaries.

A foreign secretary must also bring out the best in his officials; he is less likely to achieve that if he is too abrasive, as were Lord Curzon (1919–24), George Brown (1966–68) or David Owen (1977–79). On the contrary, foreign secretaries who treat their officials well are naturally liked and respected. Officials also respect foreign secretaries who win battles in Cabinet and who carry weight with the Prime Minister; no one wants to see Foreign Office policies rejected or chopped up. The Foreign

ABOVE *A gathering of the great, the good in July 1990, to celebrate the refurbishment of the Foreign Secretary's Room. In the front row, from left to right, are six foreign secretaries – Lord Pym, Lord Carrington, Dr David Owen, Douglas Hurd, Lord Callaghan and John Major.*

Secretary most popular within the department in the years covered by this book was Ernest Bevin (1945–51), whose bust (left) sits by the Grand Staircase.

The key officials in the Foreign Office, apart from the Permanent Under Secretary, are the Chief Clerk, who looks after administration, the Deputy Secretaries, who oversee wide areas, and the Under Secretaries, who are the specialists in particular fields. The pivot that connects the Foreign Secretary to the Foreign Office and to the rest of Whitehall is the Private Office, situated immediately to the south of the Foreign Secretary's Room. Never has the atmosphere been better described than by Nicholas Henderson in his splendid book on the Private Office: '[It] is the place where politics and diplomacy come together; ministers and the machine interlock, home and abroad meet, a clearing house for papers, a meeting-point, a bedlam.'

LORD PALMERSTON (1784–1865)

As we have seen in Chapter 2, Palmerston was responsible for the Foreign Office building taking the form it did. Educated at Harrow and Edinburgh University, he succeeded his father as 3rd Viscount Palmerston in 1802. He accepted the post of Secretary at War in 1809, which he kept for 20 years. He earned the nickname 'Cupid' for his many affairs, and it was no secret that Lady Cowper's younger children were his; he married her in 1839, after Lord Cowper's death. He joined the Cabinet as a Tory in 1827, and as a result of a speech attacking Wellington in 1829, the Whig Prime Minister Lord Grey offered him the post of Foreign Secretary in 1830, which he was to hold three times: 1830–34, 1835–41 and 1846–51. Until 1834 Grey kept strict control of foreign policy, but when Melbourne became Prime

Minister Palmerston had more scope, and steered Britain through Russia's threat to the Ottoman Empire, and civil wars in Spain and in Portugal.

Despite doubts over whether he was a true hardliner, and a growing gap between himself and Queen Victoria, Palmerston became a national hero after a triumphant and patriotic speech in 1850. But his fall swiftly followed: public approval of the second French Republic (without consulting either Queen Victoria or the Prime Minister) led to his resignation from the Foreign Office and a transfer to the Home Office in 1852. However, the outbreak of the Crimean War in 1854 saw his recall, and in 1855 he became Prime Minister which, except for a short break in 1858–59, he remained until his death in October 1865, sitting in his office with a half-completed letter in front of him. He did not live to see the India and the Foreign Office buildings he had battled over so long and hard.

BELOW Queen Victoria's last Cabinet. When Salisbury was Prime Minister he held Cabinet meetings in the Foreign Office – this event may well have taken place in one of the three Locarno rooms. The bearded Salisbury is on the left, his left arm on the table. Behind him is his nephew and successor Balfour.

LORD SALISBURY (1830–1903)

Robert Cecil, 3rd Marquis of Salisbury, dominated foreign policy in the last third of the nineteenth century, as Palmerston had in its middle third. Secretary of State for India twice, from 1866–67 and 1874–78, he was four times Foreign Secretary between 1878 and 1900, and for much of the time was also Prime Minister. Educated at Eton and Christ Church, Oxford, he hated Eton so much that he refused all invitations in later life to return as guest of honour. Moody and highly strung, his intellectualism made him appear even more withdrawn from peers from the same background. By the age of 22, he had decided he was unfit for all the conventional careers for young men of his station: politics, the Church or the Bar. Yet he decided to enter Parliament the following year, 1853, and rose rapidly through the ranks.

Elevated to Foreign Secretary in 1878, he accompanied Disraeli to the Congress of Berlin the same year. Although it was seen as a triumph primarily for Prime Minister Disraeli, who was keen to ensure that Russia's ambitions were contained, it also bore the stamp of Salisbury's input. Obsessed by Britain's relative weakness in Europe and the necessity of avoiding war,

ABOVE *The formidable Lord Salisbury, in a photograph dating from the mid- to late 1880s.*

∞

RIGHT *Lord Palmerston, who could 'express himself perfectly in French, very succinctly in Italian, and understood German'.*

Salisbury strove to limit the cost of Britain's imperial and overseas commitments while attempting to establish good relations with Germany that nevertheless fell short of a full alliance.

Salisbury remained an eccentric figure throughout his life. At one point during the Congress of Berlin Lady Salisbury admitted that her husband knew no more about the individual clerks at the Foreign Office than he did about the housemaids at Hatfield, his home. He did, however, know a great deal about the intellectual and professional qualities of Whitehall officials – and this was especially evident when it came to making senior appointments. But he could surprise them. Normally he initialled suggestions for promotions with a plain 'S'; once, however, a proposal concerning a figure of no great note came back in his box, not with the usual 'S' but with 'Mr A. beats his wife. S.'

Salisbury preferred working at the Foreign Office to Number 10. Even after he became Prime Minister, he continued to work from Scott's building, leaving Number 10 to others, including his nephew Arthur Balfour. Cabinet meetings, it seems, were held not in the Cabinet Room at Number 10 but in one of the State Rooms in the Foreign Office, which he particularly liked.

By the late 1890s Salisbury was finding the strain of doing one job, let alone two, very testing. He said in 1898: 'The work of the Foreign Office is very heavy and is getting heavier. When I first became Foreign Secretary in 1878 there was no Egypt – except diplomatic – no West Africa – no Uganda – no Zanzibar – no China to speak of!' The world had indeed multiplied in the 20-year period. A lift was installed in the Foreign Office to spare the 3rd Marquis climbing the never-ending Grand Staircase. The lift's speed matched his own pace of life. Yet, like other Secretaries of State before and after, he clung on to the job he loved. As he said in an outburst of what Andrew Roberts described as unaccustomed vanity: 'In this country there are only two extremely important appointments; one is that of Prime Minister, the other that of Foreign Secretary. For all the rest any fairly competent person will do equally well!'

Following the 'khaki' election of 1900, Salisbury was at last induced to give up the Foreign Office by the combined efforts of his senior Cabinet colleagues Balfour and Akers-Douglas, and of Queen Victoria. Akers-Douglas told Balfour in October 1900 that the Queen 'shirks from having to ask him to go', so his two Cabinet colleagues accepted the assignment. Doctors' advice and family pressure also played their part in getting him finally to consent to go. Salisbury was comforted by the fact that his son was to become Parliamentary Under Secretary, and that all telegrams and despatches would be submitted to his son before Lord Landsdowne, the new Foreign Secretary, was allowed to send them off.

EDWARD GREY (1862–1933)

Edward Grey, 1st Viscount Grey of Fallodon, occupied the Foreign Office without a break for eleven years from 1905–1916 – a stint unequalled in the twentieth century. He built on Lord Lansdowne's Anglo-French entente of 1904 and was criticised by some of his own Liberal party for merely continuing Tory foreign policy and not championing detachment from overseas alliances. But Grey, like Lansdowne and Salisbury before him, was fearful of Germany, and in 1907 he moved Britain closer to Russia. In the years leading up to the First World War Grey was criticised for secrecy and for his pro-French policy. A sense of foreboding can be detected in his famous statement looking out of his window on the eve of war. Once war came, he found his position and his authority eclipsed by Number 10, and his strength was further undermined by failing eyesight.

Alec Douglas-Home, who himself became Foreign Secretary in 1960, recalled one touching scene which encapsulates the character of the gentle Grey:

> My father greatly admired Lord Grey of Fallodon . . . When he was becoming blind, we used to go and see him taming the birds which he loved. He would sit with infinite patience until they were brave enough to come to him for food . . . The last time I visited Fallodon he had lost his sight completely and was bed-ridden. The red squirrels used to come down the chimney to visit him, and their sooty footprints were all over the sheets.

LORD CURZON (1859–1925)

The career of Marquis Curzon of Kedleston, like that of Lord Salisbury, was grounded in India. He served as Viceroy from 1898–1905, was in Lloyd George's War Cabinet in 1916, and

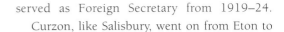

ABOVE *A portrait of Sir Edward Grey, 1915.*

served as Foreign Secretary from 1919–24. Curzon, like Salisbury, went on from Eton to Oxford, where he gained a fellowship at All Souls. An intellect, he was also frail, suffering from a painfully weak spine which needed constant surgical support. His appointment as Viceroy of India fulfilled a lifelong dream and the royal Durbar of 1903 was the high point of his personal and imperial aspirations. Two years later, after a sharp clash with Kitchener, he resigned in bitterness over the control of the Indian army.

During the decade that followed he mourned his wife and felt isolated, personally and politically. His career appeared to take off again when he was appointed Foreign Secretary, but he was only to endure further disappointments. Tensions ran high between the Foreign Office and Number 10 as Lloyd George attempted to dominate postwar foreign policy at the Paris Peace Conference and after. Lloyd George's pro-Greek policy in particular antagonised Curzon, and he was only able to display his considerable abilities fully after Lloyd George had fallen – notably at the Lausanne Conference in 1923.

Curzon, like Salisbury, had a patrician attitude towards his officials. One diplomat recalled rushing to see him, eager to relay news of the conclusion of the Anglo–Persian Agreement in 1919, only to find his enthusiasm crushed:

> I hurried to Carlton House Terrace to convey tidings which I knew would be delightful to my Chief. Lord Curzon was in his bath and refused to curtail his ablutions. I sat in the hall downstairs and wrote him notes on small pieces of paper. A footman conveyed them to the bathing statesman. They returned with damp comments. I went back to Surrey.

Curzon's relationship with his first Permanent Under Secretary, Lord Hardinge, was particularly poor, and Hardinge was mortified when Curzon succeeded Balfour as Foreign Secretary. Robert Vansittart, who himself became Permanent Under Secretary in 1930, wrote:

> To Hardinge in particular the change was grievous. He was an ex-Viceroy; so was Curzon and they detested each

other. Now the one sat as Secretary of State in the room above the other, a mere Permanent Under-Secretary. They were connected by a broad old speaking-tube, and when George blew down, Charlie blew up. The combination could not last long; thunder was too often in the air.

RAMSAY MACDONALD (1866–1937)

MacDonald was the Labour party's first foreign secretary and prime minister. A staunch critic of the Liberal government's foreign and defence policy before and during WWI, he initially aroused alarm in Whitehall when he decided, in January 1924, to combine the role of foreign secretary with that of prime minister. But the left wing had high hopes of a new direction in foreign policy and had indeed put pressure on MacDonald to take charge of the Foreign Office himself. The Russian revolution had taken place only six years earlier. Would he seek to realign British foreign policy in a Socialist direction? In office MacDonald proved more radical abroad than at home, recognis-

ing the Soviet Union. A particular success was his settling of the reparations crisis which had led to the French occupation of the German Ruhr in 1923. He also succeeded in improving relations with Italy as well as with France and Germany.

One failure, however, concerned the channel tunnel. The proposal had been in circulation since the 1880s and came to the fore again in the summer of 1924. MacDonald was personally in favour of connecting England and France but realised that the issue aroused strong emotions; he convened a meeting in London on July 1st, to which he invited all former prime ministers and Britain's most senior military leaders. Balfour, Asquith, Lloyd George and Baldwin were among those leaders who attended.

The military were of one mind: the proposal was preposterous. They argued that a tunnel would lead to the disappearance of the cross-channel steamer service, thus damaging the Royal Navy, and would inhibit the growth of the embryonic cross-channel air service, thus damaging the Royal Air Force. The top brass further argued that a tunnel would excite public fears of

ABOVE *Ramsay MacDonald, Labour's first foreign secretary, with patriotic Union Jack behind him.*

❧

LEFT *Lord Curzon by the steps leading down from Downing Street, on the north-west corner of the Foreign Office, 1922.*

invasion from marauding foreigners popping up on the English side, and the army would have to station large numbers of troops near the entrance in order to allay these fears. MacDonald noted privately:

> Presided over meeting of Committee of Imperial Defence with ex-Premiers present on subject of Channel Tunnel. Amazed at military mind. It has got itself and the country as well in a rut where neither fresh air nor new ideas blow. Like old women who seals doors & windows to keep her from shivering. My burdens are so heavy & so many that I cannot take up the Tunnel at present, but it must be taken up. Meeting most unsatisfactory.

The strain of combining both offices was beginning to tell. MacDonald had spent most of July and the first two weeks of August working without a break. On August 18th his Private Office reported to Buckingham Palace that the 'strain upon the Prime Minister during the last few weeks has been terrible' and that he had left for his home town of Lossiemouth in Scotland 'very tired'. The rest did not bring him much respite. He wrote later: 'everyday despatches and papers came and the sun forgot to shine . . . It was one of the worst summers I remember. Not once did I lie out in my whins and sun myself.' The autumn of 1924 proved no happier, and the government fell in humiliating circumstances that November. When he returned as Prime Minister in June 1929, MacDonald wisely decided to let one of his ablest lieutenants, Arthur Henderson, move into the Foreign Office. Never since has a prime minister attempted formally to combine both jobs.

AUSTEN CHAMBERLAIN (1863–1937)

Eldest son of the great imperial Liberal Unionist, Joseph Chamberlain, Austen was born with a political spoon firmly wedged into his mouth. So too was his half brother Neville, Prime Minister from 1937 to 1940.

Austen's mother died at his birth, which affected him and his relationship with his father deeply. Brought up first by grandparents and then by his father's second wife (Neville's mother), tragedy struck again when she too died in childbirth. He entered the House of Commons in 1892 and the early part of his career was spent under the shadow of his dominant father. Chancellor of

ABOVE *Arthur Henderson, Labour's second foreign secretary, having to carry his own bags and without detective support.*

'Eyre Crowe, "The Bird" [was] red-headed, crinkled, dowdy, meticulous, a conscientious agnostic with small faith in anything but his brain and his Britain.'

ROBERT VANSITTART

the Exchequer 1903–05, he first worked in the FCO building as Secretary of State for India from 1915–17, and returned to it as Foreign Secretary when Baldwin appointed him in November 1924.

'I am Secretary of State for Foreign Affairs,' he wrote. 'My garden will go to ruins and you need not expect to get a letter from me for the next four years if I survive so long.' He did indeed survive even longer, until June 1929. But it was the Locarno Treaties in his first year in office which were to be his crowning achievement. Rewarded with the Nobel Peace Prize and made Knight of the Garter for his work, he never again rose to such heights.

The initialling of the Treaties at Locarno in October 1925 was the culmination of several months of diplomacy. Despite disagreements with France almost everywhere else in the world, Britain found a way to secure France's eastern frontier against future German aggression. Germany was happy to sign, and to be welcomed back into the community of nations as an equal partner. The Locarno Treaties set up a system of mutual guarantees against aggression, and owed much to the foresight and tenacity of a remarkable Permanent Under Secretary, Eyre Crowe (1920–25), who died just months before negotiations were completed. Concluded in the small lakeside resort of Locarno in Switzerland and ratified in December in London, the agreements struck contemporaries as a wondrous event, coming so soon after the end of the Great War. Chamberlain wrote to a government colleague:

ABOVE *Austen Chamberlain pictured in 1929. He was awarded the Nobel Peace Prize after the triumphant signing of the Locarno Treaties in 1925.*

I rub my eyes and wonder whether I am dreaming when the French Foreign Minister invites the German Foreign Minister and me to celebrate my wife's birthday, and incidentally talk business, by a cruise on the Lake in a launch called Orange Blossom, habitually used by wedding parties.

Chamberlain and French Foreign Minister Aristide Briand both wept with joy during the ceremonies; the Italian fascist leader, Mussolini, kissed Mrs Chamberlain's hands; crowds danced in the streets; church bells rang out; and fireworks were vividly reflected in the lake. Baldwin wrote to Chamberlain to say that whereas November 1918 might mark the end of the Great War, October 1925 would mark the beginning of the 'great peace'. When the circus moved to London at the end of the year for the formal signing in the Foreign Office, and the tired state rooms were hurriedly prepared for the occasion, the euphoria of the Locarno spirit swept through the country. 'This morning the Locarno Pact was signed at the Foreign Office,' wrote George V in his diary. 'I pray this may mean peace for many years. Why not for ever?'

LORD HALIFAX (1881–1959)

The Locarno 'spirit' was not, alas, to last. By the late 1920s the atmosphere in Europe was beginning to darken, while under the impact of recession the voices of democracy and moderation came under attack from extremists on both the left and the right. While this sad dance was being acted out, Halifax (as Baron Irwin) was enjoying the most creative period of his life as Viceroy of India (1926–31). When he returned to Britain he would have preferred to devote himself to fox hunting and to his alma mater, Oxford, of which he became Chancellor in 1933, but he let himself be persuaded to return to politics – though it might have been better for him and for his country had he remained in Yorkshire chasing foxes.

He became Foreign Secretary in February 1938, amid talks he would be dominated by others. The Labour politician Herbert Morrison predicted that Halifax was 'a weakling who will merely be the servile instrument of an ignorant and reckless Prime Minister [Neville Chamberlain]'. Halifax had certainly done himself no favours by a meeting with Hitler in late 1937, at which he allowed himself to be impressed by the German Chancellor. The admiration, however, was not reciprocated: in 1942 Hitler told Martin Bormann that he regarded Halifax as 'a hypocrite of the worst type, a liar'.

Halifax accepted Number 10's line on appeasement and did little to press the case for rearmament. Too late in the day did he

cont. p 120

LORD HALIFAX

ABOVE *Lord Halifax photographed in 1936, in informal mode. He had a passion for hunting and country sports.*

Halifax did not always help himself in relations with colleagues and peers; in a remark that was meant flippantly but was nevertheless dutifully recorded by an assiduous private office, he told his Private Secretary on his appointment that he was 'very lazy and disliked work. Could he hunt on Saturdays?' He was in fact a hard, if spasmodic worker, though even in times of crisis he found time to leave the Foreign Office for the comfort of a good lunch. The Savoy Grill, Le Normandie and the Dorchester were favourite haunts. When unable to escape from the office he would have periodic picnics with his wife on the great desk in the Foreign Secretary's Room. Staying in was not such a great sacrifice; he liked the Foreign Office and felt at home there, surrounded by so many of his former Eton schoolmates. Not everyone felt the same. His junior minister, Rab Butler, complained of 'the old FO team where PPSs, Ministers and officials had all got OE ties and called each other by their christian names and had exactly the same brains'.

A vivid and sympathetic portrait of Lord Halifax was penned by one of his Private Secretaries at the Foreign Office, Valentine Lawford:

When Halifax moved he could be graceful and grave and shy simultaneously, like a tall water-bird wading in the shallows . . . Architecturally, the upper half of his head resembled a dome which, since it rested on more that usually jutting ears, appeared elusively to taper towards the apex.

The loftiness of the face as a whole could not cause one quite to forget an ever-present, questioning look in the eyes; and beneath a long upper lip the line of the mouth itself was expressive less of wit and irony than of a controlled and philosophical melancholy, innate and instinctive rather than acquired . . . his back and legs were magnificently straight and he looked his best astride a horse. And for one who combined proconsular talents with a reputation for almost medieval saintliness, he seemed always . . . refreshingly human and outdoor . . . Halifax's clothes were well cut, well cared for . . . and even when they were new they were slightly dated . . . though his suits were sober he was not above brightening them discreetly with a spotted tie or a patterned silk handkerchief half falling from the pocket.

LEFT *Halifax presiding over a meeting in the Foreign Office with British representatives of European capitals, 1940.*

∞

BELOW *A portrait of Lord Halifax at his window in the Foreign Secretary's Room, by Cecil Beaton, 1940.*

realise his error. He had increasing doubts, but let Prime Minister Neville Chamberlain sway him, but also Horace Wilson, the Prime Minister's influential foreign policy advisor.

Halifax greeted the coming of the Second World War, which he had sought to avoid, with stoicism. On the evening of September 2nd, with violent thunderstorms raging outside, he attended the Cabinet meeting in Number 10 which was debating the ultimatum to be sent to Hitler. He returned to the Foreign Office at 1:30 am on September 3rd, and according to Ivone Kirkpatrick, one of his senior officials, 'seemed relieved that we had taken our decision . . . he called for beer, which was brought down by a sleepy Resident Clerk in pyjamas'. He arrived at the office at 10:00 am the next day, and wrote in his diary: 'There was nothing to do'. As his biographer, Andrew Roberts, writes: 'This is an astounding remark for the British Foreign Secretary to make exactly one hour before the outbreak of the Second World War.'

Halifax would have made an appalling choice as Prime Minister in May 1940, though he was indeed a candidate to succeed Neville Chamberlain. However, Halifax declined the job. Churchill, on the other hand, accepted, and decided at first to keep Halifax at the Foreign Office. Halifax accompanied the new

Prime Minister to France on the 13 June 1940 to meet the French Supreme War Council for the last time, in an effort to stiffen their resolve. The party crossed the English Channel from Weymouth to the Channel Islands, and then on to Tours. They arrived in a thunderstorm to find the airfield had been heavily bombed the night before. The plane toured the airfield, avoiding the craters, in the hope of finding some life. As Martin Gilbert wrote: 'The Prime Minister got out and introduced himself. He said, in his best French, that his name was Churchill, that he was Prime Minister of Great Britain, and that he would be grateful for a voiture.'

The British and French delegations eventually met up, but Churchill refused to bow to the French request to make a separate peace with Germany. One account of Halifax during this desperate encounter described him as 'immensely tall, debonair, thin and loose-limbed . . . His general attitude conveyed as it always does, an impression of extreme courteousness and attention. His expression seemed slightly tinged with scepticism. I thought this was how this High Anglican would listen to a sermon on modern miracles in a Roman Catholic church'.

No divine inspiration was to save Halifax's plummeting career. Within months, Churchill was urging him to become Ambassador in Washington. Halifax suspected he was being pushed. Loyal to the end of his long fingertips, he agreed to go. He was sad to leave London, and the Foreign Office. But Washington was a wonderful embassy.

ANTHONY EDEN (1897–1977)

Anthony Eden succeeded Halifax as Foreign Secretary on 22 December 1940. He had already served as Foreign Secretary from 1935–38, was to remain at the Foreign Office throughout the war, returned as Foreign Secretary from 1951–55, and finally acted as de facto Foreign Secretary for much of his 20 months as Prime Minister (1955–57). The son of an unstable and emotionally stunted baronet father and an eccentric yet beautiful mother, he was prone to tantrums and to shouting at his officials. Poor health dogged his career, especially during the 1950s, and he suffered from years of frustration as Churchill's favoured son and heir apparent. Eden ruined his reputation by his poor judgement and deceit during the Suez Crisis in 1956. He resigned, a broken man, in January 1957, wrote three long volumes of memoirs with shiny white covers, and also a wonderful book about his childhood and the First World War, *Another World 1897-1917*, which explains, and allows one to forgive, much.

ABOVE *Anthony Eden at his desk in the Foreign Secretary's Room, photographed in 1941.*

ERNEST BEVIN (1881–1951)

ABOVE *The bust of Ernest Bevin, one of the Foreign Office staff's most favoured foreign secretaries.*

If Eden and George Brown (1966–68) were the Foreign Office's least-liked Secretaries of State since the Second World War, there is no doubting who was in pole position: Ernest Bevin. The Old Etonians and other public school diplomats had their doubts when he arrived at the Foreign Office in July 1945 as a member of Attlee's Labour government. Not only had he been a trade union leader, worrying enough in itself, but he also appeared to know nothing about foreign affairs. So why did he become such a revered figure? Donald Maitland, an admirer, explained it as follows: 'First, he carried authority; second, he listened; third, he read his papers and would write just three or four words at the bottom: fourth, diplomats realised before long that they had a world statesman.'

Born illegitimate and fatherless, Bevin grew up in extreme poverty. His mother died in 1889 when he was aged eight. Leaving school at eleven, he took casual jobs before becoming heavily involved in the Church and then in labour organisations. A brilliant negotiator and organiser, he rose through the ranks of trade unions and entered Parliament in 1940, becoming Minister of Labour until 1945. Few foreign secretaries make much difference to the course of British foreign policy, though

ABOVE *Ernest Bevin at work, surrounded by his aides, in the Foreign Secretary's Room.*

∞

RIGHT *The Foreign Secretary's Room today, with the conference table in the foreground,* aide-mémoire *on top.*

many claim to have done just that, and their biographers make the same claims. But Bevin did change the weather, and was to prove pivotal in building up a series of alliances in western Europe, culminating in the formation of NATO in 1949. He stood up to the Soviet Union and brought the United States back into Europe after the war, ensuring that Marshall Aid became an economic reality. He did not succeed in all parts of the globe; the Arab–Jew problem proved particularly intractable, even to his immense negotiating abilities.

Bevin loved the job. The first Foreign Secretary to occupy the ministerial flat on the second floor of 1 Carlton Gardens, he would rise with the birds at 4 or 5 am and work there, free from noise and disturbance. After a hearty breakfast, he would be driven across the park to arrive at the Foreign Office at about 10 am, where he worked through telegrams and papers and held meetings. After lunch he would often curl up for a nap on the notoriously hard and uncomfortable sofa, under the watchful eye of the portrait of George III. To any American visiting him he would point up and say, in mock provocation, 'you see, 'e's my 'ero'. Afternoons were often spent in the House of Commons,

'We took off from Northolt. Bevin arrived rather late and puffing a great deal. He had never been in an aeroplane before in his life and he found great difficulty first of all in getting into his seat, and even more difficulty in fastening his seat belt round him because it wouldn't go.'

NICHOLAS HENDERSON ON THE DELEGATION TO POTSDAM, 1945

but in the evenings he was keen to restrict the number of social engagements, only occasionally consenting to dine at a foreign embassy or attend an official party. On Saturdays he would work in the office until 2 or 3 pm, before going off to lunch. The Private Office always found Saturday mornings a good time to catch his attention as he was not under such heavy pressure. He didn't enjoy going to Chequers: 'You don't get enough to eat, they give you sherry in glasses the size of thimbles and the only warm room in the house is the lavatory.'

Years of hard work took their toll. By 1949/50, his weight and lack of fitness were beginning to tell. He could not fly without endangering his breathing; he would slip pills into his mouth during conferences to keep himself going; and he became irascible and illogical.

Attlee saw the end had come, and told him that he must hand over the Foreign Office to his arch enemy, Herbert Morrison, in March 1951, on Bevin's seventieth birthday. To mark the event, the Foreign Office gave him a party, described by Francis Williams:

It was a party unique in the long history of that great office of State for it was contributed to by the sixpences of all the staff: sixpence from the Permanent Under Secretary of State and from the Deputy Secretaries, from Ambassadors and Ministers and Heads of Departments. Sixpence from the messengers and typists and telephone operators and clerks. From every one of them the same: the dockers' tanner that was symbolic of so much, to a Foreign Secretary who had made himself not only admired but loved by every person in a Department of State commonly regarded as one of the most aloof and exclusive in the world.

'It was a very jolly party,' he said. 'We all stood together and enjoyed ourselves and blew out the candles and had a good time.' He was immensely touched. 'I don't think it's ever happened before,' he told me once, and then a second time when I saw him. 'You know,' he said, 'it was a wonderful thing.'

Bevin bitterly resented having to quit. As his Private Secretary wrote: 'Altogether his last few days at the Foreign Office were an unhappy time. As I saw him off the last time from the park door he looked old and frail and miserable. There was nothing I could say which could offer much comfort.' Five weeks later, in mid-April, he died in his flat while Mrs Bevin was out watching a football match.

HERBERT MORRISON (1888–1965)

At the Foreign Office, as elsewhere, it is a mistake to follow a great figure into office; one can only look pale by comparison. Herbert Morrison admittedly had little going for him; he was a towering domestic politician but rarely has any incumbent been more ignorant of the substance of foreign policy or of the methods of the diplomatic world. Harold Nicolson, the Labour politician and diarist, wrote to his wife, Vita Sackville-West, on 1 August 1951:

I am worried about Morrison. Dick Law [son of Tory Prime Minister, Bonar Law] told me that his speech on

ABOVE *Herbert Morrison in the Foreign Secretary's Room. He was a great domestic politician, but lacked expertise in foreign affairs.*

Foreign Affairs on Monday was absolutely deplorable. Everybody squirmed in agony. He pronounced the first syllable of 'Tigris' to rhyme with 'pig', and he called the Euphrates the 'You Frates', in two separate words. Now, I do not mind people pronouncing foreign names incorrectly, but to pronounce the Tigris and Euphrates in that way indicates not only lack of education, but also the fact that one has never heard the Middle East discussed by men of experience. It is that which is so terrifying.

Morrison didn't like hard work, and resented having to wade through his ministerial boxes. One of his private secretaries complained that 'He particularly resented the nightly "Box" and asked me to try to reduce the volume of reading material that went into it. This was just not possible if he was going to do the job properly, as I did not fail to point out.' Fortunately for this country, Attlee called a general election for October 1951, lost, and Morrison was out of the Foreign Office.

SELWYN LLOYD (1904–78)

Selwyn Lloyd became Foreign Secretary to the Conservative government in December 1955. He never recovered from having been Eden's junior minister when Eden was Secretary of State at the Foreign Office (1951–55). As Foreign Secretary under Eden when Eden was Prime Minister he supported the latter's belligerent and secretive diplomacy over Egypt during the 1956 Suez Crisis, despite the fact that only two of his senior officials, Ivone Kirkpatrick and Patrick Dean, agreed with the policy. Most Foreign Office officials were kept in the dark about the details of the Suez operation, and violently opposed it when the truth came out. Having allowed himself to be patronised by Eden, Selwyn Lloyd was then dominated by Harold Macmillan, who followed Eden into Number 10 in January 1957.

Lloyd was a private man who found personal relations difficult. After six months in the job, he asked one official in the Private Office, 'Why do you all dislike me?' At a meeting in Bermuda to try to repair relations with the Americans just after the Suez Crisis, he became convinced that the key lay in warming up the American Secretary of State, John Foster Dulles. He was told that Dulles liked to take an early morning swim in the sea so decided to slip on his trunks and join him. The Secretary of State was not pleased to find he had a bathing companion and Lloyd did not repeat his morning gambit.

Macmillan would describe Selwyn Lloyd as 'just a middle-class lawyer' and affected to despise him. Yet Selwyn Lloyd was loyal to a fault and worked longer hours than many foreign secretaries. By worrying away at the nuts and bolts of foreign policy, he achieved several successes, including resolving problems in Cyprus and the Formosa Straits. His five years at the Foreign Office witnessed two changes: the ending of Saturday morning work in 1956 and the demise of the bowler hat. Selwyn Lloyd was the last Foreign Secretary to come regularly into the office wearing a bowler.

GEORGE BROWN (1914–85)

Any Labour foreign secretary was bound to feel that he or she was operating under the shadow of the great Ernest Bevin. Several tried to emulate some of his traits; George Brown (1966–68) unfortunately chose the wrong trait to imitate.

ABOVE *Selwyn Lloyd at his desk in the Foreign Secretary's Room. He lacked confidence but was devoted to the job.*

∞

RIGHT *George Brown photographed during one of his more sober moments, at that famous desk.*

Bevin liked to begin his weekends, as early as Friday lunchtime, with glasses of Harvey's Bristol Cream sherry dispensed to all and sundry and, as Nicholas Henderson described it, 'plenty of follow through'. As he entered the Foreign Secretary's lift one day (a mechanism only just capable of encompassing his massive frame) he was heard to boom out: 'I'd like to make the whole darned Foreign Office tight.' George Brown was fond of his sherry. Unfortunately, he could not take it. Even one or two glasses were sufficient to render him incoherent. Private secretaries would try in vain to keep the drinks cupboard locked.

Shouting at underlings was another of his failings. If Brown happened to find something that displeased him in his ministerial box he would phone Donald Maitland, his Principal Private Secretary, at 2 am and proceed to berate him. The next day, he would appear in the office, red-faced and full of remorse. His most celebrated rudeness took place at the Paris Embassy when he told Lady Reilly, in the presence of the French Foreign Minister, that he thought her unfit to be the

Ambassador's wife. He seemed incapable of striking the right note with women, and would either appear gratuitously offensive or inappropriately amorous. Each morning, his private secretaries would gather to discuss the latest George Brown horror story. One recalled:

George was notorious for his habit of peeking down the bosom of his diplomatic hostess when, as all too often, he dined out at one of the Embassies in London. On one such morning, nobody came to report anything . . . perhaps, this time, it was too awful even for us to know. I made enquiries. It transpired that the evening before, George had dined at one of the Scandinavian Embassies; the Swedish, I think. George had caused enormous offence there. The Ambassadress in question was not

young – and George had not troubled to peek down her bosom. Prepared for the experience, she had been deeply mortified by his failure to come up to scratch.

Brown's relationship with his Permanent Under Secretary, Paul Gore-Booth, was as bad as it gets. Gore-Booth, a dignified Christian Scientist and an Old Etonian, was antithetical to Brown. He wore what the Americans call 'striped pants', and came from a different world to Brown; they shared nothing in common. Brown treated him accordingly, and when drunk would try to humiliate him in front of subordinate officials.

Brown's treatment of Gore-Booth and officials in general, on top of disparaging comments in his memoirs, *In My Way*, provoked an unprecedented protest from a diplomat in a letter to the *Times*, which said, among other things: 'The Foreign Service

ABOVE *Anthony Crosland, a man of great charm and high intelligence, but with little grasp of foreign affairs.*

LEFT *The young Alec Douglas-Home, carrying gas mask, with Sir Archibald Sinclair in 1940.*

ABOVE RIGHT *Geoffrey Howe (right) with Antony Acland unveiling a plaque at the Foreign Office in memory of members of the Diplomatic Corps who died in the line of duty, 1985.*

suffered grievously from Mr George Brown.' The author was Evelyn Shuckburgh, whose own published diaries were later clinically to dissect Eden.

Brown despised and distrusted his Prime Minister, Harold Wilson, and after one tantrum too many Wilson accepted Brown's resignation and replaced him with the reliable Michael Stewart, an underrated Foreign Secretary whose amusement on long plane journeys was to set himself mathematical problems.

LORD HOME (1903–95)

A richer contrast could scarcely be found in the Conservative Scottish aristocrat Alec Douglas-Home, whose two periods in the Foreign Office (1960–63 and 1970–74) provide dignified, elegant bookends to Brown's louche paperback foreign secretaryship. Working in harmony with Number 10, first under Macmillan and latterly under Heath, was not the least of Home's achievements. He was a man who knew foreign policy from the inside, having served as Neville Chamberlain's Parliamentary Private Secretary, and having travelled to Munich with him

to meet Hitler. He had also been junior minister at the Foreign Office in Churchill's 1945 caretaker government, then Secretary of State for Commonwealth Relations (1955–60), all of which made him one of the best prepared of all foreign secretaries since 1868.

Home was a man of tremendous charm and the Foreign Office loved him. He was decisive, courteous and knew how to enjoy himself. Fishing and shooting were two of his greatest passions. When shooting, he would arrange for one of the beaters to be at the railway station at 7.30 am to collect the boxes sent up by the Foreign Office. His Private Secretary would discuss these with him before the morning shoot and they would meet again during the picnic lunch on the moors for what colleagues described as 'reviewing the Cold War over the cold turkey'. At the end of the day, Home would spend a further hour and a half on his boxes so the telegrams could go back to London for processing overnight. Seldom has there been a more balanced or urbane foreign secretary, even if the major issues of the day – relations with the USA and the Soviet Union under Macmillan and entry into the EC under Heath – were in fact handled at the top level by Number 10.

IN MEMORY OF
MEMBERS OF H.M.
DIPLOMATIC SERVICE
VICTIMS OF TERRORISM
WHILE SERVING
THEIR COUNTRY

CHRISTOPHER EWART-BIGGS
CMG. OBE.   DUBLIN 1976
SIR RICHARD SYKES
KCMG. MC.   THE HAGUE 1979
PERCY NORRIS
OBE.   BOMBAY 1984

Tony Crosland (1918–77)

Following Wilson's surprise resignation from Number 10 in the spring of 1976, Foreign Secretary James Callaghan became Labour Prime Minister. Tony Crosland was Callaghan's choice to succeed him at the FCO. An intellectual and outstanding domestic minister, Crosland was nevertheless to prove a poor Foreign Secretary, who came in knowing little about foreign affairs and showing little determination to learn. Officials complained that he treated policy decisions like an academic exercise, assembling all the evidence and then reaching a logical conclusion. 'Foreign policy isn't like that,' said one private secretary, 'It is far more intuitive and quick decisions are often needed that don't allow for a long thought-process.' By the time of his sudden death in Oxford in February 1977, Crosland was beginning to enjoy the work and might well have turned into an effective Foreign Secretary, but nine months in office was not enough, and Callaghan reflected at the time that the biggest surprise and disappointment in his Cabinet had been Crosland.

David Owen (1938–)

At 38 David Owen was the century's youngest foreign secretary. It was a brave appointment by Callaghan but one in a sense forced on him. Other candidates had ruled themselves out by being too ardent or antipathetic to the European Community, while the most experienced candidate, Denis Healey, was ensconced at the Treasury.

Owen had the makings of a great Foreign Secretary. He had in many ways the most creative mind of any incumbent of the previous 40 years. But it was to be a traumatic two years, in which relations within the FCO as a whole reached a very low ebb. Owen was partly to blame. He was insecure and needed more help and support than he let on. He appeared often graceless and failed with the small courtesies and 'thank yous' which go down well in the Foreign Office and at embassies abroad. Naturally combative, as was his wife, the literary agent Deborah Owen, his rebarbative manner went down badly with the smooth FCO mandarins. 'They were used to foreign secretaries placidly agreeing with papers put up to them and they found it difficult to adjust to someone who questioned everything,' said one diplomat. Few in the FCO knew that Owen was up many nights looking after his seriously ill child.

Nor did the FCO handle Owen well. Michael Palliser, the Permanent Under Secretary, was an old-style mandarin who was affronted by Owen's manner. Policy over Rhodesia was the biggest issue that divided Owen and his officials. Owen pursued his own radical policy and felt that the FCO had failed to back him up: 'At the Ministry of Health,' he was heard to say, 'officials acted on my policy; here they don't.'

ABOVE Lord Carrington, as Foreign Secretary, flanked by Margaret Thatcher and Douglas Hurd.

He mellowed barely at all over the two years he was in office and the atmosphere in the FCO remained tense. But he had a good relationship with his Private Office. As one private secretary said, 'It took me three months to realise that actually he was a very decent man who insisted on behaving like a shit.'

GEOFFREY HOWE (1926–)

Two relatively short-lasting Secretaries of State came between Owen's departure and Geoffrey Howe's appointment as Foreign Secretary in 1983. The first was Lord Carrington, who presided over the Zimbabwe settlement. A man of honour, he resigned over the failure to anticipate the Argentine invasion of the Falkland Islands in 1982. Carrington had ambitions to restore the splendour of the Foreign Secretary's Room, but was sidetracked from the task by the demands of monetarist economics and achieved little more than replacing Owen's puritanical portrait of Oliver Cromwell by the painting of a Nepalese prince.

Carrington was as businesslike as Owen but knew how to charm people and lighten the atmosphere. After an oleaginous and immaculate senior mandarin had left his office, he sighed, 'If only that man would have had a hole in his sock.' He had mixed feelings about Mrs Thatcher and when asked 'What might happen if Mrs Thatcher should be run over by a bus?'

replied: 'The bus wouldn't dare.' He was followed by Francis Pym, one of the more laid-back foreign secretaries, who disliked Mrs Thatcher, and she him.

Geoffrey Howe was appointed after the Conservative general election of 1983. He had been a successful and courageous Chancellor of the Exchequer since 1979 and had forged a very close working relationship with Mrs Thatcher. Like Selwyn Lloyd he was a meticulous lawyer and loyal to a fault, but unlike Lloyd, he had a creative mind and a surprising charm. He and his wife, Elspeth, loved entertaining and they used their country home Chevening to particularly good effect. Officials liked him and admired his grasp of detail. His Private Office was amused when his red boxes, brought over from Carlton Gardens in the morning, were opened, to find that his neat annotations in red ink (a foreign secretary's privilege) would occasionally slide in a straight line off the page. He had presumably fallen asleep at that point. Regularly awake at 2 am in the morning, Howe would relish overnight flights as a chance to catch up on work.

His achievements were many: in Hong Kong, the Near East, Southern Africa and in the improving relations with the Soviet Union. But relations with Number 10 were worse than during

ABOVE Queen Elizabeth II with Foreign Secretary Francis Pym and a young Douglas Hurd, then Minister of State, who would go on to hold Pym's post, in the Foreign Secretary's Room.

any protracted period in the postwar world. Mrs Thatcher became increasingly uneasy with Howe's pro-European views and was irritated by his style of business which she considered ponderous, overly legalistic and cautious. She humiliated him in Cabinet and in meetings with guests, and by the late 1980s had lost confidence in him. Charles Powell, the Private Secretary for Foreign Affairs at Number 10, made matters worse; preferring to keep the reins in his own hands, he had no interest in bridging the widening gulf across Downing Street and by the late 1980s few officials from the FCO were being invited across into Number 10 to meet the Prime Minister. Attempts from the highest levels of the Civil Service to move Powell on were repelled by Thatcher, and it was left to Antony Acland, then Permanent Under Secretary at the FCO, to salvage what he could of the relationship with Number 10. A head-on clash was inevitable

and it came over Europe. Howe's resignation and his courageous speech to the Commons were mortal blows that played their part in felling Thatcher a few weeks later.

DOUGLAS HURD (1930–)

Hurd had entered the Foreign Office as a young diplomat in 1952 and served for 14 years until leaving the service in 1966 to join the Conservative party. As Political Secretary at Number 10 from 1970–74 he became one of Heath's most influential aides and held a variety of ministerial posts under Mrs Thatcher,

though she had held out against giving him the one job he craved: the FCO. So it was with some interest that observers watched his performance over his first two months. No one doubted his command of foreign affairs or his considerable skills as a minister, but would Mrs Thatcher be able to work with him? The answer was 'yes and no'. Relations between Number 10 and the FCO had already improved during John Major's three months' stint in the job in the summer of 1989. They continued to thaw under Hurd, but Mrs Thatcher's fixation with Europe and her growing bunker mentality did not make the bonding exercise easy.

ABOVE *Queen Elizabeth II on the Grand Staircase during her visit to mark the bicentenary of the Foreign and Commonwealth Office in 1982. Next to her is Francis Pym, Foreign Secretary at the time.*

Hurd was more of a broad-picture man than Howe; he would leave the detail to others if he trusted the official or minister concerned. Having already worked in the Foreign Office, he came in with none of the suspicions or the macho need to prove himself that had encumbered some of his predecessors. His mind was unusual – as one might glean from his penchant for writing thrillers with names like *The Smile on the Face of the*

ABOVE *Foreign Secretary Robin Cook, pictured with his wife Gaynor.*

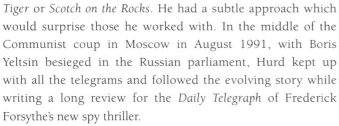

RIGHT *An example of the Foreign Secretary's engagements for one day in 2000.*

Secretary of State's Engagements

Thursday 17 February

0800	Breakfast with EU High Representative for Foreign and Security Policy, Javier Solana [1CG]
0915	Attorney General and Defence Secretary [FCO]
1030	Cabinet [No 10]
1145	Russian Ambassador Fokine [FCO]
1415	Bosnian High Representative Wolfgang Petritsch [FCO]
1445	Danish Foreign Minister Helveg Petersen[FCO]
1600	Bilateral with Prime Minister [No 10]
1700	Deputy Prime Minister John Prescott [Room 21a, HoC]
1900	/// TO VOTE

Tiger or *Scotch on the Rocks*. He had a subtle approach which would surprise those he worked with. In the middle of the Communist coup in Moscow in August 1991, with Boris Yeltsin besieged in the Russian parliament, Hurd kept up with all the telegrams and followed the evolving story while writing a long review for the *Daily Telegraph* of Frederick Forsythe's new spy thriller.

Hurd liked personal diplomacy, which means he liked talking to people. He would frequently be on the phone to his opposite numbers abroad and would meet people face to face when he could. In his first year in office, he travelled 130,000 miles by air. He became a connoisseur of embassy swimming pools: 'The pool at Washington was rather nice. Then there was the Cairo pool, the Abu-Dhabi pool, the Pretoria pool . . . the Roman swimming pool was built by Hitler. The Germans were in the Embassy and Hitler became fed up hearing his Ambassador complain about the heat.' Amidst all this he found time to become a close personal friend of John Major, and after Chris Patten's appointment to Hong Kong in mid-1992 became the Prime Minister's most trusted aide. Major left most foreign policy issues to Hurd, though not East–West relations nor Ireland. Relations with the EU and discussions over the Balkans dominated much of Major's premiership, and here both men shared responsibility.

ROBIN COOK (1946–)

Robin Cook is the longest-serving Labour foreign secretary since Bevin, a man he admired so much that he moved his hero's bust from 1 Carlton Gardens, where it had been carefully placed in the conservatory during the 1990s renovation, into his room in the FCO.

Cook became one of the steadiest performers in Blair's first team. He clearly relished the job, and with his incisive mind, cut through the work quickly. The Foreign Secretary currently has six red boxes for his papers, of which at least four are in use at any one time. Within the box are a number of coloured folders. One contains a daily briefing and a schedule for the following day's appointments, another contains material from GCHQ/MI6, labelled 'Top Secret', another letters for signature and a fourth, on Wednesday nights, contains Cabinet papers for the next day and the most important telegrams, placed there by the Private Office. On one occasion Cook worked through to the bottom of his box to find a dried-up piece of mangetout. He wondered if this was a device used by the Private Office to test whether he had finished all his work! Interim assessments are notoriously difficult: time alone will tell whether Cook will fit more readily into the successful, the colourful or the eccentric box.

CARLTON GARDENS

BRITAIN'S MOST SENIOR CABINET MINISTERS are given official London residences during their tenures of office. The Prime Minister has Number 10 Downing Street and the Chancellor of the Exchequer Number 11 next door, symbolic of their close relationship. But the Foreign Secretary has the best perks of office. Not only does he have the most palatial office and department of the three, but his residence, 1 Carlton Gardens, easily eclipses that of the Prime Minister and the Chancellor, both for its pleasing unity of design, and for the space and comfort of its private accommodation. The house has been the Foreign Secretary's official residence since 1947.

NASH'S BUILDING

ABOVE *The impressive State Dining Room, furnished in Regency mahogany. The chairs date back to King George III.*
PREVIOUS PAGE *The Entrance Hall, oddly reminiscent of Number 10.*

John Nash, architect and town planner, was born in London in 1752. He is remembered especially for designing and building houses in London faced with stucco. His career blossomed with his close association with the Prince Regent, and in 1815 he began work remodelling the 'Marine Pavilion' (later the Royal Pavilion) in Brighton. Regent's Park, from 1811, and Regent's Street were two of his main London projects, though nothing remains of his Regent's Street except All Souls at Langham Place, the church of the BBC. Nash's career peaked late in life when the Prince Regent came to the throne as George IV (1820–30). Alterations to Clarence House were followed by the extravagant redevelopment of Buckingham Palace. However, after George's death his career declined, and he died in 1835, aged eighty-three.

Carlton House Terrace was built to the designs of Nash between 1827 and 1830. Carlton Gardens was added between 1830 and 1833, at its western end.

The two immense Regency terraces face St James's Park, on the north side of the Mall between Trafalgar Square and Buckingham Palace. They can be seen in their context on the old and contemporary aerial photographs on pages 38–9. Four semi-detached houses were erected behind the terraces, surrounding ornamental gardens, as part of the redevelopment of the area hitherto occupied by the Prince Regent's residence, Carlton House.

By 1820 Carlton House, dilapidated beyond retrieval, had been superseded by Buckingham Palace as the Royal Residence. Numbers 1 to 4 Carlton Gardens were built of similar three-storey design, but with individual details. Numbers 1 and 2, for example, have graceful bow windows which allow their principal rooms to look across to Westminster.

EARLY OWNERS

Carlton Gardens was built for Sir Alexander Cray Grant, a prominent member of Parliament. In 1827 the Crown Estate Commissioners instructed Nash to 'start at the ground' and furnish Sir Alexander with 'copies of the design, plans and specification to be adopted for your intended house'. He insisted on elements of individuality for Number 1, including 'extending the first-floor balcony beyond the bow of his house', and the addition of a portico entrance. After all his fussing about the contract, Sir Alexander was to occupy the house for just one year before it passed to Lord Goderich, the former Chancellor of the Exchequer, in 1831. Goderich's family was to occupy the house until 1885, and during this time the house was leased to Prince Louis Napoleon when in exile from France, 1839–40.

The house was altered periodically by a succession of owners over the next 100 years. One notable change was the building in 1859 of a conservatory over the porch, occupying the full height of the first floor, with a glazed canopy ceiling. In 1911 Lord Inchcape purchased the house for £20,000; his modernising changes included the building of a projecting bay on the western elevation to house a four-passenger 'Waygood' lift serving all floors. In 1918 the newspaper tycoon Alfred C W Harmsworth, later Lord Northcliffe, bought the house for £32,000. By 1922 he had become seriously ill, and the house became a 'one patient hospital'. To provide some solace, friends suggested erecting a 'revolving shelter' on the roof to enable him to enjoy the air and view of London. But the roof was found to be unsuitable for the unusual structure, and it was erected on the roof of Number 2 Carlton Gardens instead. Harmsworth died in August of that year, and the house was again put on the market, described thus:

RIGHT *Detail of the main staircase. Perhaps the most striking feature of the house is the balustrade, with its elaborate acanthus scrolls made of bronze and brass.*

※

BELOW *The beautiful tapestry and side table in the Entrance Hall.*

A corner residence commanding an uninterrupted view over the gardens of Clarence House at the rear and having a private garden at the front. The accommodation is situated on three floors and comprises: Lounge, 5 Entertaining Rooms, 14 Bedrooms and Dressing Rooms, 5 Bathrooms and offices. Offers £45,000.

Considerable interest was shown in the property. After further changes in ownership, the house was in the possession of Lord Bearstead when it suffered bomb damage in 1940 during the Blitz. High explosive bombs damaged every floor and a hole was left in the roof. When the RAC Club in Pall Mall was hit by high explosives on 16th November, the bedrooms of 1 Carlton Gardens facing it had their windows blown in and walls and ceilings cracked. The front of the house suffered particularly badly, with the first-floor canopy partially blown in and the stucco facing badly cracked. Lord Bearstead moved out and the house was pronounced unfit for habitation until repairs could be completed. The Ministry of Works, the government department responsible for official buildings, took over temporary tenancy of the house while its future could be settled. Parts of the building were used by the Wireless Corps, and it also provided space for the Free French government, under General de Gaulle. In February 1944 Number 1 again suffered bomb damage, though the French, undaunted, continued to use the rooms (and also Numbers 2 and 3 Carlton Gardens), until 1946.

THE FOREIGN SECRETARY TAKES OVER

While the war was still raging, the question was raised as to where the Foreign Secretary should live in London when peace came. The time was deemed right to provide the Foreign Secretary with an official residence. The Ministry of Works began a search, noting that Britain had 'never provided our Secretary of State with a house'. Various properties, including Lord Courtauld-Thomson's Dorneywood, given to the country in 1942, were considered. The search was spurred on by Ernest Bevin (Foreign Secretary 1945–51), who considered his flat at the top of Downing Street grossly inadequate. What was required was 'an equivalent of Number 10 Downing Street'. In June 1946, 1 Carlton Gardens came available, and the Ministry of Works duly reported to the Government that the house would provide 'very dignified accommodation for official entertaining', and that the third floor could be adapted to provide 'quiet and comfortable living accommodation'. By August 1946 work had already begun on the 'shrapnel-pitted house'.

Extensive structural damage, caused not least by the bombs, meant the work had to be urgently carried out. Seventy men were employed on the project, and it was completed on time, if not within budget, for Bevin to take up residence in January 1947. The top (third) floor was greatly changed to create the private residence, and a new staircase constructed in place of the former linen cupboard to provide secluded access. A third bathroom was put in, and new bedrooms created and modernised. The second floor received even more extensive alteration, and a new entrance to its official rooms was built. The former principal bedroom became the Dining Room, the south-facing Corner Room was restored to its original size to form the Drawing Room, and the Dressing Room became the Study. A new wood-block floor and carpets replaced the existing flooring. Much work was carried out on the kitchens and sanitary facilities to cater for the large number of anticipated visitors. Apart from some minor changes in the 1970s, the house was to remain largely unaltered until the 1990s.

ABOVE *One of a pair of George III side tables, with gilt-wood mirror above.*

∽

LEFT *An English neo-classical chimneypiece in the Blue Drawing Room.*

The house into which Bevin moved had the staircase as its principal feature, as it had been when the house had been built. The balustrade was made of bronze with brass enrichments, and is very similar to Nash's grand staircase in Buckingham Palace. The State Dining Room led off to the left, and was furnished in mahogany. Opposite the fireplace, a pair of veneered doors with ormolu mounts leads off to the Small Dining Room – in unconscious imitation of Number 10, which also contains large and small State Dining Rooms (the work of John Soane, dating from the 1820s). On the first floor, the Smoking Room contained an array of antiques. Next door was the Blue Drawing Room (originally the Great Drawing Room), decorated in powder blue and picked out in gilt. The decoration gave the room a Georgian feel, in contrast to the smaller White Drawing Room, reached through double doors, which took one back to the reign of Queen Anne. Bevin relished the specially altered house, and found it eased his life considerably. According to his Private Secretary, Roderick Barclay, Bevin found the house:

pleasantly furnished and equipped by the Ministry of Works and was, of course, conveniently close to the Foreign Office. It was very useful for informal meetings with British and foreign colleagues out of normal office hours . . . The ground floor and first floor of the house

were available for luncheon and dinner parties or receptions, and these too became very familiar. The flat was to be the Bevins' home until after his death . . . Mr Bevin normally began his day's work at between 4 and 5 am and reckoned to spend three hours or more on his papers before breakfast . . . every evening a messenger from the Foreign Office would take over to Number 1 Carlton Gardens a black box containing the latest telegrams and all the papers he needed for the work of the coming day.

Although Bevin's brief successor, Herbert Morrison, did not occupy 1 Carlton Gardens, preferring instead to remain, with the permission of the Prime Minister, Clement Attlee, at 11 Downing Street, most foreign secretaries since have taken advantage of the official residence.

On the fall of Edward Heath's Conservative Government in 1974, the builders moved back in. Most of the work concentrated on the private residence – partition walls were removed and modernisation undertaken. The house remained unoccupied until 1979.

RIGHT *The ceiling, door panels and skirtings in the Blue Drawing Room are all Victorian. The panelling and cornice have been placed there later in an attempt to make it look more Georgian.*

ABOVE *View from the State Dining Room into the Small Dining Room, which is furnished in Georgian and Regency style. The furniture includes 14 walnut chairs and a kingwood cabinet.*

ABOVE AND RIGHT *Details of the Smoking Room showing the beautiful plasterwork. On the mantelpiece are copies of the famous Wedgewood Portland vase, brought to England by Sir William Hamilton, George III's Ambassador in Naples.*

In 1979 Lord Privy Seal, Ian Gilmour, and not the Foreign Secretary, became the new occupant; returning to the practice of earlier and more aristocratic years, Lord Carrington (1979–82) preferred to live and entertain from his own London home. The status quo was re-established after Francis Pym became Foreign Secretary.

Geoffrey Howe was Foreign Secretary from 1983 to 1989, after having been Chancellor of the Exchequer:

> *I didn't find 1 Carlton Gardens as useful as Number 11 because Number 11 was physically closer to the Treasury. I couldn't summon people across to meetings as I did in Number 11: it was just too far. Its relative distance and seclusion across the park, however, did mean it was useful for more discreet meetings. It was also a good place for entertaining, especially on a more intimate basis than at the Foreign Office or Lancaster House. It was also a little more exclusive than Number 11, being physically separated from Number 10, and not giving one the feeling of 'living above the shop'. I would have my boxes brought over at night and would work on them until they were all done.*

Douglas Hurd formed a deep affection for the house and lived there during the week with his young family.

> *It was a marvellous place, I worked at my desk in the Dining Room. I had a '1 o'clock rule': I just had to go to bed. The first two floors were used for official business, not family, although on my son's sixth birthday we played cricket in the Blue Drawing Room, hugely dangerous with all the pictures and all the glass. But it was just about the right length for a child's cricket pitch, I am afraid to say, and it was too good an opportunity to pass by.*

Hurd was particularly close to John Major when the latter was Prime Minister. Major would periodically come across the park for discussions over breakfast: 'He could never understand how we ever managed to concentrate with all the hubbub of the children being packed off to school.'

ABOVE *The conservatory, with its recently restored domed glass roof. The busts of Bevin and the Duke of Wellington were placed here during the 1990s restoration.*

Robin Cook moved into the house in May 1997. In the conservatory he noticed a glint of metal which turned out to be a bust of Bevin. He has now had this taken across to the Foreign Secretary's Room in the Foreign Office. Cook is much keener on exercise than his illustrious, if generously proportioned, predecessor, and walks across St James's Park each morning to the office, a journey that takes him seven minutes. The amount of foreign travel involved is just one of the changes in a foreign secretary's life over the last fifty years: Cook has to be out of the country on average two working days out of every five; he thus relishes all the more the time he is able to spend at Carlton Gardens.

1990s REFURBISHMENT

A report into the building in 1990 concluded that 'the property had never been fully repaired or restored following the bomb damage it suffered in the Second World War'. The report found the level of repair and maintenance to be inadequate, and that layers of paint 'disguised' fundamental problems. The basements were of particular concern, and the build quality of Nash also came under attack. A memo to Douglas Hurd soon after his arrival in office proposed some fundamental work on the building to restore it to health but also to make it more elegant by removing some fairly coarse Ministry of Works adaptations. Hurd responded enthusiastically, but little appreciated how much his life was to be disrupted, with builders working for two years round him and his family. At one point he telephoned David Brown, the FCO official overseeing the work, to enquire when the work might be completed on their private bathroom, as one of the workers had just drilled through the bathroom wall.

The house eventually emerged, structurally more sound, treated for damp, its fireplaces restored and window sashes repaired. The doors had the paint stripped off back to the walnut and other wood surfaces. The grand staircase was repainted the correct dark green instead of black, and the spindles repaired. Outside, in keeping with the original intent, a courtyard with a gateway was created. Now the Foreign Secretary even had his own gates to rival those protecting the Prime Minister at the entrance to Downing Street.

HOME AND ABROAD

IN THE DAYS BEFORE the telegraph and the train, in the early nineteenth century, Britain's ambassadors in far-flung posts would take decisions as if they were the monarch, or later the government, especially in times of crisis or where speed was of the essence. In the 1950s jet aeroplanes and telephone diplomacy speeded up communications between national leaders. From the 1990s immediate electronic information exchange in 'real time' became possible. This did not, however, render overseas embassies or high commissions (as they are called in Commonwealth countries) redundant. Although instructions can now be received instantaneously, this has not nullified the value of personal diplomacy.

THE LIFE OF THE AMBASSADOR

Having 'our man' or 'our woman' (an increasing number) on the spot, helps ensure that British interests will be advanced in the overseas country, and ensures that a regular flow of information of importance to Britain's national interest flows back into the FCO. Overseas posts provide a platform for entertaining, showing off and conveying to the host country a sense of Britain's status, history and importance. They allow face-to-face lobbying, giving diplomats on the spot the chance to talk confidentially to politicians and other influential figures. The Ambassador or High Commissioner can argue Britain's case in the national media, defending it in the country's language. Increasingly, embassies and high commissions advance Britain's commercial interests while the British consulates provide vital assistance for subjects abroad. Much of the work of embassies and high commissions is, in fact, with the Treasury and Trade departments in London, and with the Ministry of Defence; not just with the FCO.

Posts vary in size: from Minsk, where two people are employed, to the British Embassy in Washington, which employs 58 FCO-funded staff and 186 local people. Washington has been the career goal of many diplomats. It is an enticing, high-profile appointment, and though no longer rated the most senior overseas post – which is that of the UK Representative to the European Union in Brussels – it comes second equal in the hierarchy, alongside Paris, Berlin and the UK representative to the UN in New York. Washington and Paris, are not, however, typical of most missions abroad. Many are not at all grand, and the descriptions in this chapter are by no means representative.

ABOVE *Lutyens was commissioned to create an embassy with an English feel but which would be able comfortably to accommodate the ever-increasing numbers employed there.*

THE BRITISH EMBASSY IN WASHINGTON

The first full British ambassador to Washington, Lord Pauncefote, was appointed in March 1893. He lived in a modest embassy, situated in a Washington unrecognisable today but described by Harold Nicolson as still recapturing 'the charm of a provincial, almost a county, capital', while 'the house, with its balconies, its bow-windows and its sun-blind, produced the effect of a large villa at Newport'.

Henry Hopkinson, a diplomat, described the Embassy:

The British Embassy which I knew was a large white Victorian building dating from 1874 at the corner of Connecticut Avenue and N Street. It had big rooms for entertaining and a vast ballroom. A small wing consisting of my office and three small rooms had housed the whole chancery in days gone by, but now the office's lay across a courtyard at the back and looked like a wartime camp with two long wooden army huts and a brick entrance. It was high time the whole thing came down.

Almost as soon as the embassy had been chosen, it became clear that with America's mounting importance, and the growing potential for Anglo–US relations, the Embassy was inadequate for its task. The decisive entry of the United States into World War I in 1917, the Washington Conference of November 1921–February 1922, and the United States' retreat into isolationism, all suggested the need for a grander British presence in Washington. As Nicolson wrote:

It was felt after the first war that this gay but suburban residence did not correspond to the ever-increasing importance assumed by our representation in the United States. Sir Edwin Lutyens was entrusted with the task of designing an Embassy which, while providing office accommodation for an expanding staff, would at the same time be English in character and afford opportunities for lavish entertainment.

Hopkinson describes inspecting the site for the new embassy:

The ambassador decided to take a last look at it before finally signing the purchase deed. It lay alongside the

ABOVE, RIGHT AND BELOW *The embassy that Lutyens built is a fine red brick stone-faced building in the early Georgian style. Lutyens was a stickler for detail and applied utmost attention to every facet of the embassy complex. These photographs date from 1930.*

already heavy traffic of Massachusetts Avenue below the Naval Observatory. Surprisingly the whole area was still covered with thick scrub and bushes. We found that the only way he and I could reach it comfortably was on horseback, pushing the branches out of our faces as we went up the narrow path.

Shortly after Edwin Lutyens was commissioned by the Baldwin Government in 1925 he visited the site in person. Lutyens' reputation was at its height. He was working concurrently on the design and construction of the Viceroy's Palace and offices in New Delhi, and had recently completed the Cenotaph outside the Home Office in Whitehall. Although in his career he was responsible for over 300 buildings across the world, this was to be his only building in the United States. He took to the commission with relish, despite all his other assignments. By 1927 he had completed 68 sheets of drawings, and the following year travelled to Washington to witness the laying of the foundation stone.

Hopkinson describes Lutyens' intent:

Lutyens was full of charm but quite determined to stick to his own ideas of what the Embassy should be – a grand English country house inside and out. It was to be a fine red brick stone-faced building in early Georgian style. The front was to look out in a straight line across the White House to the Capitol. He insisted that no bedroom should have direct access to a bathroom and the interior wall heating on which he also insisted would make this impossible to change. The Ambassador's loo was so built that his successor, Sir Ronald Lindsay, who was six foot seven, had the greatest difficulty in making use of it at all. The garage was long enough to house the old embassy Cadillac but not Sir Ronald's new Rolls-Royce.

Not until after 1940, however, did the new embassy fully come into its own. America's isolationism between the wars had reduced the need for international diplomacy. After F D Roosevelt's re-election in November 1940, and the US entry into

the war in December 1941, the British Embassy became a throbbing centre of activity. There was a rapid shift from London to Washington of many key war decisions; military, scientific, intelligence and economic collaboration bound the two countries closely together. The Embassy was the hub of this unique collaboration, and by 1945 there were 9,000 personnel working for it. But the pattern of the future imbalance in the relationship was already discernible during the war. As Eden wrote on 10 September 1943, hinting also at the tensions between the Foreign Office and Number 10 that runs as a leitmotif throughout the years:

I felt depressed and not very well all day, partly, I think, because of the exasperating difficulty of trying to do business with Winston over the Atlantic . . . I am most anxious for good relations with the US but I don't like subservience to them and I am sure that this only lays up trouble for us in the future. We are giving the impression, which they are only too ready by nature to endorse, that militarily all the achievements are theirs and W [Churchill], by prolonging his stay in Washington, strengthens that impression.

After 1945 the British wanted the relationship to remain; Washington was less convinced of the need, though the Embassy was to play a seminal role in concluding the North Atlantic Treaty in 1949. Nevertheless, when Churchill travelled to Washington shortly after returning as Prime Minister in October 1951, he stayed, indicatively, not at the White House as he had done during the war, but at the Embassy. His first day in Washington saw him on the Potomac River on President Truman's yacht. Churchill's doctor, Lord Moran, wrote: 'when he returned to the Embassy in the small hours, [we] were startled to find something like the Winston Churchill we had half forgotten. He was full of the evening. "Oh, I enjoyed it so much; we talked as equals".'

But three days later, the razor-sharp British Ambassador, Oliver Franks, had discovered Churchill's egalitarian feelings were not reciprocated: '. . . the Ambassador put his head through the door. He began by saying he was afraid he had been a poor host, and then he came to the point. He does not want the PM to outstay his welcome in Washington.'

> '*I have spent most of the day preparing for Francis Pym's visit (he arrives on the 15th) about which I am probably over-fussy having an idée fixe about the attention MPs and ministers expect from Embassies. What ministerial, parliamentary and official visitors require of an Embassy is not only advice or analysis about the political scene or expertise on this or that topical subject, but transport, food, drink and newspapers.*'
>
> NICHOLAS HENDERSON, AMBASSADOR IN WASHINGTON 1979–82, ON MORE HUMDRUM ASPECTS OF LIFE.

Anglo–US Relations reached an all-time nadir during the Suez Crisis in 1956, not helped by the extraordinary, though preplanned, departure of the emollient Ambassador Roger Makins (1952–56) in October, and by the decision of his novice successor Harold Caccia (1956–61) to travel out by sea, the month before fighting broke out in Egypt. The Americans sabotaged the British military strategy, and the Embassy was frozen out. Only when Macmillan succeeded Eden as Prime Minister in January 1957 did the relationship once again begin to improve.

A high point of embassy influence arrived when David Ormsby Gore was made Ambassador to the USA following Kennedy's becoming President in January 1961. Ormsby Gore, of whom Kennedy said 'I trust David as I would my own cabinet', became a frequent visitor at the White House and to the Kennedy's family retreat on Cape Cod. His advice during the 1962 Cuban Missile Crisis was crucial to the outcome.

The Embassy lost its pivotal position after Kennedy's death in November 1963, after which Ormsby Gore became a marginal figure. Replaced by Patrick Dean in April 1965, he died later in a car accident. Anglo–US relations were not close under either Prime Minister Wilson (1964–70) or Heath (1970–74), and were affected, too, by British coolness to America's involvement in the Vietnam War, which for ten years dominated US foreign policy.

With Mrs Thatcher's arrival as Prime Minister in May 1979, and Ronald Reagan's as President in January 1981, the relationship warmed considerably. During the Falklands War of 1982, British Ambassador Nicholas Henderson (1979–82) worked

BELOW *On the main staircase in the Entrance Hall are placed several chairs which are covered with the same blue damask that was used in Westminster Abbey for the coronation of Queen Elizabeth II.*

hard with the UK's Representative at the UN in New York, Anthony Parsons, to keep the Americans on side. Henderson's championing of British policy in the US media at this time was particularly effective.

Mrs Thatcher loved to visit Washington and to stay at the Embassy. Ambassador Oliver Wright (1982–86) recalled how when she flew into the Embassy late at night with her exhausted staff she would want to settle down and talk long into the night. 'When Denis was there he would help get her to bed at a sensible time.'

BELOW *The most impressive features of the Dining Room are the cascading chandelier, and the stunning mahogany table.*

The Anglo–US relationship flared into life again during the Gulf War. George Bush had felt lukewarm about Mrs Thatcher but enjoyed the company of John Major, and the shared objectives of the war, its conduct and ending, helped the relationship. As Antony Acland (Ambassador, 1986–1991) put it, the Gulf War showed the Americans that 'when the chips were down, there was only one wholly reliable ally!'.

London–Washington relations cooled during the Major–Clinton years, with differences over Northern Ireland and the Balkans coming to the fore. The Embassy became pivotal once more under Ambassador Christopher Meyer, after the way had been paved for the close Blair–Clinton relationship by Jonathan Powell, Blair's Chief of Staff, who served at the Embassy 1991–95.

The British Embassy, with some 20 subsidiary missions across the United States, is always active, working to advance British interests there, but experience shows how often it is personal chemistry and inclinations that decide how central the Embassy is to be in the Washington community.

The site chosen for the Embassy occupies just 1.6 ha/4 acres below the Observatory summit of Massachusetts Avenue, and it lies in one of Washington's most exclusive residential areas. Lutyens unquestionably created the grandest building on the street, which contains many other diplomatic buildings. After the Second World War, it became apparent that more space was needed, and in the late 1950s the Embassy offices were transferred to a new and unacceptably pedestrian building in the grounds next door. The space vacated was converted into staff apartments and rooms for visitors.

The Residence is one of the grandest of any British Ambassador. Lutyens' design is like a smaller version of the Viceroy's palace in New Delhi, with many similar features and fittings, including door handles, mirrors, columns and high ceilings. But it also had distinct echoes of his beloved English country house and garden style, reminiscent of the Queen Anne period.

BELOW Looking south through the ballroom and out to the garden. The room can accommodate several hundred guests and has been the scene of some of Washington's most glittering social events.

Lutyens was a stickler for detail. The red bricks on the exterior elevations were of non-standard size and had to be specially made in Pennsylvania to resemble those used in Britain in the sixteenth century. The high roofs, crowned by tall brick chimneys bearing the royal cipher, are one of the building's most distinctive features. Lutyens joined the Residence to the original offices by a bridge which carries the Ambassador's Library and also serves as his study, and this is one of the glories of the building. Part of the Residence's success lies in Lutyens' skill in designing a building perfect for entertaining on a grand scale but one which the Ambassador and his wife would feel was their home.

Many ambassadors have left their mark on the building. The last major redecoration of the Residence took place under Lady Henderson, wife of Nicholas Henderson. Six interior designers and many British manufacturers helped her create 'the British Embassy showcase', which was formally opened by HRH Princess Alexandra in May 1982. The custom has now grown up for one major room or area to be redecorated each year.

Entering the Residence, the most striking impression is of the flying arch formed by the twin limestone staircases that lead up to the main floor and reception rooms. The largest room upstairs is the Ballroom, with its four columns at one end painted to resemble scagliola, a composition marble used extensively in great eighteenth-century houses. In this room, Queen Elizabeth II gave a banquet for President Bush during her state visit in 1991. The Ballroom is also used for large receptions for up to 500 people, for dinners, concerts, lectures, press conferences and dances. The Drawing Room has a typical Lutyens mantelpiece as well as Chippendale mirrors, and the Dining Room has walnut chairs and a mahogany dining room table which can seat 34. The silver cutlery and candelabra were once in the British Embassies at Lisbon and The Hague, and were brought to Washington in 1893 when the legation was upgraded to an embassy. The bedrooms and sitting rooms are all named after former ambassadors, beginning with Sir Esme Howard (1924–30), the first to live in the Residence. Some of the eight principal bedrooms have their own sitting rooms, and most rooms have oil paintings, watercolours or prints lent to the Residence, principally by the families of two former ambassadors, Lord Bryce (1907–13) and Lord Halifax (1941–46).

The formal gardens were also designed by Lutyens, though they bear the influence of his collaborator, Gertrude Jekyll; the straight paths, stone steps and an enclosed rose garden are typical of their partnership. The Rose Garden is famous in Washington, not least for its striking splashes of colour created

ABOVE *The Chancery.*

ABOVE *An external view of the Library.*

∞

LEFT *The beautiful Drawing Room has a typically Lutyens-style mantelpiece and elaborate Chippendale mirrors. The carpet has panels of Islamic script with quotations from Persian poets.*

by grouping varieties together. The bronze statues are by Barbara Hepworth and Elisabeth Frink; Frink's sleeping horse is particularly effective on the lawn. By the gates, lions (a typical Lutyens feature) growl at passers-by. Just outside the Embassy, on Massachusetts Avenue, a bronze statue of Winston Churchill, with hand aloft making a 'V-sign' for victory, stands astride the boundary between the property of the British Embassy and the US District of Columbia; it symbolises both Churchill's Anglo–American parentage and his award of honorary citizenship of the United States. The statue was unveiled by US Secretary of State Dean Rusk in April 1966, the year after Churchill's death and on the third anniversary of his grant of US citizenship. For 20 years, whatever the season, flowers or other greenery were mysteriously placed in Churchill's hand. In 1985 this activity suddenly ceased; no one ever discovered the identity of the admirer.

THE BRITISH EMBASSY IN PARIS

The Washington Embassy may be the largest of any British overseas post, containing virtually a replica of Whitehall, but Paris is undoubtedly the most historic, elegant and stylish. A successful ambassador to France requires a big personality, as well as an unusually socially confident wife, to make the Embassy the focal point in French life that is expected.

Since 1814 the Embassy has been located in the Hôtel de Charost – the former home of the Duc de Charost, governor of Louis XV; of the Compte de La Marck, friend of Marie Antoinette; of Princess Pauline Bonaparte-Borghese, the younger sister of Napoleon; and of the Duke of Wellington, Ambassador to France from 1814–15, who initiated the purchase of the house in October 1814. Wellington described the house, built in 1720 by Mazin, as 'in excellent repair . . . completely furnished, and admirably calculated for its purpose'.

The Hôtel de Charost has indeed made a splendid Embassy, one of only two

ABOVE *An artist's impression of the British Embassy in Paris, dating from 1871.*

buildings in the prestigious rue du Faubourg Saint Honoré to have survived largely unaltered since the early eighteenth century. The other is the Elysée Palace, home to the French President. Throughout the nineteenth century, when Anglo–French relations were the pivot on which world politics turned, discussions of the greatest import were held in the Embassy's rooms. Cultural and social events also took place within the portals: in 1836 William Thackeray married Isabella Shaw in the house, and regular visitors have included Marcel Proust and Marc Chagall. Architecturally, the building is striking in that it manages to be both very French and very English. The furniture for which the house is now famous is, for the most part, from the First Empire, as are the chimneypieces and cornices in the Salon Vert and the Ambassadress's Bedroom. The decoration of the Ballroom, Throne Room and State Dining Room, and the chimneypieces in the Victoria Room, Duff Cooper Library and Salons Rouge and Bleu is all High Victorian and Second Empire. The Entrance Hall and Private Dining Room are in the Louis XV revival style of the Edwardian period, while the Duff Cooper Library is in the First Empire revival style of the late 1940s.

When the allies entered Paris in April 1814 Napoleon abdicated. Pauline Bonaparte-Borghese, realising the danger of her position, gave instructions for the house and its contents to be sold. However, for three months Francis I, Emperor of Austria, chose to live in the house, and only when he moved out could a purchaser be found: the Duke of Wellington, who arrived in Paris that August to take up his appointment as Ambassador. Wellington lived there only briefly, but it was his successor, Charles Stuart, who agreed the terms of the sale. Pauline wanted 1 million francs for the house and contents, but was beaten down to 800,000 francs, and the British government finally agreed to pay, in instalments, 500,000 francs for the house, 300,000 francs for the furniture, and 61,600 for the stables.

The Paris house was described as 'stuffed from floor to ceiling with the emblems of French imperialism . . . among the most

extravagant, theatrical and feminine houses in Paris'. Charles Stuart was initially so mesmerised that he did not dare anglicise or change it. A visitor to the house in 1817 was surprised to discover that . . . '*rien n'y changé que ceux qui l'habitent . . . on y retrouve toute la splendeur qui brillait dans les palais que donnaient aux personnes de sa famille la vanité et la prodigalité sans bornes de Bonaparte*'. (Nothing changes but the occupants. Here we find all the brilliant splendour of the palaces that Napoleon would, with his boundless generosity, bestow upon the members of his family.) Stuart soon proved himself a bon viveur in the tradition of many of his successors. He filled the building with stunning French art and furniture and entertained on a scale more lavish than any former ambassador to Paris. A contemporary observed:

'Dinners, balls and receptions were given in profusion throughout the season. In fact, Sir Charles spent the whole of his private income in these noble hospitalities.'

Much of the money was spent on lighting: Stuart's receptions were renowned for being brilliantly lit, which was costly because gas was not introduced until the 1850s. Of one ball, on the occasion of George IV's birthday, a guest wrote, 'there is nothing in the world like these diplomatic balls on the Continent, for brilliancy, and the gathering of strange and remarkable people; and this, on the whole, was one of the most splendid and most picturesque I ever saw'.

The building saw alterations under successive ambassadors, and by the time that Lord Normanby left, in 1852, little remained of the interiors of the 1820s. In their place were rich chintzes, wallpapers, velvets and silks. Lord Cowley succeeded Normanby as Ambassador in 1852, the year that the Embassy sent the first telegram from an overseas post to the Foreign Office and, although presiding over a brilliant ambassadorship, Cowley destroyed much in the building that should have been preserved, and turned it into a mixture of a Victorian mansion and a Second Empire palace. However, when Queen Victoria, accompanied by their Royal Highnesses Prince Albert and the Princess Royal, visited in 1855, 'Her Majesty . . . was graciously pleased to express several times her gracious satisfaction of the Residence, furniture, etc.'

A second royal visit in 1868 was less happy. On the morning of her arrival, Queen Victoria received a visit from the Empress Eugénie in place of her husband, Napoleon III, who was absent from Paris. The Queen did not realise that protocol required her to return the Empress's visit, and the Empress was left waiting at the Elysée Palace for a monarch who failed to transpire. Victoria's dress sense also attracted some rather wry comment from the cognoscenti of Parisian fashion. Full-length portraits of Napoleon and Eugénie now hang on the Muses' staircase in the Foreign Office.

Two years after Victoria's visit, Paris was besieged by the Prussians early on in the Franco-Prussian War of 1870–71. The long-serving British Ambassador, Lord Lyons, was ordered to join the French government which had fled to Tours, where he was promptly arrested on suspicion of spying. Lyons' indignity was kept an official secret. Meanwhile, those remaining in the Embassy were suffering from the effects of the siege, especially after the bitter winter set in. Just after Christmas, the Embassy's livestock, which included two horses and a cow, was confiscated by the Paris authorities, and by the time the siege ended in February 1871, Embassy staff were living off rats and mice.

Further tribulations were to come during the Communard uprising which followed in March and April of that year, when the Embassy came under fire from the government troops who counter-attacked against the mob on April 21. According to one witness, 'a great deal of damage has been done to the Embassy house by six shells falling on the roof and knocking down a large chimney'. The army also blasted a hole

LEFT The Pauline Room. The famous bed was moved from the Ambassadress's bedroom to the Pauline Room so it could be shown off without embarrassment.

ABOVE *The rich and opulent Salon Jeune was first hung in yellow silk in 1904–5. In recent years it has been used by ambassadors as a formal drawing room.*

through the wall in the Embassy garden, and government troops burst into the grounds.

The beginning of the twentieth century saw a determination to consolidate a new era of friendship with France. Edward VII, a lover of French art and architecture, visited Paris in 1903 and stayed several days at the Embassy in the first-floor apartment overlooking the gardens. The King was concerned by the drab interiors that he found during his visit and, on his return to England, persuaded the Foreign Office to restore and redecorate the Embassy. The work was to be a celebration of the Anglo–French Entente Cordiale of 1904, which was a key plank in Britain's new policy of forming overseas alliances.

The building work at the Embassy was directed by the English architect Vye Parminter, and the Residence was restored in what was described as 'a manner consonant with its history and tradition and gratifying to the artistic sentiment of the nation to which our premier embassy is accredited'. Louis XV

cont. p 158

THE DUFF COOPERS IN PARIS

ABOVE *A portrait of Lady Diana Cooper by Cecil Beaton.*

BELOW *The Duff Cooper Library. The opulence of the room is in keeping with the rest of the Embassy, with bookcases rising right up to the gold cornice.*

T HE DUFF COOPERS' RESIDENCY at the British Embassy in Paris was surely one of the most glamorous. 'On 13 September 1944, Duff Cooper, the first British Ambassador to France for four years, flew across the Channel in a Dakota escorted by four squadrons of Spitfires,' wrote his granddaughter, Artemis. 'It was a magnificent beginning to what was to be the most enjoyable appointment of his career.'

On their arrival at the Embassy the Duff Coopers were met by Christie, one of the four porters left behind from 1940; it is said he was standing on the front steps wearing a top hat and a purple frock coat. Duff Cooper and his wife, Diana, were certainly the most charismatic and one of the most influential couples to preside over the Embassy in the twentieth century. Duff Cooper had been Churchill's Minister of Information and was the biographer of Talleyrand, while Diana Cooper, an actress and socialite, was a lady of surpassing beauty and charm. They filled the Embassy with beautiful objects and people. Two particular legacies were the Duff Cooper Library, which contains many books donated by Duff Cooper himself, and the re-designed bathroom adjoining the Ambassadress's bedroom.

RIGHT *Diana Cooper, pictured clutching a bunch of carnations, onboard a steam ship. She was one of the most beautiful and desirable women of her generation.*

BELOW *The heavily gilded Salon Bleu, showing the magnificent chandelier of 24 lights and 4 candelabra fashioned in bronze and gilt-bronze. It has now been moved to the Grand Salon Vert et Or.*

revival interiors were created in the Ante Room and the Small Dining Room. The Entrance Hall and Conservatory were '. . . remodelled to the style end-Louis XIV . . . the Salon Blanc et Or was stripped of its yellow damask hangings and panelled in the First Empire manner'. Much else took place besides, including the removal of large numbers of potted palms. Although some original features were destroyed, the redecoration was, in general, a success, and was one of the most important during the long period of British occupancy.

During the First World War, many staff were called up and the Embassy was left with only a skeleton staff. Francis Leveson Bertie (Ambassador 1905–18) recorded in his diary in September 1914, 'Between 6 and 7 pm I heard the hum of an aeroplane; it passed over the house and dropped a bomb, somewhere near the Place de la Concorde, I think I heard the explosion and then continuous sniping at the machine by the soldiers.' With the Germans acting out the Schlieffen Plan and advancing fast on Paris, the French government withdrew to Bordeaux. Bertie had to follow them, as Lyons had done in 1870. When the German advance was halted by counter-attacks by the French and British Expeditionary Force at Mons and the Marne, Bertie returned to the Embassy. For the rest of the war, the Embassy endured regular enemy bombardments. Shunning the safety of shelters, Bertie sat out air raids in the Salon Vert. In April 1918 he was relieved by Lord Derby. Paris again came under threat during the powerful German Spring Offensive, and by June 1918 panic had set in. With fears that the Embassy would be sacked and looted, Derby arranged for all but the chandeliers and firedogs to be shipped to England, where they were safely stored in a London underground station.

The most brilliant of the interwar British ambassadors was thought to be Lord Tyrrell (1928–34), in post at a time of mounting economic and political instability. Lady Tyrrell, however, ranks as one of the more unconventional of ambassadresses. She had set herself the demanding assignment of writing a history of the world, beginning in the year 2000 BC, and purporting to show exactly what had happened in every part of the globe at the same moment. However, not even the inspiration found writing in a tree in the Embassy garden was sufficient to allow her to conclude her *magnum opus*. A footman was instructed that if a visitor wanted Lady Tyrrell he should discreetly position himself at the foot of the tree without looking up, and whistle.

When war broke out again in September 1939, the Embassy swelled in size. The incoming Ambassador, Ronald Hugh Campbell, found that the Ballroom had already been occupied by members of the Information Division. Events leading to the evacuation at Dunkirk in May 1940 were watched with mounting horror by those in the Embassy. On June 8 the incineration of official papers began, the most important classified documents being burnt in a central heating furnace. On June 9, with the Germans fast advancing on the city, Churchill arrived in Paris for talks with the government and stayed overnight in the Embassy. Lady Campbell led a host of Embassy wives in a fleet of cars to Le Havre and a boat to England, and on June 11 Campbell himself left to join the French government in Touraine.

When the Germans arrived in Paris only four staff were left at the Embassy. Before leaving, Campbell had guaranteed the protection of the Embassy by the Americans, who fixed seals and notices to the front of the building. When the United States entered the war in December 1941 the Swiss Consulate was asked to take over the protection. Despite several attempts by the Germans to enter the building, they never succeeded, and when, after the Liberation of Paris, the advance British party arrived in September 1944, the seals were found to be intact.

Although the Embassy never perhaps recaptured the glamour of the Cooper post-liberation years, several distinguished couples have occupied it since, including Gladwyn and Cynthia Jebb (1954–60), Christopher and Mary Soames (1968–72), the son-in-law and daughter of Winston Churchill; Nicholas and Mary Henderson (1975–79); and Ewen and Sara Fergusson (1987–92). In 1981 Lord Carrington (Foreign Secretary 1979–82) decided the Embassy should again be restored. Work continued until the late 1990s and today it fully deserves its reputation as one of the most elegant of all Parisian houses.

> '*Lord Lyons . . . was consumed with so great a shyness that, as he dared not look his servants in the face, he had to recognise the footmen by their stockinged legs. He kept the finest carriages in Paris, a good cellar though he never drank wine, an excellent chef. Some compensation for loneliness was found in excessive enjoyment of food which, together with a dislike of exercise, contributed to his vast dimensions. The farthest he was known to walk was to and from the church over the road, and even for this brief excursion away from British territory he never failed to carry his passport.*'
>
> CYNTHIA GLADWIN ON LORD LYONS, BRITISH AMBASSADOR IN PARIS 1867–87

ABOVE *Christopher Soames, Britain's Ambassador in Paris, escorts Princess Anne, 18, at a ball given at the Embassy in June 1969. The ball was in honour of Soames' two children, Nicholas and Emma.*

The Embassy took centre stage when Britain attempted to join the European Community. When he became Prime Minister in June 1970 Edward Heath persuaded Christopher Soames to remain as Ambassador in France in order to help negotiate the difficult British entry into the EC. Like Heath, Soames was a passionate European, and he fully justified the confidence placed in him by the Prime Minister. At the height of negotiations, in May 1971, President Pompidou met with Heath for lunch at the Embassy – a rare compliment in diplomatic protocol for a president to come to lunch with a mere prime minister. Heath wrote:

Christopher and Mary Soames were the hosts at lunch in the British Embassy on Friday, to which the President and Madame Pompidou came, together with all living former French prime ministers and others prominent in public, industrial and artistic life. The British Embassy is one of the loveliest houses in Paris . . .

Another dramatic moment came in November 1990 when Mrs Thatcher, her leadership under severe threat, had flown to Paris for a meeting of the Conference on Security and Cooperation in Europe. Aides in Westminster phoned to say that she was just four votes short of outright victory in the first round of voting for the leadership of the Conservative party. It was in her room in the Embassy that her hapless aide Peter Morrison broke the news: 'Not quite as good as we had hoped,' he intoned.

THE BRITISH EMBASSY IN BERLIN

ABOVE *The front of the new British Embassy in Berlin.*
The architects who worked on the buildings were
Michael Wilford and Partners.

Following the unification of Germany in 1871, the British Embassy was established in Berlin. It was closed down at the advent of war in 1939, and after the Bonn Conventions were signed in 1952 it moved to the new capital of the Federal Republic of Germany in Bonn. The building that became the Ambassador's Residence in Bonn had been requisitioned in 1945 by the American forces and used as a transit base; after renovation it was taken over by the United States High Commission; and when the Americans moved to larger premises in 1952 the house was bought by the British government. Three years of building preceded the arrival in 1955 of Frederick Hoyer-Millar as Ambassador.

Succeeding ambassadors made various changes, but despite the importance of the post, it was never the most entrancing of residences and the Embassy offices were dull. So too, in comparative terms, was the social life in Bonn. In the 1980s the small Aubusson Drawing Room was converted into a Library and the main guest bedroom, known as the Reingold, restored to its original oval shape. During Christopher Mallaby's tenure (1988–93) the Music Room was refurbished. The expectation, with the Embassy back in Berlin, is that the style and elegance that characterised German Embassy life before 1939 will be rekindled. The new Embassy certainly has a panache that the old Embassy lacked, and within a few years will surely rival Paris and Washington for the prestige of the posting.

*Above and right *Details of the interior of the new Berlin Embassy.*
The building has been designed to maximise space and light.

∞

*Left *The old Berlin Embassy.*

ABOVE *The courtyard of the Kharitonenko mansion*
where the old stables and offices were situated.

∞

LEFT *The corner of the Ballroom, the largest room in the*
house. The three large windows face the Kremlin, a fact
that was much disliked by its Communist incumbents.

THE BRITISH EMBASSY IN MOSCOW

Until the Russian revolution of 1917 the British Embassy was located in St Petersburg, at the end of the long courier trail from London via Berlin and Warsaw. The Bolsheviks transferred the capital from Petrograd (as St Petersburg became in 1914) to Moscow in 1918, and when diplomatic relations were restored in the 1920s the need arose for a suitable Embassy for Esmund Ovey, the first British Ambassador to the new Soviet Union. The Commissariat for Foreign Affairs decided it would help to secure 'for the English Ambassador premises which would accord with his prestige and conditions of work' and the former Kharitonenko mansion was chosen.

The Kharitonenko mansion, formerly owned by a sugar merchant, had been in the front line of fire during the revolution. After the Kharitonenko family fled from the Bolsheviks in the summer of 1918, the Danish Red Cross, the only foreign mission to remain in Moscow, moved into the house.

The mansion was later acquired by the Bolshevik Ministry for Foreign Affairs and thus avoided the fate of many other large houses in Moscow of being divided up into small crowded apartments. The English connection with the house had begun with nannies to the Kharitonenko family, and continued after the revolution with the English wife, Ivy Low, of Maxim Litvinov, the Deputy Commissar for Foreign Affairs. The writers H G Wells and Arthur Ransome both stayed in the house at different times in the 1920s.

Diplomatic relations with the new Soviet regime had been damaged when British troops, landing at Murmansk and Archangel in the summer of 1918, had intervened in support of the White Russians. But at the insistence of Lloyd George, Britain became one of the first major powers to reopen diplomatic relations with Russia – de facto relations were established in 1921, and Russia was formally recognised in 1924.

Esmund Ovey moved his residence and office into the Kharitonenko mansion above the river Moskva, opposite the Kremlin, in 1931. Establishing good relations with the Soviet regime over the narrow water was not easy, and in 1933 Ovey was withdrawn for 'consultations' to London, not to return. A thaw did come, however, in 1935 when Litvinov invited Anthony Eden, then Lord Privy Seal, to Moscow. Eden became the first western leader to meet Stalin, and the first British minister to visit Moscow since 1917. Despite a visit to the Bolshoi Theatre to see Swan Lake, Eden found Moscow depressing:

ABOVE *A front elevation of the Kharitonenko mansion on the Sofiiskaya Embankment, on the southern banks of the river Moskva.*

ABOVE *A view of the Kharitonenko mansion from the back garden. The garden has a tennis court at the back, which is used as a skating rink in winter.*

LEFT *A corner of the Dining Room in the Moscow Embassy. The two cartouches above the doors are by François Flameng.*

∞

ABOVE *A corner of the gothic first-floor landing.*

LEFT *The fireplace overmantel in the Dining Room.*

∞

RIGHT *The Red Room, looking into the Ballroom. The room opens out onto the balcony and gives a view over the River Moskva.*

The dismal two mile drive from the station to the Embassy left a lasting impression on me. Large, drab crowds, unsmiling, poorly dressed and ill-fed by our standards, went disinterestedly on their way. The weather, the streets, the people, all seemed grey, sad and unending. I was surprised when the Ambassador told me that conditions were better than they had been even a year or two before. They must indeed have been pitiful. Our party stayed in the British Embassy, in the ugly grandeur of a former sugar merchant's house, but with a splendid view of the Kremlin across the Moscow river. Elegant in its lovely soft rose colour, there are few more beautiful sights in the world.

Eden met Stalin at the Kremlin and was struck by the 'short, thick-set man with hair *en brosse*. He was in a grey tunic, with rather baggy dark trousers and calf-length black boots . . . Though I knew the man to be without mercy, I respected the quality of his mind and even felt a sympathy which I have never been able entirely to analyse,' wrote Eden later.

Anglo–Soviet relations deteriorated again when Stalin launched the Great Terror. Russian members of the local

ABOVE *A view of the gold cupolas of the Kremlin, seen from the Kharitonenko mansion. Eden proclaimed it one of the most beautiful sights in the world.*

Embassy staff began to disappear without explanation; Fitzroy Maclean, then a young diplomat in the Embassy, recalls how his cook suddenly vanished. The Nazi–Soviet Pact of 1939 made relations even worse: attempts to alert Stalin of the imminent Nazi invasion in 1941, based on intelligence gained from Bletchley Park, were rebuffed. But after Hitler launched Operation Barbarossa in June 1941, Britain and the Soviet Union formed an alliance. As the German army drew close to Moscow, the Embassy staff were evacuated to the Volga and during the bombing that autumn, many of the Embassy's windows were blown in. After the Soviet victory at Stalingrad in 1943, the Embassy was able to return to Moscow.

Churchill had visited Moscow in August 1942 for a first meeting with Stalin, but had quarrelled over the opening of a Second Front in Europe. He returned in October 1944, with relations much warmer. Stalin even accepted Churchill's invitation to dine at the Embassy. As Churchill writes in his war memoirs:

In the evening of October 11th Stalin came to dine at the British Embassy. This was the first time that the British Ambassador had succeeded in making such an arrangement. Every precaution was taken by the police. One of my guests, M. Vyshinsky, on passing one of the NKVD armed guards on our staircase, remarked, 'Apparently the Red army has had another victory. It has occupied the British Embassy.' Till the small hours of the morning, we ranged over the full field of discussion in an informal atmosphere. Among other topics we discussed the next General Election in England. Stalin said that he had no doubts about the result: the Conservatives would win. It is even harder to understand the politics of other countries than those of your own.

Churchill's feelings towards Stalin are expressed in a letter he wrote to his wife, Clementine, on October 13: 'I have had vy nice talks with the Old Bear. I like him the more I see him. Now they respect us here & I am sure they wish to work w us.' He was wrong, just as Stalin was wrong about the outcome of the 1945 general election.

As the war was ending, it was Clementine's turn to stay at the Embassy. The highlight of her visit was her meeting with Stalin, to whom she gave a gold fountain pen: 'my husband wishes me to express the hope that you will write him many friendly messages with it,' she said.

Churchill's hopes for a close postwar relationship did not transpire; instead, the Cold War set in. At its height, in the late 1940s, only seven Soviet guests out of three hundred invited attended a birthday party at the Embassy in honour of George VI. Stalin's death on 5 March 1953 changed much, and in June that year a ball to mark the coronation of Elizabeth II saw Russians arriving in their hundreds; it lasted all night. The following year, a Labour party delegation, headed by Clement Attlee, passed through Moscow on its way to China. With the turmoil in the leadership following Stalin's death, it was difficult for Ambassador William Hayter (1953–57) to know which Soviet leaders to invite. Hayter recalled:

BELOW *Embassies are often the focus for political demonstrations. Here, demonstrators outside the British Embassy in Moscow protest against alleged British intervention in the Middle East, 1967.*

DIPLOMATIC PASSES

TRIPARTITE MEETING
FOREIGN MINISTERS OF FRANCE, UNITED KINGDOM, UNITED STATES
NEW YORK, NEW YORK, SEPTEMBER, 1950

NAME ___ Sir F. Hoyer-Millar ___ *174*

OF ___ United Kingdom ___

TITLE ___ Adviser ___

SIGNATURE

CHARLES W. YOST
SECRETARY GENERAL
BY
SECURITY OFFICER

S ir Frederick Hoyer-Millar rose to become Permanent Under Secretary at the Foreign Office from 1957–62. He began his diplomatic service in 1922 and worked for a year in Brussels, later serving in Cairo and Washington before rising to become Britain's first representative to NATO and Britain's Ambassador to the Federal Republic of Germany. Hoyer-Millar was a gentle-mannered Scot. He was elevated to the House of Lords, as Lord Inchyra, and lived in a beautiful retreat, Inchyra House in the Lowlands of Scotland. Here we see samples of his conference passes, including the one he took to the Peace Conference in Paris in 1946.

BERLIN 1954
БЕРЛИН 1954

No. **28**

Sir F. Hoyer-Millar

Name / Nom

Имя и фамилия

Signature of bearer
Signature du titulaire

Authorized
Autorisé
Разрешено

U. K.

Delegation of the
Délégation de la
Делегация

предъявителя сего

COUNCIL OF
FOREIGN MINISTERS

Lancaster House · London SW1

SEPTEMBER 1945

СОВЕЩАНИЕ МИНИСТРОВ
ИНОСТРАННЫХ ДЕЛ

Берлин, 1954

В ЗАЛ ЗАСЕДАНИЯ

Фамилия ___ Sir F. Hoyer-Miller ___

Должность ___ United Kingdom ___

Делегация

Делегация СССР

No. **106**

FLOWER CONFERENCE
LONDON, SEPTEMBER 1954

DELEGATE'S PASS

Name ___ Sir F. Hoyer-Millar ___

Delegation ___ United Kingdom ___

The London Conferences

24th April to 17th May, 1950

Admit to
Foreign Office (King Charles Street)
and Lancaster House

PASS
No. **328**

C. A. E. SHUCKBURGH
Secretary-General

245

PEACE CONFERENCE
Paris, July 1946

Admit the Bearer of this Pass to the Offices
of the United Kingdom Delegation

Bearer's Signature

NOT TRANSFERABLE

H. M. G. JEBB

Stalin had once dined at the Embassy during the war, and then the whole building was taken over by the secret police. There were no special precautions this time. It all looked very fine, the big dining room with its painted ceiling and red silk walls on which hung huge royal portraits (it was always necessary to explain to Russian guests that the portrait of George V was of him and not of the last Tsar Nicholas II, his first cousin whom he so closely resembled).

As part of the new spirit the theatre director Peter Brooke brought *Hamlet,* with Paul Schofield, to Moscow – the first cultural visit of this kind since the Revolution. In 1959, when Macmillan visited Moscow – the first British prime minister to do so in peacetime – Khrushchev took dinner with him at the Embassy.

During the Cold War MI6 were obsessed by security in the Embassy buildings in Moscow; there were innumerable attempts by the KGB to eavesdrop on proceedings. Their solution was to create a room secreted deep within the Embassy and protected from all possible 'bugs'; it was here that the daily ambassador's meeting with senior staff took place. By the 1970s the Soviet authorities were putting pressure on London to vacate the Embassy, not least because they took offence at having the Union Jack flying so close to the Kremlin. However, Mrs Thatcher held out and managed to persuade Gorbachev to let them remain. The Kharitonenko mansion was to become the residence of the Ambassador.

Parvel Ivanovitz Kharitonenko had chosen a site boasting one of the finest views in Moscow: across the river to the Kremlin and to the 30 gold cupolas of the fifteenth- and sixteenth-century cathedrals that stand out against the sky. The house, built in 1893, contains many fine rooms, including the Ballroom, also known as the White and Gold Room, lit by three windows facing the Kremlin, and the Picture Gallery, now the Dining Room, which faces south over the garden. It is here that the portrait of George V, that so disconcerts the Russian guests, is situated.

The mansion remains in British hands, though the staff have now moved to their new offices (below), opened in May 2000.

BELOW *A view of the new British Embassy in Moscow, situated on the Moskva river.*

COLONIAL HOTELS

There are many famous hotels associated with the British Empire: the Peninsula in Hong Kong, the Ledra Palace in Nicosia, and the King David Hotel in Jerusalem are three of the best known. Most celebrated of all, perhaps, is Raffles Hotel in Singapore, opened in 1887. One of its first guests was Joseph Conrad, then a seaman, plying the Eastern seas. Rudyard Kipling was another early guest, who dined there and wrote *Feed at Raffles*. The interwar years saw visits from many of the world's most famous figures, Somerset Maugham, Charlie Chaplin and Noel Coward. In 1942, Singapore surrendered to Japan as British colonials gathered at Raffles Hotel to dance and sing 'There Will Always Be An England'.

RIGHT *The King David Hotel, bombed by Jewish terrorists after the Second World War.*

THE BRITISH EMBASSY IN ROME

In 1870 the British Government acquired a beautiful mansion set in luscious gardens just inside Michelangelo's splendid gate at Porta Pia. During WWII the Villa Wolkonsky, which was the Ambassador's Residence, was occupied by the Gestapo. They spilled out into huts in the gardens overlooking the aqueduct. It is said Hitler was so fed up hearing of the Ambassador complaining about the heat, that he ordered a pool to be built. In 1946, the Embassy was seriously damaged in a terrorist attack by a Jewish freedom organisation. Embassy functions were moved to the Villa Wolkonsky until May 1963 when the reconstruction of a new building was approved. In June 1971 Basil Spence designed the modern palazzo. Though expensive and thus attracting some criticism, the size of the new embassy provides an ideal working space for the increased workload that came from Britain's entrance into Europe in 1973.

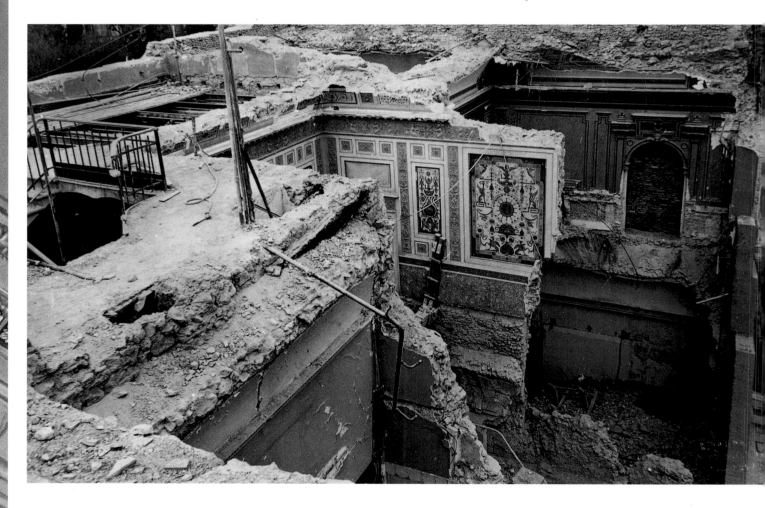

TOP, ABOVE AND RIGHT *Three views of the modern British Embassy in Rome. The Embassy was designed by Basil Spence and completed in 1971. Here we see the Embassy entrance facing Via Venti (top), a detail of the rear elevation, showing the ornamental lake (above) and a view from the Embassy garden, in the snow (right).*

LEFT *The old legation compound on the south-east of the Forbidden City, first occupied by the British in 1860.*

BELOW *The main entrance gateway in the old legation compound, viewed from within the compound. Marines guard against intruders. Both photographs date from 1899.*

THE BRITISH EMBASSY IN BEIJING

The British diplomatic presence in China did not get off to an auspicious start. The Treaty of Nanjing, which concluded the Anglo–Chinese (or First Opium) War in 1842, officially established diplomatic relations between Britain and China, but it took another 18 years before Chinese obstruction could be overcome and the legation established under Frederick Bruce, in October 1860. The Chinese were obliged to provide accommodation and assigned the British a palace to the south-east of the Forbidden City. An early description of the British legation compound, as it became known, came from a British army doctor, Dr Rennie:

> [it] may be described as consisting of two sets of quadrangular courts, running parallel to each other, north and south, with a covered passage between them. These courts contain blocks of buildings, built in the ordinary Chinese style of architecture. The set of squares on the eastern side form the palatial portion, and contain the state apartments.

In September 1861 an additional plot of land was purchased to provide accommodation for a hospital and for junior diplomats. Extra plots of land, much repair work and considerable new building took place in the 1860s and 1870s.

Life in the compound remained unchanged until the Boxer Rising in 1900. Foreign missions in general had been slow to recognise the xenophobia spreading across north China. As usual, the British legation celebrated Queen Victoria's birthday on May 24, when supper in the small theatre was followed by dancing on the tennis courts to a Chinese band. But within days missionaries and other foreigners were beginning to relay alarming tales of aggression and extra forces, including British Marines, were summoned into the legations. By early June, Britons living in outer Beijing began to flood into the legation for sanctuary. Telegraph and railway lines were cut, and Beijing found itself isolated from the outside world.

The Fifty-Five Days siege began on June 20. The previous day the Chinese authorities had ordered all diplomats and

BELOW *The front gate of the legation compound,*
in a photograph dating from 1900.

other foreigners to leave Beijing immediately, and had guaranteed their safe conduct. However, when the German minister went to check the validity of the guarantees, he was shot dead by an imperial soldier. As soon as the ultimatum expired on June 20, troops began firing on the legations, choosing the flagpole on top of the main gate of the British legation as a particular target.

The British compound was the largest and most central of the foreign legations in Beijing. As Jim Hoare, the historian of Britain's far eastern missions, points out, it was also, with its high walls, good wells, canal on one side and Imperial Carriage Park on another, the easiest to defend. Many westerners took refuge there, and numbers rapidly swelled to 1,500. Life inside was hard, but all attempts to enter or burn the legation were repelled and after heavy bombardment on the nights of August 13 and 14, relief finally broke through the next day. Roger Keyes, one of the earliest into the legation, expected to find many dead; instead he found the occupants dressed as 'though for a summer garden party'. All the buildings in the compound had, however, suffered from shells or fire.

The compound expanded to over four times its original size as a result of the negotiations which followed the uprising, and buildings were modified and extended and services improved. By 1916 electricity and water closets had been introduced in all the main buildings. Some of the extra land was used for barracks. During the 1911 revolution the compound again came under fear of attack and the guard was retained until the 1930s.

China's decision to join the allies in WWI in 1915 helped cement good relations and life in the compound was relatively calm both during and after the war. In 1928 the nationalist government of Chiang Kai-Shek (Jiang Jieshi) moved the capital from Beijing to Nanjing, and in 1936 the incoming Ambassador, Hughe Knatchbull-Hugessen, decided to keep the legation compound in Beijing but move the Ambassador's headquarters to Nanjing. Three months after the celebrations to mark George VI's coronation, while travelling from Nanjing to visit the British community in Shanghai, the Ambassador's car was

strafed by Japanese aircraft. The car had been clearly marked with a British flag. The Foreign Office debated how to respond, and awarded Knatchbull-Hugessen £5,000. According to Neville Chamberlain, Prime Minister at the time, the gift was '. . . to show the Japanese the value placed on an Ambassador', which, as the injured diplomat commented, was a curious way to put things.

When the Japanese invaded Nanjing, the British Embassy moved to Shanghai, where the Chancellery remained until the Pacific War began in December 1941.

In 1945 the British returned to Beijing and found the compound, which had been looked after by the Swiss consul-general, in surprisingly good condition. Most of the Embassy staff settled back in Nanjing, until the capital returned to Beijing.

Diplomatic relations suffered under Chairman Mao's communist regime and in 1954 the British were told that the communist government intended to repossess the legation compound. In the midst of all the turmoil, Douglas Hurd became a Third Secretary at the Embassy in the mid-1950s and was captivated:

I really think I liked the old legation compound more than anywhere I have ever lived in my life. It really was magical. I lived in a little bungalow in the compound opposite a rather attractive whitewashed two-storey house which was used by language students. It was a great big compound, lovely trees, a scarlet pavilion, and a Chapel with bells. You were right in the middle of the city. Sparrows took refuge in the trees away from the Red Guards, who had a campaign against them.

In January 1959 the bombshell exploded: the British were ordered to leave the compound within a few months. Temporary accommodation was provided by the government for the Embassy, opposite the Albanian Embassy, with the Residence next door, and the compound had to be rapidly cleared. The royal coat of arms, which had hung over the main gate on the Imperial Canal, was shipped to Hong Kong where it graced the ballroom at Government House until the British departure in 1997.

The British moved into their new modern offices and Residence with reluctance. Mrs Winifred Stephens, one of those forced to move, complained about her new flat being 'more or less a Council house' with the servants 'on top of one'. But in some ways life was to improve: the central location was a boon and the foreign community in Beijing was growing in size – though the staple diet remained Scottish country dancing, film shows and Christmas carols.

The onset of the cultural revolution in 1966, which saw the destruction of much of China's heritage, ushered in one of the grimmest periods for the British diplomatic community. In May 1967 a million demonstrators paraded in front of the British mission and an effigy of Harold Wilson, the Prime Minister, was burnt. That summer, the offices had their windows broken and Chinese attackers shouted 'Sha, Sha [kill, kill]' – the same cry they had uttered during the Boxer Rebellion. By dawn on August 23, the office was burnt out and the Residence looted; although all British personnel managed to escape with their lives, many were beaten up, some seriously.

By 1969, however, the Chinese government realised they had gone too far and in February 1970 began the process of rebuilding the office and Residence and clearing them of the forest of slogans. In 1972, 23 years after the 1949 revolution, full diplomatic relations were finally established between Britain and Communist China, and John Addis became Ambassador. Alec Douglas-Home (1970–74) was the first British foreign secretary to visit Beijing. He was moved to tears when, in the Great Hall of the People, the orchestra struck up one of his old school songs, in a scene almost too incongruous to imagine: the Eton Boating Song.

Embassy staff have continued to live and work in the same 'temporary' accommodation they were given in 1959, and have always accepted and made the best of it. The Embassy remains a cramped and unattractive building, but in Beijing terms the Residence verges on the palatial. Steady improvements have come, including redecoration with silk wallpaper (and new lavatories!) to mark the occasion of the visit of the Queen and Prince Philip in 1986. The Tianamen Square crackdown in 1989 has been the main blight on generally good Sino–British relations since the late 1960s, when again Embassy staff found themselves destroying secret documents in a hurry lest the offices be entered.

The old legation compound still stands today, though entry to it is forbidden. The famous main gate remains firmly closed and a shop, incongruously selling security equipment, now graces the archway.

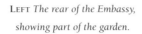

LEFT *The rear of the Embassy, showing part of the garden.*

∽

BOTTOM LEFT *The Dining Room, showing the silk wallpaper that was put up for the visit of Queen Elizabeth and Prince Philip in 1986.*

ABOVE *The bell that was originally erected in the old legation compound to mark Queen Victoria's Diamond Jubilee in 1897.*

∽

LEFT *A brass eagle lectern given to the Embassy by the American community in 1900 as an expression of its gratitude for the use of the legation during the Boxer Rebellion.*

THE GOVERNOR'S RESIDENCE IN HONG KONG

In 1841 Captain Elliot took possession of Hong Kong island and in 1843 Hong Kong became an official British colony. Its first governors were housed, to their displeasure, in either government shelters or rented mansions. This was not good enough for Hong Kong's third Governor, Samuel George Bonham, who insisted on a proper Government House. After several unsuccessful overtures, the Secretary of State for the Colonial and War Departments, Lord Grey, finally relented: 'I think a house absolutely necessary,' he said. 'I am not able to judge what it ought to cost but it would be very bad economy not to build a good one.'

Construction began in October 1851. An exceptionally beautiful site which overlooked Hong Kong harbour was chosen for the surveyor-general Charles St George Cleverly's pillared, neo-classical mansion on Upper Albert Road facing Victoria Peak. As it was to be built on a slope, two-thirds of the building would have a basement connected to the outlying kitchens and stables. Cleverly designed the house to be surrounded by verandas: on the ground floor they would encircle the Drawing Room, Dining Room, Library, double-storied hall and offices; on the first floor a higher veranda would encircle the bedrooms, nursery and drawing rooms. The house, owned by the Hong Kong Government, was finally ready for occupation in 1855; extensions were made in 1887 – a new building formed a wing on the eastern side, housing a ballroom, billiard room, smoking room, and 'other conveniences'; and the now-famous azaleas were planted in the gardens for the first time in the early 1920s.

ABOVE *The neo-classical mansion of the former Governor's Residence enjoys a beautiful and tranquil setting.*

∞

LEFT *The south-east view of the former Governor's Residence in Hong Kong, seen from the stable yard.*

Government House survived countless typhoons, but it did not emerge from the Second World War unscathed. When, in September 1941, Mark Young arrived as the new Governor, he found that Government House was beginning to fall down because of an air raid tunnel dug under the house. Three months later, Japan bombed Pearl Harbor and attacked Hong Kong, wiping out the airfield at Kai Tak. Churchill sent Young a message to say that every day that Hong Kong held out was of value to the allies. The aerial bombardment intensified. At 3.15 pm on Christmas Day the white flag was flown over Government House. That evening the Governor surrendered the colony in person to Lieutenant General Takashi Sakai, Commander-in-Chief of the Japanese forces in South China. Young became a prisoner of war and all those remaining were taken into captivity.

The Japanese appointed Lieutenant General Isogai as Governor, who decided not to chose to live and work at Government House, partly because the building was cracking open. As a Japanese official said to one of the senior British captives: 'Your Governor must be a very brave man to have lived in a building in that condition.'

Isogai brought in a young 26-year-old engineer, Seichi Fujimura, to erect a new building on the site. Instead, he retained part of Cleverly's mansion, including the Ballroom Annexe, scrupulously retained the original ground-floor plan, and seamlessly constructed a new central tower, replacing the roofs with a Japanese-style tiled roof. The floors were replaced with tatami mat floors, and sliding paper screen doors installed. The result was a striking blend of eastern and western influences. The rebuilding was complete by 1944, and on April 29 the Emperor of Japan's birthday was celebrated there with bows towards Tokyo and a pledge to redouble the war effort.

After the Japanese surrender of 15 August 1945 Government House was handed back for the use of the British Governor. He lived there until the colony was returned to China in 1997.

One of the lesser-known sagas of Government House concerns feng shui, the ancient Chinese custom of ensuring that objects interact with the environment to create optimal conditions to maximise health and happiness, longevity and fortune. Governor Murray MacLehose (1971–1982) recognised that although the Residence was extremely well-placed in terms of feng shui, permitting a flow of good energy or 'chi' to pass into it, the back door directly opposite the front door was allowing good energy to pass straight out again! So MacLehose decided to place a large table in the centre of the hall to block the flow, and keep it inside the house. As far as we know, the table did the trick.

Governor Edward Youde (1982–1986) did not believe in feng shui, and the 'unlucky' changes that he made to the house were perceived by the Chinese staff as contributing to his untimely death in 1986. Youde had ordered an oblong pond to be constructed in the gardens, rather hurriedly, for a visit from the Queen, and since the steps below the pond were crumbling, he had had them repaired and transformed into a gentle waterfall falling away from the house. As soon as Wilson was appointed Governor on Youde's death he consulted a feng shui expert who turned off the water running down the steps. In Cantonese, the character for water is also that for money, so to have water running downhill away from the house, and then disappearing, was seen as an extremely bad omen. He also altered the shape of the pond. Oblong shapes are considered very unlucky (being the shape of a coffin), so it was made into a circular pond with a fountain in the middle (moving water brings good fortune).

The feng shui expert then pronounced that the house was like a cat, with its forepaws outstretched. The tower was its head, and the Ballroom was its forepaws. But the cat was extremely unhappy as it didn't have anything to play with. So Wilson constructed a 'mouse' in the garden, with a pagoda as its head, a pergola as its body, and a curved stone walk as its tail. It was situated exactly between the Governor's office and the recently erected Hong Kong Shanghai Bank building, to prevent a clash of energies.

Another external force that played a key role in the renovations of the house was the prominent Hong Kong landmark, the Bank of China building. The Chinese population considered it to have bad feng shui and, worst of all, the edge of the pyramid-shaped tower was pointed directly towards Government House – a knife point aimed at the heart of the British. To counter this force, two soft shapes were erected in the garden between the 'knife' and the house in the form of willow trees.

LEFT The large table placed in the main hall in the Residence by MacLehose to stem the flow of energy through the house.

ABOVE A view of the Drawing Room, once avidly enjoyed by the occupying Japanese governors.

The last British Governor was Christopher Patten, who arrived on 9 July 1992 with his wife, Lavender, to oversee the final five years of British rule. Government House was the centre of frantic diplomatic activity. It was a traumatic and emotional period for Patten, which concluded with the ceremony on 30 June 1997, attended by Prince Charles and Prime Minister Tony Blair, at which the British flag was lowered for the last time. Patten, accompanied by his wife and their three daughters, boarded *Britannia* and sailed for home down the harbour into which Captain Elliot had sailed 156 years before.

DORNEYWOOD & CHEVENING

RAB BUTLER, TORY FOREIGN SECRETARY, was asked on a visit to the Paris Embassy if he would like to visit the Jeu de Paume, the gallery full of the works of the French Impressionists. 'Oh no,' he said, 'we have quite enough of those at home.' With his country estate and grand house, Stansted Hall in Essex, Butler was harking back to an earlier age. Most foreign secretaries since the Second World War have lacked the means, or the birth, to own gracious country homes in which to entertain foreign visitors on a grand scale and to relax in style. In 1 Carlton Gardens the Foreign Secretary had acquired an elegant town house: from 1955 he took possession of a country residence first at Dorneywood and from 1981 at Chevening.

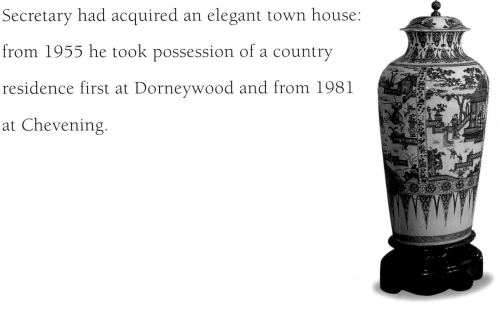

DORNEYWOOD

Dorneywood and later Chevening have gone some way to compensate for foreign secretaries no longer possessing country estates, and have also provided an excellent showcase for giving overseas ministers and officials first-hand experience of British style. Britain may not have equivalents of Versailles or the Homburg, but it does have its country houses: the Prime Minister has had the use of Chequers, the equivalent of the American President's Camp David, and the Foreign Secretary has had Dorneywood and Chevening. As Nicholas Henderson, the diplomat, put it: 'Foreign Secretaries have always had a slight feeling of being patronised when they go to Chequers. They never really feel at home there. It is important for their self-esteem to have a country house of their own.'

Chequers, in Buckinghamshire, had been given to the Prime Minister by Lord Lee of Fareham as a country residence in 1917, but it was an expensive house to run, and its running

ABOVE *The Dorneywood Garden Room. Both the east and west sides of the room give views of the beautiful garden.*

∞

BELOW *The Music Room (with bow window) was added in 1920. Here we see the sunken oval lawn, thought to have been a marl pit.*

ABOVE *The staircase in the hall, showing Rex Whistler's front porch mural (which was created to overcome a draught).*

ABOVE AND RIGHT *A pair of 18th-century Venetian blackamoors on marble stands flank the piano at the opposite side of the Music Room to the bow window. At the room's south window stand another pair of Venetian blackamoors, 'evoking memories of Tiepolo and Longhi'. (COUNTRY LIFE, 14 DECEMBER 1951)*

costs soon exceeded the revenue from its endowments. Realising that escalating costs might ultimately make Chequers prohibitive, a businessman, Lord Courtauld-Thomson, decided to act. In 1942 he donated his home, Dorneywood, at Burnham Beeches to the west of London, for use after his death as an alternative residence for the Prime Minister. The gift came with a generous endowment from the Dorneywood Trust to cover all foreseeable expenses, including 'motors'. Courtauld-Thomson was a prodigious benefactor. During the war he entertained over a thousand officers from across the empire who had come to England on leave or to convalesce, and he wished this hospitality to be perpetuated for the enhancement of the country's standing in the future.

The deed of gift was handed personally by Courtauld-Thomson to Winston Churchill at Number 10 in 1942. To heighten the sense of occasion, Churchill moved into the Cabinet Room and sat down in the Prime Minister's chair to receive the title deeds from the owner. The gift stated that if the Prime Minister did not personally require the house, he should make it available at his discretion to one of the five Secretaries of State or the Minister of Defence, and if none of these was to occupy the house, it should be offered to the Lord Mayor of London or to the American Ambassador so he 'may entertain his fellow countrymen and guests in an English country home'.

Dorneywood is within sight of Windsor Castle and Eton College (where Courtauld-Thomson had been at school) and is less than an hour's drive from London. One Cabinet Minister in the 1980s was driven back to a Downing Street emergency meeting in nineteen minutes. The house, dating back to the sixteenth century and earlier, was partially destroyed by fire in 1910 and was later rebuilt and restored in Edwardian style. At the time of the gift, the house contained seven principal furnished and fitted rooms and twelve (now ten) bedrooms. The buildings are surrounded by two hundred and fifty acres of woodland, as well as farming land, next to Burnham Beeches, whose groves were said to have provided the pikes and staves for Oliver Cromwell's soldiers.

The house is mainly Georgian in style. The inner porch was decorated by Rex Whistler, who lived close by and who has other paintings in the house. The Library has an Adam chimneypiece, and the shelves hold inscribed books by authors including Thomas Hardy, Rudyard Kipling and J M Barrie. The largest and grandest room in the house is the Conference Room (originally the Music Room), which occupies most of the ground floor on the

ABOVE *A rather empty space on the first-floor landing was transformed into a tent of Indian cottons. The curtains can be drawn to give a private room.*

east wing and has two oriental carpets that came in 1988 from 11 Downing Street. At one end is a bow window overlooking the garden, which can also be seen from the loggia, or Garden Room which, with its simple furniture, has a farmhouse air about it. There is the inevitable Games Room for snooker and table tennis, and a famous bagatelle board with a scorebook in which guests can compare their skills with those of illustrious visitors such as Winston Churchill and Lord Mountbatten of Burma. A signed certificate records that 'at 4.00 pm on Sunday 6 December 1942, Mr Churchill scored 1,015 points at bagatelle . . .'.

The grounds contain a row of picturesque brick-and-timber staff cottages, built originally for farm workers and since restored. They are approached by a brick-paved, flower-edged path known as 'the street'. The National Trust has developed the garden since the original gift, and features include a rose garden, a sunken dell and herbaceous borders.

Courtauld-Thomson died at Dorneywood, aged eighty-nine, on 1 November 1954. In February 1955 Churchill, then in his last months at Number 10, chose to offer the home to Anthony

Eden, his Foreign Secretary and heir apparent. So began a tradition, and over the next 22 years, six successive foreign secretaries had use of Dorneywood. Several found its proximity to London's Heathrow airport a convenience, as overseas visitors could be easily brought in, as at Chevening, without drawing press attention.

Alec Douglas-Home, the longest-serving foreign secretary of the period (1960–63 and 1970–74), enjoyed the house and found it a valuable enhancement to office; both he and his wife, Elizabeth, were naturally sociable. Douglas-Home had served as Commonwealth Secretary from 1955 to 1960, and found Dorneywood to be an excellent place for entertaining old Commonwealth friends and others. However, he was at heart a countryman and a sportsman, and whenever he could, he liked to get away to his home on the Scottish borders, the Hirsel, where he fished, and to Castlemains, where he shot. The Douglas-Homes were always loved by their staff, and when Labour won the general election in 1964, and Patrick Gordon Walker became Foreign Secretary, his wife complained that the housekeeper kept on saying how wonderful it had been under the Douglas-Homes, and that she reminded her of Mrs Danvers in Daphne du Maurier's *Rebecca*.

When a subsequent Foreign and Commonwealth Secretary, Tony Crosland, died suddenly in February 1977, Prime Minister James Callaghan decided to offer the house to Home Secretary Merlyn Rees rather than to his comparatively junior new appointment as Foreign Secretary, David Owen. For the first time the sequence of foreign secretaries using the house came to an end.

RIGHT *An impressive view of the beautiful country setting of the Dorneywood estate.*

CHEVENING

Since 1981 foreign secretaries have had the use of a country residence at Chevening in Kent, to the north-west of the town of Sevenoaks, twenty miles from London. While Chequers and Dorneywood are both large country houses; Chevening is a small stately home. To many, it eclipses Chequers.

Chevening is in fact privately owned, and is administered by its own Board of Trustees. The upkeep is entirely paid for from revenue from the 3,500-acre estate and tied cottages. Chevening thus has an independence which helps give it its special atmosphere.

A manor house existed on the site as early as the reign of King John (1199–1216), owned by one Adam de Chevening. The house went through many changes before being extensively rebuilt between 1616 and 1630 to a design attributed to Inigo Jones. In 1717 the house and its estate were sold to James, 1st Earl Stanhope, the son of the then British Ambassador in Madrid (and later the Hague). James Stanhope was the founder of the modern house; he added the extensions on its east and west flanks and built the two pavilions on either side of the front of the main building, and the structures joining them to it. He also enclosed the forecourt with the wrought-iron railing. On his death in 1721 he was succeeded by the 2nd Earl, who took up residence in 1736 after completing a Grand Tour of Italy, and laid out in the Main Hall the splendid array of weapons that can be seen today (right).

The 3rd Earl Stanhope succeeded in 1786, and is remembered for some unsuccessful alterations to the house. He was also responsible for the construction, at his own expense, of new roads to afford greater privacy for the house, obviating the need to use the Pilgrims' Way, which ran close by the house, and the London road. When the 4th Earl Stanhope succeeded in 1816, Chevening was described as an 'unwarmed ice-house in winter with raging draughts at every corner'. The new Earl spent nearly £5,000 on the house between 1817 and 1821, installing some hot water pipes but not notably improving the creature comforts: the large house still contained only one bathroom and two water closets. It was left to the 5th Earl Stanhope, after 1855, to modernise the house: he introduced gas lighting, installed heating in the hall and main passages, and improved the meagre sanitation. Lady Stanhope was a great social hostess, and held many literary dinners and weekend country house

RIGHT *The impressive Grand Staircase leads from the hall to the second floor. It is made of deal cased in Spanish oak.*

parties. The 6th Earl enjoyed a successful political career, but devoted increasing time to Chevening after he succeeded his father in 1875. It was he who extended the hot water system to the top floor in 1894, and introduced electricity in 1912.

The 7th and last Earl Stanhope was born in November 1880. Educated at Eton and Magdalen College, Oxford, he spent his holidays at Chevening and celebrated his twenty-first birthday there in 1901 with a glittering week of balls and entertainment. His marriage to Eileen Brown, daughter of the Marquis of Sligo, was happy, although she knew she could never bear her husband children. During the 1920s and 1930s, the Stanhopes made Chevening a centre for political and social activity. Winston Churchill, a friend, was living just four miles away at Chartwell. Stanhope's career flourished in the 1930s: he founded the National Maritime Museum at Greenwich in 1934, and as a Cabinet minister, from 1936, supervised the coronation ceremonies of George VI in 1937. (Stanhope had taken the future king's side during the abdication crisis of 1936, and had

invited him down to Chevening during the episode.) Then in 1938 he became First Lord of the Admiralty, responsible for overseeing the Royal Navy.

Lady Stanhope died in the autumn of 1940, and Stanhope decided to give up politics. He withdrew to Chevening, but managed to avoid being killed when a Luftwaffe bomb fell on the house in 1941. Having no children, he decided, shortly after his wife's death, to leave the house and estate to a trust so that it could be preserved for the nation in perpetuity. In 1959 Parliament passed the Chevening Estate Act which gave effect to the Earl's wishes, and the Earl continued to live quietly in the house until he died in August 1967.

The Trustees soon found that they had a major task on their hands. The building was stripped down to close to its original roofline, and extensive work was carried out throughout the house. The renovation, paid for from the Earl's will, was not completed until 1973.

The 1959 Act gave the Prime Minister of the day responsibility for nominating the occupant of the house, who could be either the Prime Minister, a member of Cabinet, a widow or lineal descendant of George VI, or a spouse, widow or widower of such a descendant. If, after a number of years, it was found impractical to nominate the occupant from any of these groups, the house and estate should be offered first to the Canadian High Commissioner, then to the United States Ambassador, and, if neither accepted, the house and estate should pass to the National Trust. Both Dorneywood and Chevening could thus, theoretically, be occupied by the American Ambassador.

The first two ministerial occupants of the house were nominated by Prime Minister Edward Heath (1970–74), but neither Anthony Barber nor Lord Hailsham were to live in the house for more than a few months. Following the Conservative defeat at the February 1974 general election, the incoming Prime Minister, Harold Wilson, nominated the Prince of Wales (as a

cont. p 195

THE LETTERS

Geoffrey and Elspeth Howe used Chevening extensively for entertaining foreign ministers, ambassadors and other guests and friends from overseas and home, who visited them during their six years at the house. Guests were invited to pen rhyming poems of appreciation in the 'bread and butter' tradition of Disraeli's letters to Lady Stanhope. Here is a selection:

A redoubtable Welshman named Howe
Has never shown fear in a row
So in Tokyo, Beijing and Moscow
He is always received with a bow.
But Elspeth his spouse is far braver,
And conferred to his friends a great favor,
She invited to lunch
A very large bunch
Her good food and good talk to savor.

CHARLES McC MATHIAS, JR,
FORMER US SENATOR

'It was a splendid afternoon. Our thanks – and warmest wishes –
For your genial welcome, prodigious introductions and exquisite dishes.
We much enjoyed our lunch, the tour, the talk,
The house itself, the library, the walk
Around the pewter lake, the hundred ways
It took us to get into, and then out of, that infernal maze.
The outing really raised our peckers –
Such a nicer class of place, and people, than at Chequers,
As you observed. The trip was educational what's more:
You told us of Disraeli and that man who used to work at Channel 4
And how it's not enough that thank you letters should be written and despatched on time.
We've learned that bread and butter notes should really rhyme.'

SARAH AND NICK ROSS, BBC

Dear Elspeth and Geoffrey,
I don't write to every
Kind lunch host
In verse, but the toast
Of the Isaacs is Chevening and Howe
Not for butter and bread but splendiferous chow
And a gallery groaning with prints
And a lake, and the tints
Of the autumn on trees in the park,
And a memory warm to take home in the dark
Of a house – this on paper with crest at its head –

That our Patron once took, but shortly instead
Charles chose to move on, as all Princes will do,
And left Chevening, and its contents, to you.
And therefore, as ink and inventiveness fails,
Let us all drink the health of our good Prince of Wales.
Consigning these lines to the care of the posts
Once again I give thanks to our generous hosts.

JEREMY ISAACS, ROYAL OPERA HOUSE

'The invitation came by post, complete with Crest:
"It doesn't matter greatly how you're dressed
But be at Chevening for lunch at one",
We read: and travelled Kentwards in the morning sun.
We were greeted by our charming hostess, Lady E
And, ourselves informal, were relieved to see
Relaxed and kindly, in his shirtsleeves, Britain's Kissinger
(You see we'd turned up with a suited High Commissioner).
In introducing us Sir Geoffrey's grasp of things mnemonic
Stunned us all – especially me, but I'm moronic
When it comes to names; and just about the best
That I could do was memorise the functions of each fellow guest.

JOHN SIMPSON, BBC

'The luncheon, I need hardly say, was worthy of Escoffier.
And my wife's rapture was completed when it transpired that she'd been seated
next to the master of the house. She felt as timid as a mouse,
but he soon put her at her ease, and by the time we reached the cheese
he found himself obliged to sit through strictures on Child Benefit!
(Let's hope these none-too-subtle digs went unrecorded by Lord Briggs,
for surely such a great historian should save himself for Things Victorian.)
Meanwhile I cannot tell you how delightful I found Mrs Gow – a pianist but no prima donna.
To meet her was a real honour.'

EDWARD MORTIMER, EX-FINANCIAL TIMES

LEFT *The Dining Room, in which can be seen the portraits of the seven Earls of Stanhope and their wives. Over the fireplace hangs the portrait of James, the 7th and last Earl, in Garter Robes, painted by James Gunn in 1947.*

lineal descendant of George VI). His occupancy terminated in June 1980, and in May 1981 Margaret Thatcher nominated Lord Carrington, beginning a tradition that has continued to this day of foreign secretaries having use of the house. One diplomat recalled: 'Lord Carrington loathed it because it was on the wrong side of London for him: he had his own house at Bledlow and on the one occasion we used Chevening to entertain the French Foreign Minister we all froze to death!' Lord Carrington's resignation following the Falkands War in the spring of 1982, and the dismissal of his successor Francis Pym after the general election in June 1983, meant that both occupancies were brief. Pym also had his own country house and had little need of a country retreat. But Chevening came into its own with Geoffrey Howe, who was appointed Foreign Secretary in June 1983.

Geoffrey and Elspeth Howe quickly formed a great affection for the house and its gardens. Because the lease on their house in their Surrey East constituency expired about this time, Chevening provided an ideal base, just four miles from the borders of the constituency. Howe had earlier fallen for Chevening when he was Chancellor of the Exchequer (1979–83), and had asked Lord Carrington if he could use the house in January to help prepare for his 1982 spring Budget. The setting provided the ideal mix for serious thinking and light-hearted relaxation:

Our first visit was dramatically beautiful, since the Kent countryside was thickly covered with fresh snow. This added to the drama of the parkland walks, which my Treasury team only sampled but which our wives enjoyed to the full. In these conditions the famous 'keyhole' – a rectangular aperture in the line of trees along the ridge of the North Downs above the house – was startlingly visible, looking more like a huge memorial stone, almost in the sky. On the Saturday evening I began to rediscover my army taste for billiards. But even after subsequent years of practice on the Chevening table my standard never approached that of Peter Middleton and Terry Burns [senior Treasury officials] at that first weekend.

Howe spent another 'pre-Budget weekend' in the house in January 1983, and was delighted when Margaret Thatcher nom-

inated him as incumbent when he became Foreign Secretary. As he wrote,

It was for us and our family an enchanting second home. Gradually it came once again to exude a lived-in atmosphere, after many decades without children. I have subsequently been teased, I know, for having played too much the part of the country squire, who revelled in showing off this borrowed home. But, after we had been made so welcome there by both village and staff, it would have been difficult as well as churlish to avoid identifying ourselves with such a magically historic place.

Howe found the combination at Chevening of family home, grand house for entertaining as Foreign Secretary, and constituency base more than he could have hoped for. The Howes were both highly hospitable, and they also treasured Chevening church, where they worshipped every Sunday when they were down. The Archbishop of Canterbury preached there. Howe also took a great interest in the restoration of the library, and in overseeing the publication of a booklet about it. In the Howes, the house found a couple who showed what value the house and gardens truly had.

John Major succeeded Howe as Foreign Secretary in July 1989, but never visited the house as Foreign Secretary. However, Douglas Hurd, who took over from Major three months later, found the house ideal. Although the Hurds had a country home in Oxfordshire, in Hurd's Witney constituency, they managed to spend one weekend a month at Chevening. Hurd said:

We liked to entertain there, and it was a marvellous place for Christmas: we spent four out of our five Christmases there. We went boating on the lake and had huge fun there. The rooms were light, with lovely portraits on the wall. We didn't spend as much time there as at 1 Carlton Gardens because the children didn't have all of their toys there. I felt extremely lucky to be living there. I much prefer it to Chequers: it is much more genuine. My favourite room is on the first floor, overlooking the lake, with a slightly preposterous fireplace.

Howe found Chevening particularly useful when forging relationships with new foreign ministers: 'We would meet them at Gatwick and bring them over and I'd sit and relax with them in front of a log fire until late into the night.'

ABOVE *The Tapestry Room, showing the tapestries presented in 1708 to General James Stanhope by Frederick I, King of Prussia.*

Malcolm Rifkind, Foreign Secretary 1995–97, made good use of the house despite busy weekends visiting his Scottish constituency, and travelling on foreign secretary's business. Robin Cook became Foreign Secretary on the Labour election victory in May 1997, and despite the demands of foreign travel being greater than ever on a foreign secretary, Cook still managed to spend on average one weekend a month at Chevening:

> *To me, Chevening means peace and solitude. It is a place secure from the outside world, secure from the press. I can get through a phenomenal amount of work there, while mentally pretending that I am on a weekend holiday!*

The secret of Chevening's success and popularity with foreign secretaries lies in part in its proximity to London (less than an hour by car), but also in the way the house can be used both for official entertaining and as a family home. Relative seclusion is another key. One senior diplomat highlighted the value of being able to collect France's Foreign Minister Roland Dumas secretly from Gatwick in the mid-1980s for key discussions which helped resolve the great EC Budget row then raging. The media never found out he had been in the country.

Chevening's imposing hall has a sweeping, semi-circular staircase dominated by the array of guns (carbines rather than mus-

kets) placed there by the 2nd Earl Stanhope. The wood-panelled Dining Room can comfortably accommodate 18 or 20 guests around the single table, though further tables are set up for larger occasions. The Drawing Room rivals any room at Chequers in grandeur, and over the fireplace hangs Thomas Gainsborough's portrait of the 4th Earl of Chesterfield. The Print Gallery with its curved walls links the Drawing Room with the Library Wing and the Billiard Room. The principal Library Room can be used for official meetings of up to twelve. The five rooms of the Library Wing contain some 20,000 volumes. When the house was bequeathed to the nation in 1967, the Library was placed in the care of the National Art Library of the Victoria and Albert Museum. Among many of the items of cultural and historic interest is the dispatch box of William Pitt; Robin Cook wryly remarked on first seeing it that the work of the Foreign Secretary had grown exponentially. Pitt's box was comparatively small, whereas he might find himself arriving at Chevening with four or five boxes, stuffed with official papers to read and process.

The gardens date from at least the late seventeenth century. A thermometer-shaped canal was originally laid out by the 1st Earl Stanhope, but it has since been broadened out into a lake, with

ABOVE *The uniquely curved and richly decorated wall of the Print Gallery.*

∞

BELOW *The 'broderie' or Spot Garden on the west side of the house, as it was replanted by the Trustees in 1983.*

a boathouse and two rowing boats. Most of the earls proved enthusiastic gardeners and left their mark. The 4th Earl would bring home seeds of exotic plants from his travels, and it was he who planned the two Italian gardens and planted the maze. So partial was he to the estate that he even added a codicil to his will:

> *Having during many years and much expenditure greatly improved and adorned the gardens, the pleasure ground, parks and woods of the family mansion at Chevening, it is my most solemn injunction to every person who may here-after possess the same, to leave unaltered the sight and arrangement of the said gardens, pleasure ground, parks, woods and plantations.*

The Trustees of the estate took the spirit of the words very much to heart, and from 1980 undertook an extensive restoration of the gardens to their former glory.

Dorneywood and Chevening play an essential part in the lives of foreign secretaries, and their work at the Foreign and Commonwealth Office. An understanding of the importance of these two houses is necessary for full comprehension of the more public aspects of the Foreign Secretary's role.

A SECRET WORLD

MUCH OF THE FOREIGN OFFICE'S WORK is conducted in secret. Foreign governments have always wanted to gain access to this information and discover the contents of communications travelling between the nerve centre in London and overseas posts. Similarly, the Foreign Office has been interested in knowing what foreign governments have not wanted them to know, expressly where it affects British interests. In this game of cat and mouse, the Foreign Office, throughout its history, has resorted to devices from invisible ink to the most sophisticated cryptology to try to keep its secrets from prying eyes.

EARLY DAYS

When the Foreign Office was established as a separate Department of State under Charles James Fox in 1782, the methods of communication had changed barely at all since the medieval period. John Adams wrote in his diary in 1770, 'Pen, ink and paper and a sitting posture are great helps to attention and thinking.' In 1783 Anne Cheese, the housekeeper at the Foreign Office, described one of her tasks as providing the Foreign Office with paper and disposing of old office pens. In 1786 parchment, vellum and paper began to be supplied by the Government Stationery Office, which acquired its monopoly in 1823. In 1795 the staff of nine at the Colonial Office used over 2,000 quills in the one year. Steel pens were being mass produced in Britain from the 1820s, but many of the staff in the Foreign Office and Colonial Office, throughout the nineteenth century and even beyond, preferred to use quill pens. In 1919 Lord Curzon spoke contemptuously of the inkstand he found on his Foreign Secretary's desk: 'This contraption,' he said 'was merely brass and glass'. The Foreign Office Librarian, Stephen Gaselee, used quills dipped into his favourite inkstand, which had formerly been used by the Cabinet, up until his death in 1943.

MESSENGERS, POST AND DIPLOMATIC BAGS

Britain's first overseas posts were faraway places. Travel to and from them was long and often dangerous. Until the middle of the nineteenth century there were two methods for sending communications abroad: by messenger and by post. Messengers would carry letters and documents between the monarch and the ambassadors in the field, but travelling – by sailing ship, horse and coach – was arduous and often dangerous.

The most sensitive material would go by messenger. Official couriers had been in existence since 1485, but the corps of 'King's Messengers' (or 'Queen's Messengers') see themselves as descendants of a line given particular blessing by the future Charles II when in exile in the Netherlands during the Protectorate, and they have been busy carrying confidential material ever since.

In 1780 a journey by a King's Messenger from London to St Petersburg cost £459.3.4d. It was a particularly difficult route: in 1820 a King's Messenger named Thomas Brown died of fatigue after a continuous journey of 23 days and nights. In 1824 the service was reorganised by George Canning, and brought under the control of the Foreign Office. Two basic routes were introduced: a southern one to Constantinople via Paris and Vienna, and a northern route to St Petersburg via Berlin and Dresden. Being a King's Messenger was no sinecure. William Kaye, for example, in the space of one year went from Paris to London once, Paris to Calais and back twice, London to Madrid and back, London to St Petersburg and back twice, and from St Petersburg to Hamburg and back five times. In 1859 the corps was reviewed in the light of rising costs; the Queen's Messengers were reduced to 15 in number and given an expense allowance of 2s 6d for days spent abroad; a rota system was also introduced. One messenger obtained permission from the Chief Clerk to go on leave to Monte Carlo where he was surprised to receive a telegram: '[Your wife says] you are fast and dirty, return at once.' On his return he found that his wife had indeed sent the telegram, but that it had been garbled in trans-

ABOVE *Sir Stephen Gaselee, Librarian and Keeper of the Papers, 1929. The slate-lined safe was kept in the old Foreign Office Library, which was under the Grand Locarno Reception Room.*

mission from its original, which had read: 'You are the first on duty, return at once.'

King's or Queen's Messengers carry special burgundy passports with their status emblazoned on the outside cover, and on the inside cover the words that the bearer has been 'charged with dispatches'. The corps is still, in the year 2000, under the control of the FCO, although it now carries sensitive material around the world for all government departments. Numbers in the postwar period have fluctuated between 30 and 50, and messengers are often former officers from the armed services. The corps' historian, Lt Col John Kimmins, wrote: 'The corps has never had a traitor in its ranks, and in over 300 years, never knowingly failed in its duty.'

Less important material would go by the mail and take its chances with the ordinary post, though it would often be enciphered, i.e. written in a code known to the recipient, who would then decipher the message using the same code. Some messages were written in invisible ink, a technique that was surprisingly effective, so long as the recipient knew how to restore the visibility and where to look.

Until 1830, one man collected all the outgoing mail from the Foreign Office and from two other government offices, and took it all to the Lombard Street post office for the 8 pm coach. As he frequently arrived late, the coach was often held up. Poor weather and the unpredictability of sea voyages meant that mail was often further delayed or even lost. After 1830 stricter controls and a more streamlined system were introduced.

The diplomatic bag, or pouch, still forms the principal method used by embassies from all countries to send material between their outposts and their governments at home. Until the 1963 Vienna Convention on Consular Relations, customs officers had the right to challenge a bag they believed contained inappropriate material or perhaps guns. Bags were supposed to contain only documents or other bona fide items of diplomatic import such as code books. But since 1963 the diplomatic bag has been inviolate and cannot be challenged, even when customs officers have good intelligence reasons for searching the bags. The year after the Vienna Convention, however, the customs authorities in Rome took the law into their own hands and violated the Egyptian bags' immunity for the solid reason that they heard moans coming from within. A drugged and kidnapped Israeli was found inside. It is not the only time in the last 40 years that the privileges of immunity have been abused: drugs, parts of guns, and explosives have all been smuggled in diplomatic bags, and customs officials, even when they have known what was inside, have had to wave the bags through.

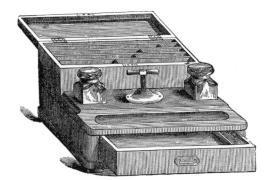

COPYPRESS

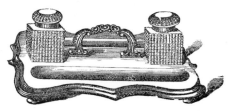

INK STAND

STATIONERY CABINET

ABOVE *These drawings of old machinery and stationery gadgets are from Harrison's Stationery Catalogue which was printed at the back of the Foreign Office List (a yearbook of personnel).*

TELEGRAPH, CABLE AND WIRELESS

One of the earliest forms of telegraph was the semaphore system devised by the French engineer Claude Chappe near the end of the eighteenth century. By the late 1830s Berlin was close to being linked to St Petersburg by a chain of semaphore masts. The introduction of the electric telegraph, however, made semaphore's further development redundant. In Britain, the first cable for the transmission of telegraph was set up in 1838–39

ABOVE *The bags were carefully checked to see that they had not been opened or tampered with.*

LEFT *Sorting through the hundreds of dispatches that would arrive daily at the Foreign Office in diplomatic bags from all over the world.*

ABOVE *A 1941 photograph clearly showing the seals on the dispatches, as they were emptied out of their bags.*

alongside the Great Western Railway from Paddington to West Drayton. The telegraph had the benefit of speed and reliability, and lines rapidly spread across Britain. In 1850 the first cross-Channel cable was laid, using copper wire enclosed in an insulating sheath. Twenty-seven miles of cable were paid out from a steam tug from Dover and landed at Cap Gris Nez in France. The first electric message across the Channel was sent that August to President of the Republic Louis Napoleon (who had himself been a brief tenant at 1 Carlton Gardens, the future Foreign Secretary's home, in 1840). The *Times*, marvelling at the cross-Channel link, declared:

> *The jest of the scheme of yesterday has become the fact of today. The wildest exaggeration of an Arabian tale has been outdone by the simple achievement of modern times … [and] the first and obvious effect of this instantaneous communication between the two most civilised and powerful nations of the world will be to unite them so closely in community of interests as to secure their cooperation in all designs that may promote the advancement of humanity and maintain the peace of the world.*

In 1858 a third attempt to lay a telegraph cable across the Atlantic (from Ireland to Newfoundland) proved successful, and on August 5 Queen Victoria and President James Buchanan of the United States exchanged messages. More durable cables were laid by I K Brunel's iron ship, *The Great Eastern*, between 1866 and 1874. In 1859 cables were laid connecting Britain with Constantinople and Suez, and by 1870 the new India Office was linked by telegraph cable to the government in India. Messages which could have taken many weeks to arrive now took just hours; the modern era of diplomacy had truly arrived. At first cables of commercial companies such as The Electric Telegraph Company and the Submarine Telegraph Company were used, but it was understood that government messages took priority (and were prefaced by the words 'clear the line, clear the line').

As tension in Europe mounted in the run-up to the First World War, concerns were raised about the ease with which the cables could be cut by the enemy. Increasingly, thoughts turned to the advantages of radio. In 1911 Marconi proposed establishing a chain of high-power wireless telegraphy stations linking Britain to its empire, and that May the government decided to

proceed with Marconi's idea, but to bring it under public ownership from the start. Then, in 1928, the Cable and Wireless Company was set up, which for the first time fused into one body all the cable and radio interests involved in communications between Britain and the empire.

TELEGRAMS

Telegrams have long been the standard mode of communication in the Foreign Office. Manuscript letters began to be superseded from the moment when, in December 1852, the Paris Embassy became the first mission abroad to send a telegram to the Foreign Office. The following year, telegraph communication was established with Berlin, Vienna and Florence. Edmund Hammond, the long-serving Permanent Under Secretary, was not convinced about the new technology; he told a Parliamentary Committee in 1858: 'No, we do not have the Electric Telegraph in the office; provision was made to admit of its coming in, [to the planned new Foreign Office building] because it was right and proper to make it, but I hope it will never come in.' Hammond thought it would be 'a very inconve-

ABOVE *In the telegraph distribution room all the confidential materials were locked in red leather-covered dispatch boxes.*

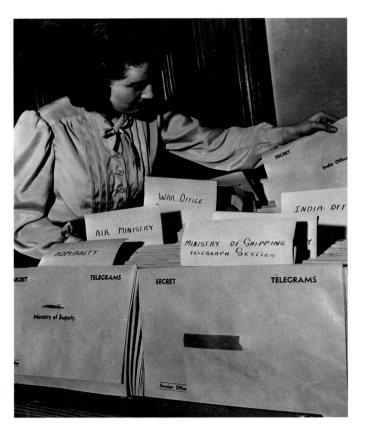

ABOVE *Most of the correspondence you see here concerned state secrets. It had to be filed carefully in the telegraph distribution room, now the Grand Locarno Reception Room.*

RIGHT *During the war the Locarno Conference Room was filled with clerks coding and decoding messages of key importance.*

nient and very expensive arrangement' and he feared that, with some prescience, 'I think the tendency of the telegraph is to make every person in a hurry, and I do not know that with our business it is very desirable that that should be so.' By the time the new building was occupied in 1868, staff all took telegrams for granted. When, in 1870, the government-owned Post Office took over from the several commercial telegraph companies, the Foreign Office's growing problem with security was eased. Telegrams were produced in capitals and traditionally bore the Foreign Secretary's name on outward journeys, and the name of the Ambassador of the relevant Embassy when telegrams came in. The first telegrams were sent *en clair*, and even when they were ciphered it was still difficult to guarantee security with different private companies.

When Scott's new building was first occupied, telegrams that came in during the day would be delivered to departments like ordinary post, and telegrams received out of office hours were distributed by the Resident Clerk, who provided 24-hour cover. In 1884 the telegraphic address PRODROME (from the Greek *prodromos* meaning precursor) was registered: PRODROME

LONDON was the address for diplomatic telegrams being sent into the Foreign Office and PRODROME, followed by the name of the mission, for telegrams going out of the office.

In 1923 the Communications Department was set up for ciphering and dispatch. Since enciphering and deciphering all took time, the advice to staff was : 'Telegrams should be written as from a miser to a fool.' All incoming telegrams were copied in the Communications Department's distribution room and circulated as required; the most important would be seen by the Monarch, by the Prime Minister and by the Foreign Secretary. Pressure increased on the outbreak of war in 1939 because of the extra flow of traffic, and the Ciphering Branch spread itself into the Locarno Suite, though problems and frustrations occurred because of its distance from the Communications Department. Work around the clock was the order of the day throughout the war, and the lights never once went out.

ABOVE *Female Foreign Office staff hard at work in the telegram copying room, 1941.*

ABOVE *The top-secret cipher, used for decoding confidential messages from all over the world, was kept securely in this strong room.*

LEFT This particular cipher, spread out on the floor, was used to report the progress of the Congress of Vienna.

BELOW LEFT *Detail of an old cipher, from 1809.*

By 1950 there were 225 Foreign Office staff working on ciphering and deciphering, and sending out and receiving telegrams. A one-page telegram of 400 words would take from 40 minutes to 2 hours to encipher, and cost £25 to transmit to Lima, though only £3 to Cairo. At the height of the Gulf crisis in 1990–91, 12,000 telegrams came in and out of the FCO every single day.

Even in an age of instant on-screen news, with Reuters, ceefax and CNN, the telegrams from embassies abroad are still valued, for their specifically British perspective on events. The world may know that Prime Minister A has resigned, but the telegram from the embassy in the country concerned will advise the FCO what the consequences for Britain will be, and what appropriate action should be taken.

PRINTING, COPYING AND TYPEWRITERS

The Foreign Office has had an official printer since 1800, when a salary of £150 was paid to James Harrison whose family was to be connected with the Foreign Office's printing well into the twentieth century. The printing presses in the Downing Street office had to be shifted down to the basement in the 1820s as the vibration was affecting the stability of the fragile building. When they moved into the Scott building in 1868, the presses were set up in the basement below the Foreign Office courtyard. Today the work is carried out by the FCO's Print Services and Reproduction Centre.

Until the late nineteenth century copyists had been employed to make handwritten copies of all the important documents going in and out of the Foreign Office. In 1886 the Treasury concluded that typewriters in government departments would yield economies and within a few years typists using carbon paper to make copies had taken over from copyists. Miss Sophia Fulcher was the first typist to be employed by the Foreign Office, in 1889, and she and her colleagues were initially known as the Lady Typewriters. By 1905 typists were being entrusted with confidential work and had begun to type drafts and outgoing dispatches. In 1908 Edward Grey acknowledged that 'type-writing has now become essential', in both the Foreign Office and overseas posts.

The manual typewriter remained in situ for much of the twentieth century. The standard fare was a Remington model, supplied by the Stationery Office. Failure to change ribbons when necessary upset Austen Chamberlain (Foreign Secretary 1924–29), who threatened that if dispatches were not typed in sufficiently dark lettering he would make himself 'as disagreeable as Lord Palmerston'. The Foreign Office's records contain a circular issued in response to Chamberlain, making it clear that office machines had to be kept clean at all times and ribbons replaced frequently. The first electric machines were introduced in 1950 and were American Electromatic Proportional Spacing Typewriters; by the 1960s electric typewriters were the norm in the Foreign Office, although manual typewriters continued to be used for longer abroad, in part because they were considered less of a security risk.

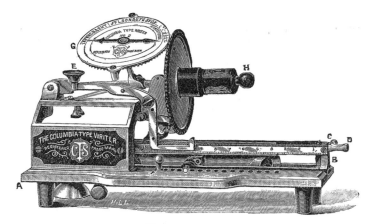

TYPEWRITER

ABOVE *Drawing of an old typewriter model,*
from Harrison's Stationery Catalogue.

TUBES, TELEPHONES, TELEX AND FAX

In the nineteenth century some Foreign Office rooms were connected by speaking tubes, most famously the Foreign Secretary's and the PUS's room immediately below. The tubes were made of rubber, and to attract the listener's attention, the person making the call would whistle down the tubes, which could be painful if the receiver had the tube pressed to his or her ear at the same time.

The first telephone line was introduced into the Foreign Office between 1888 and 1889 by the National Telephone Company; the number was Westminster 415. In 1902 demand was such that another line had to be put in; the Foreign Office's number became Westminster 211, and the Private Office Westminster 210. The telephone was so manifestly superior to the blowing tube that before long everyone was demanding one, and in 1906 the Treasury agreed to the 'installation of a system of telephonic communications in the Foreign Office' at an estimated cost of £390. The employment of a 'female Switch Clerk' (or switchboard operator) was also approved. The telephone network was installed by the Post Office which gave the Foreign Office its own private branch exchange and by July 1909 its number had become Victoria 22 or Victoria 490. On 1 January 1912 the Post Office

'I was placed in charge of the shift which worked from midnight till eight a.m. Coming on duty at midnight on August 3rd my first task was to dispatch a telegram which I had been warned would be waiting for me in a locked box. It was to go off at midnight unless other instructions were issued. I opened the box and sent off the message. It was the declaration of war on Germany drafted in Sir Edward Grey's handwriting.'

SIR HUGHE KNATCHBULL-HUGESSEN

took over all private telephone companies on behalf of the government. The celebrated Foreign Office Librarian Stephen Gaselee provided some helpful advice to users of the telephone:

Good manners normally demand that the receiver should not be replaced and the Foreign Office operator should merely be requested to put the call through to the other department . . . Remember that during the time the Foreign Office operator is 'holding on' while . . . looking up the number of the extension you require, she is unable to deal with other calls and may be keeping other people waiting.

RIGHT *Telephonists at work, 1941.*

∞

BELOW *The Tube Room. The 'tubes' are one of the more unusual methods of communicating within the Foreign Office. The system was installed in the 1940s.*

The Foreign Office switchboard, like its opposite number across the road at 10 Downing Street, soon acquired a reputation for efficiency, calm and hard work.

In 1932 the Post Office informed the Foreign Office of a new service which it called 'telex' and which was described as a form of 'typewriting over telephone wires'. The Chief Clerk initially declined this new technology but in May 1940 it was introduced and was in widespread use during and after the war. Telex fell into disuse partly as a result of the introduction and wide use of facsimile equipment (fax) from the 1980s.

Harking back to earlier speaking tube technology, in 1944 the Foreign Office introduced an internal 'pneumatic tube' system which shoots messages placed in cylinders around the building via a labyrinth of tubes. This rather charming and outmoded method of communication has survived into the twenty-first century, and was indeed extended when the Foreign Office came to take over all of Scott's building.

BLETCHLEY PARK AND GCHQ

The First World War taught the government much about the need to intercept other countries' confidential communications and the need to protect its own. The Germans learned the exact timing of the Battle of the Somme on 1 July 1916 from intercepting a telephone message to soldiers in the front line. After the war the Government Code and Cipher School (GC & CS) was established to study the methods and content of cipher communication used by foreign powers and to advise and improve on the security of British ciphers and codes. In 1922 GC & CS was put under the control of the Foreign Office and initially had 25 cryptologists plus 30 support staff. After the euphoria of the Locarno Treaties had evaporated, in the early 1930s, navy, army and air sections were added to GC & CS. Its work, carried on in various buildings around London, expanded, and the government began to look for a secure base outside London, away from the possible danger of bombs.

The most celebrated of Bletchley Park's many contributions (see over) was the breaking of the German Enigma cipher machine, an achievement of such importance to the strategic direction of the war that the whole operation had to be shrouded in the highest secrecy and was known as 'Ultra' intelligence. Cracking the enemy's codes, without the Germans realising that the British codebreakers had done so, allowed the navy to antici-

LEFT *A mid-1970s view of the Benhall site of Government Communications Headquarters in Cheltenham.*

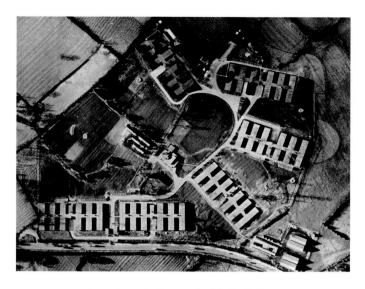

ABOVE *An early photograph of the Benhall site, taken shortly after GCHQ moved there in 1952.*

pate movements of submarines and surface ships and so protect allied convoys; it also gave the RAF advance information on the targets for Luftwaffe bombing raids, and it allowed the army to know in advance the intentions of enemy commanders in the field. Only in the 1970s did the world at large start to hear about the work and significance of Bletchley Park. Churchill knew how important the work was, and had the intelligence brought personally to him; very few of his immediate staff at Number 10 even knew of the breaking of the Enigma code.

The end of the war saw the rapid scaling down of the operation. An extraordinary collection of people had gathered at Bletchley; one of the leading lights was Alan Turing, a mathematician considered to be the father of the modern computer. The academics returned to their universities, the WRENS and others to civilian life. In 1946 Government Communications Headquarters (GCHQ) moved to Eastcote in Pinner, north London, which had been one of its sites during the war, and in 1952 it moved to two separate sites in the Gloucestershire town of Cheltenham. Its role remained that of intercepting and interpreting the secret communications of overseas governments, and advising the government on the technical security of its own communications. The secrecy of its work was carefully protected by the town, where it was known locally for many years simply as 'the Foreign Office'.

GCHQ reports to the FCO and its main findings are considered, along with reports from MI5 and MI6, by the Joint Intelligence Committee of the Cabinet. GCHQ's operations became public knowledge in 1983 when its function was

cont. p 214

BLETCHLEY PARK

When the work of the Government Code and Cipher School began to expand, the government needed a safe base outside London. Several possible sites were examined and in 1938 the decision was made to purchase Bletchley Park, a mansion to the north of London with 55 acres that had been bought in 1883 by Sir Herbert Leon. It had ample grounds, and could house very large numbers of personnel. Its situation in Bletchley on the main north–south railway line commended it, as did the fact that it had direct rail links to Oxford and Cambridge from where many of the high-powered codebreakers would come. It was also close to a main road, the A5. Captain Ridley (of MI6) duly bought it, supposedly with his own money, and began to supervise the erecting of large numbers of wooden huts and blocks of brick buildings in the grounds. Locals were told the men and women arriving in ever increasing numbers were members of 'Captain Ridley's shooting party'.

GC & CS moved in from its various London offices to Bletchley Park days before the outbreak of war. Their new, unprepossessing home was given many names, including 'War Station X', 'Room 47 Foreign Office', 'BP', the 'Park' and Government Communications Headquarters or GCHQ – the name it came to be known by. The number of those working there grew from under 100 in 1939 to over 7,000 in 1944. By the end of 1942 it was reading some 4,000 German high-grade signals each day, as well as smaller numbers of Italian and Japanese signals. Bletchley Park came to perform a service of the highest value in intercepting, breaking, interpreting and summarising key German, Italian and Japanese communications, distributing their contents to the government and to allied commanders in Britain and abroad.

LEFT *An example of the codebreaking headphones that were used during the Second World War at the wartime intelligence centre at Bletchley Park.*

LEFT *Personnel decrypting coded signals on modified British telex cipher machines in the registration room in hut 6, Bletchley Park, 1943.*

LEFT *The punch room in C Block at Bletchley Park, 1943.*

BELOW *Bletchley Park, Oxfordshire. Its rural setting is close to both Oxford and Cambridge, where some of the most important intelligence officers have been trained.*

ABOVE *Codebreaking equipment used during WWII at Bletchley Park. This photograph was taken in June 1999.*

∞

LEFT *A WREN operates the 'Colossus' computer. It helped codebreakers crack the Lorenz code, considered unbreakable by the Germans.*

revealed to Parliament, and in 1994 the Intelligence Services Act defined its role in the post-Cold War world as keeping the government abreast as new threats emerged to take the place of the old, and charged it with responsibility for the prevention and detection of serious crime. With the increasing complexity and technological sophistication of life in the twenty-first century, it is unlikely that the need for GCHQ will go away.

MI6

The two other elements of the intelligence community which are overseen by the Cabinet's Joint Intelligence Committee, and by the Parliamentary Intelligence and Security Committee, are MI5 and MI6. MI5, or more properly, the Security Service, was

set up in 1909 to counter penetration of British organisations by foreign intelligence services. It has since gained additional national security responsibilities and from the 1960s has had a major responsibility for combating Irish terrorism. MI5 reports to the Home Secretary and is only tangentially involved with the Foreign Office, whereas MI6 is very much involved with it, and reports to it.

Created in 1911, MI6 or, more properly, the Secret Intelligence Service (SIS), has as its task the undertaking of espionage activities overseas. First based in Broadway in central London, it then moved to the very ugly Century House in Lambeth, close to the Imperial War Museum, and in the early 1990s moved into its current head office (right) on the south bank of the river Thames – the £200 million Vauxhall Cross

LEFT *A four-rotor German Enigma cipher machine with a second operator display (a 'remote lampboard'), made during WWII.*

RIGHT *A three-ring Enigma cipher machine complete with a wooden transit case. With original German battery serial number A6421.*

(whose cost can be contrasted with the £108 million for restoring the Foreign Office). The 1994 Intelligence Services Act described MI6's role as 'to obtain and provide information relating to the actions or intentions of persons outside the British Islands, and perform other tasks relating to these in relation to the interests of national security'. Its focus for much of the postwar period was on the activities of the Soviet Union and its satellites. Since the end of the Cold War it has lost this clarity of focus but is operational in many overseas countries; the threats of religious fundamentalism and the risks of nuclear and biological terrorism are some of its main contemporary concerns.

RADIO AND HANSLOPE PARK

The use of radio (originally called 'the wireless') expanded considerably in the interwar period. After the fall of France and the Low Countries in May 1940, the government asked the armed forces to set up a secure radio network to communicate with Britain's remaining allies and with agents in Europe. The global network using high frequency radio and Morse code was based at Hanslope Park, a large stone mansion built in 1692 and requisitioned by the Ministry of Defence in 1941. For the next four years it assisted 'Special Operations Executive' (SOE) in the communication with agents and friendly parties abroad.

After the end of the war the Diplomatic Wireless Service took over and ran the network, which linked the Foreign Office to over 90 overseas posts. With the Cold War the need for secure communications increased and a basic machine cipher was introduced in the 1950s. In 1963 came a teleprinter-based high frequency radio system called Piccolo, which took over from labour-intensive Morse code. Piccolo revolutionised Foreign Office communications around the world, and from 1964 it offered online cipher protection for all text, greatly speeding up the processes of encryption and decryption. In 1973 the Diplomatic Wireless Service was absorbed by the FCO's new Communications Division and the first computer-based systems were installed in 1986–87. By 1990 the FCO was moving away from radio and telex as the conduits for its communications with overseas posts, and return to the public telephone network, with satellites for backup. With more than 150 satellites in orbit, all main locations in the world can be covered by the use of the FCO's portable satellite terminals, the latest of which can be carried in a suitcase for use in emergencies and in remote locations.

COMPUTERS

Although some of the country's earliest computers were in use at Bletchley Park during the war, the Foreign Office itself was slow to adapt to the use of computers, as were Number 10 and many other government departments, all of which were some ten years behind the private sector. The first word processors were brought into the FCO in the 1970s, and for the next 25 years its network was hermetically sealed within the FCO and its embassies overseas. Communication outside the Foreign Office went by post or fax. Now the FCO is in the process of combining a Windows PC-based office automation system with a global telecommunications network, which will, for the first time, unify FCO computer systems; by early 2002 the transition should be complete. Communications between the FCO and posts in more than 160 countries over the global network will use internet protocols, with data of all kinds encrypted and decrypted at both ends. But even after the move to desk-to-desk e-mail, vestiges of the great telegram will remain in the main format of communication between the FCO and overseas posts. Because it was felt important to retain the look and feel of the telegram, a specific configuration of an e-mail – an 'e-gram' – has been devised to come up on screens and be printed where necessary. The FCO is eager to preserve the same sense of authority as the traditional telegram, including the name of the Foreign Secretary at the foot of an outgoing e-gram, and of the Ambassador at the foot of incoming ones. The e-gram will, however, allow graphics and pictures to appear in addition to the words of a traditional telegram. The FCO is taking a technological leap forward as big as the introduction of telegrams in the late nineteenth century.

TRAINS AND BOATS AND PLANES

The advent of the steam train from the 1830s transformed the job of the Foreign Secretary: allowing him to attend conferences in Berlin, Geneva or Vienna without having to be away from London for several weeks. Trains also made foreign secretaries' lives easier at home. Lord Salisbury enjoyed racing from the Foreign Office to King's Cross station, his record time being 17 minutes. As Andrew Roberts, Salisbury's biographer, writes: 'A footman would be ready with his greatcoat, another would open the door of the single-horsed brougham, which would set off the moment it closed. Horse Guards Arch, Whitehall, Trafalgar Square, Charing Cross and Bloomsbury would be negotiated at speed by his coachman.' When he became Prime Minister as well as Foreign Secretary, Lord Salisbury had a private train with a single carriage permanently available to take him from King's Cross to the station near to Hatfield, where he had a private waiting-room built on the station platform. Eden recalls travelling with Austen Chamberlain to Geneva in the late 1920s:

The top-hatted stationmaster and the Foreign Office representatives at Victoria, the harbourmaster at Dover bowing us on the ship, the préfet and the mayor at Calais, then a drive across Paris and the dinner at the Embassy, the night train at the Gare de Lyon . . . finally, the arrival at Geneva, about 7.30 in the morning, the whole staff paraded to meet their chiefs at the station.

The aeroplane was to transform the life of both the Foreign Secretary and the Prime Minister from the 1930s. Neville

ABOVE *Foreign Secretary Robin Cook boards an RAF jet at Heathrow Airport before flying to the Middle East.*

Chamberlain flew to Germany in 1938 by slow propeller plane from London's Heston airport; by the 1950s jets were halving the travel time. Macmillan complained with prescience that: 'In the old days, foreign secretaries seldom left their desk in Whitehall. Today, they have become of necessity peripatetic salesmen.'

Today, the Foreign Secretary can reckon on spending two days a week abroad, and every other weekend on foreign soil or in the air. Robin Cook uses three planes: for short flights, such as his monthly visits to Brussels or to Paris for a dinner, he will take an HS125 from the RAF's 32 Squadron. Little more than a 'flying tube', it takes about eight passengers, has no facilities for hot meals, but can fly from Biggin Hill, the former Second World War aerodrome, conveniently close to Chevening. For trips of more than an hour he will use a BAe 147, which has space for about 30 passengers, its own office, and can fly out of RAF Northolt, which is closer than London Heathrow. Distance from Whitehall counts, as the Foreign Secretary, unlike the Prime Minister, does not have police 'outriders' or motorbikes to stop the traffic.

For intercontinental flights, the Foreign Secretary still uses a VC-10 from Number 10 Squadron based at Brize Norton. This plane, built in 1966 and painted in grey paint, was converted from a troop carrier in 1974 on the instructions of James Callaghan. The plane needs a long runway so the Foreign Secretary has to travel to Heathrow to use it. The VC-10 is a flying office. It has a VIP cabin for the Foreign Secretary and his wife, the Principal Private Secretary, Press Secretary and any other officials in the party; an office at the back with power points and computers; and it also has beds. The pilot has communication by radio and satellite. But as one official said: 'Not having messages constantly coming through for just a few hours can be quite a relief.' Some of Fox's calm life of 1782 can be refound.

LOWERING THE FLAG

AT THE BEGINNING OF THIS BOOK we looked at the rise of Britain as a world power, and at how she developed her vast empire. We left the story with the fall of Singapore in 1942. For a year after the fall of France in 1940, Britain and her empire had stood alone against Germany; her resources were stretched to the limit, but she nevertheless prevailed against the Luftwaffe in the Battle of Britain and her empire remained intact. But after the war the tide began to turn. Britain could no longer keep pace with other countries such as the United States and Japan, who were outstripping her economically. The remaining 55 years of the twentieth century were spent trying to adjust, and to find a new role for Britain.

THE BEGINNING OF THE END

In 1947 India and the Moslem state of Pakistan gained their independence and the lowering of the British flag had begun. Britain had become a second-rate power whose continued position in world councils owed almost everything to her past. How did this decline in Britain's standing occur so quickly and how, by the end of the century, did she succeed in reclaiming some, if not all, of her former position?

The fall of Singapore in February 1942, and the loss of Malaya and Burma to the Japanese, were huge blows, not just to the allied war effort, but also to British self-esteem. In Singapore, a garrison of 130,000, designed to repel all attackers, fell to a smaller Japanese force. It became clear that Britain was not able to protect her far-flung empire alone. The defence of Britain's Far East empire and the defeat of Japan were to owe much to the United States. It was a pattern that set the tone for the postwar world.

Although Britain and her allies 'won' the Second World War, the impact of the war on Britain was heavy, and her economic and strategic relationship with her dominions and colonies would never be the same again. By 1945 Britain owed vast sums to the United States and other overseas creditors. Dislocated by six years of total war, the British economy could no longer generate the investment nor produce the goods to restore Britain's world trading position to that of pre-1939. Two-thirds of Britain's prewar exports were lost, and her gold reserves were depleted by three-quarters. The physical damage to major cities, factories and ports from the Luftwaffe was heavy. Britain emerged from the war a weakened nation, unable to flourish alone.

Within twenty years, Britain had reached a point where barely any of her empire was still intact. No one in 1945 foresaw how quickly the flag was to be lowered. The Labour government that came to power that July certainly did not see itself as presiding over any kind of decline in British overseas power. It was determined to keep the 'Great' in Great Britain and in 1947 took the decision, in great secrecy, to build an independent British atomic bomb. Britain's permanent seat on the Security Council of the United Nations also seemed to offer the prospect that her prewar status as a great power would continue into the postwar world.

The postwar Labour Government did not, as had been feared by those on the right, move the country closer to the Soviet Union. The Cold War between East and West soon set in, and Prime Minister Attlee and Foreign Secretary Bevin rapidly concluded that Britain's future lay in re-establishing a close association with the United States. American loans and Marshall Aid were to prove invaluable in helping Britain and Western Europe rebuild their war-torn economies. Bevin's particular achievement was

ABOVE LEFT *General Percival, British Commander at Singapore, on his way to surrender the British stronghold to General Yamashita.*

LEFT British prisoners at Singapore, victims of the Japanese attack on the Philippines and on Singapore.

to bring the United States into the North Atlantic Treaty Organisation (NATO), formed in 1949, thereby ensuring that the United States did not return to the isolationism of the inter-war period. Although much of the wartime intimacy between Britain and the United States ended with the war, a close identity of interest remained. The United States, always hostile to British imperialism, was pleased when independence was finally granted to India and Pakistan in 1947. It was similarly gratified when Britain stood up against Russia in the Berlin airlift of 1948–49, when the Communists' attempt to starve West Berlin into submission was foiled. There were differences, naturally, in the Middle East and the Far East, but when the Korean War broke out in 1950, it was Britain that was to prove the closest and staunchest ally of the Americans against the Communists in the north.

The Foreign Office, more than any other department in Whitehall, had to adapt to Britain's changing postwar impor-tance. Critics were quick to point out that Britain's foreign ser-vice expanded as her power in the world declined – the vast 19th-century empire was run with a staff of 100, in London and in a handful of overseas posts. Today, with the empire gone, and Britain at best a second-rate power, it has a staff of 6,500 in two main London buildings, and overseas missions in 189 countries. The 55 years since 1945 certainly saw the prominence of the Foreign Office decline, as it lost influence to Number 10 (as the Prime Minister became increasingly involved in overseas sum-mits from the 1950s), to the Treasury and to the Cabinet Office from the 1970s, which coordinate much of interdepartmental foreign policy. Increasingly, too, other Whitehall departments have come to play major roles in overseas missions.

THE PACE OF INDEPENDENCE QUICKENS

Neither the Foreign Office nor the Colonial Office had envis-aged that independence would come for the bulk of the British Empire for many years. Palestine was an exception, where the Jewish state of Israel was established in the former British man-

BELOW *The flag is lowered in Palestine after 25 years of British rule. The State of Israel is proclaimed by the Jews, 14 May 1948.*

date in 1948. Here, as in India and Pakistan, the government felt that a British withdrawal was the only solution, given the explosive nature of internal conflicts combined with mounting pressure against continued British rule. But the empire started to unravel far more rapidly than any of the most far-sighted planners in Whitehall had foreseen.

Various factors were at play in the rapid dismemberment of an empire that had been three centuries in the building. Britain's economic decline relative to other developed countries prevented her being able to afford the cost of policing and administering such a far-flung empire. After 1945 the idea of empire no longer had the same appeal in Britain, nor was there the political will at the top to retain it by force. Within the colonies, unrest against Britain's continued presence mounted, and several Nationalist groups turned to violence in order to get Britain

ABOVE *President Banana and Robert Mugabe outside the former residence of Lord Soames in 1980. The new cabinet is sworn in.*

BELOW *Robert Mugabe and Joshua Nkomo at a 1976 meeting in Geneva on Rhodesian independence.*

to leave. Behind the scenes, the United States was increasing its pressure on Britain to decolonise. The logic was inescapable, though it took the Suez Crisis of 1956 to show Britain and the rest of the world how much things had changed since 1945.

West Africa saw the first British colony to go. Riots in the Gold Coast of Ghana encouraged some acceleration in the process of reform, and it became clear by the mid-1950s that the pressure for independence could no longer be denied. Self-government was granted in 1957, followed by the independence of Nigeria in 1960. In East and Central Africa, the government hoped to slow down the pace, not least because in these colonies lived a significant white minority who were in fear of losing their special position under black African rule should democracy come. The government tried to create federations by grouping colonies together, but was unsuccessful. Prime Minister Macmillan admitted as much when, in 1960, he went to Cape Town and spoke of a 'wind of change' sweeping through Africa. In 1961 Sierra Leone and Tanzania became independent, followed by Uganda in 1962, Kenya in 1963, and Zambia in 1964.

The white minority in southern Rhodesia became so alarmed by developments that it declared unilateral indepen-

cont. p 226

THE SUEZ CRISIS – 1956

It was the Suez Crisis that really underlined how much the map of the world had changed in the wake of the Second World War. Suez was the most humiliating experience for Britain in the postwar period. When the Egyptian leader Nasser nationalised the Suez Canal in July 1956, and after intensive diplomacy failed to resolve the crisis, Britain and France hatched a plan to invade the canal area on the pretext of separating Egyptian forces from an attacking Israeli army. Within a few days of the invasion in early November, however, British troops were forced to leave Egypt, Britain having been condemned by the United Nations. It later came to light that Prime Minister Eden had lied to the House of Commons in denying prior knowledge of Israel's attack on Egypt and that he had thus attempted to deceive the international community. The affair ended Eden's proud political career. He resigned as Prime Minister in January 1957, and spent the twenty years until his death believing he had been right to act as he did.

BELOW *Port Said troops prepare for action.*

LEFT *Nasser's sunken block ships put the canal out of action for several weeks.*

∞

BELOW *The arrival of the first United Nations troop contingent in Port Said, where it was enthusiastically greeted by the Egyptian civilians. The Suez Canal inflamed anti-British colonial sentiment, and may have encouraged other nationalists to fight Britain's continued presence.*

dence in 1965 under its leader Ian Smith. Sanctions failed to bring the Smith government into line, and for much of the next 15 years Labour and Conservative governments battled to resolve the issue. By the 1970s civil war and unrest made a settlement all the more necessary. In 1980 a resolution finally came following the Lancaster House Conference in London. Free elections were held and Robert Mugabe was elected Prime Minister.

OLD FRIENDS AND NEW

The major shift in the overall direction of British foreign policy since the war has been the move away from empire towards Europe. Britain stood aside from the discussions in the late 1940s and 1950s between France, West Germany, Italy, Belgium, Luxembourg and the Netherlands about creating a closer economic relationship. She sent only a civil servant to the negotiations which followed the conference held at Messina in Sicily in 1955. The Foreign Office was not alone in believing that Britain's future lay outside European integration. Both major political parties, much of the press and the media all clung to the idea of Britain as a great power, holding a unique position as the head of the Commonwealth, enjoying a 'special relationship' with the United States and remaining a major independent force in international affairs.

The retreat from empire was a major factor in the reevaluation of Britain's future. In 1961 the Macmillan government applied to join the Common Market, or European Community (EC), which had been ratified by the Treaty of Rome in 1957. Six countries initially belonged to the EC: France, West Germany, Italy, Belgium, Luxembourg and the Netherlands. It was France, under President de Gaulle, that was responsible for vetoing the Conservatives' application. In 1967 Wilson's Labour government again applied to join, and for a second time France vetoed the application. Ted Heath, who won the general election for the Conservatives in 1970, made entry into the EC one of his major priorities. He had led the negotiations in the first attempt to join in the early 1960s, and was a lifelong pro-European. In 1972 Britain's application was at last accepted and on 1 January 1973 Britain joined the by now European Economic Community (EEC), along with the Republic of Ireland and Denmark.

Britain was always the awkward partner within the EEC. In 1975 the Labour government, which had been returned to power in 1974, held a national referendum on whether Britain should retain its membership. The country voted positively but has become ambivalent. When Mrs Thatcher came to power in

ABOVE *Edward Heath (left) with former Prime Ministers Sir Alec Douglas-Home and Harold Macmillan in Brussels, 1972.*

ABOVE *Lord Soames, Edward Heath, Alec Douglas-Home and Anthony Barber during EEC talks in Paris, November 1972.*

∞

RIGHT *Argentine prisoners are searched by British paratroopers and Royal Marines at Port Stanley before being repatriated during the Falklands conflict.*

1979, it rapidly became clear that her attitude to further European integration lay at the opposite end of the spectrum to that of Heath. She fought bitter battles over Britain's contribution to the EEC budget and made it clear that she was an Atlanticist first and a European second. She accepted the Single European Act of 1986, and Britain's entry into the Exchange Rate Mechanism (ERM) in 1990 only with deep reluctance. Her antipathy to Europe and her bitter clashes with her senior min-

ABOVE *Smoke pours from the stricken Destroyer* HMS Sheffield *after she had been hit by an exocet missile during the Falklands conflict.*

BELOW *The Union Flag and White Ensign are raised on South Georgia after British forces recapture the island, 19 June 1982.*

isters, principally Geoffrey Howe and Nigel Lawson, played a decisive role in her downfall in November 1990.

John Major came into office a pro-European, but had to moderate his rhetoric and to some extent the substance of his European policy to accommodate his increasingly Euro-sceptical Tory party. Tony Blair, who brought the Labour party to power in 1997, and Gordon Brown, his Chancellor, are also instinctive Europeans but have played a slow hand on Britain joining the single currency, aware of profound reservations amongst the press and the electorate.

The relationship with the United States has been the most constant of the three strands of Britain's postwar foreign policy. The strength of the relationship has fluctuated, reaching its nadir during the Suez Crisis of late 1956. High points were during the Second World War, the early 1960s when Kennedy was in the White House and Macmillan in Number 10, during the 1980s when Reagan and Thatcher were in office, and again since 1997 with Blair at Number 10 and Clinton US President. Low points were when Britain's failure to send troops to

ABOVE *The Gulf Crisis — members of the 42nd squad
of the Royal Corps of Transport from Milford
outside the liberated British Embassy in Kuwait.*

BELOW *British soldiers run to a helicopter in Saudi Arabia.*

ABOVE AND LEFT *The Lion Again Roars: the 1982 Falklands War.
Men aboard* HMS Hermes *(above) take a break from the rigours
of training for a little sunbathing on the flight deck.*

ABOVE *In the middle of the Saudi-Arabian desert, British soldiers
in an armoured vehicle receive supplies.*

Vietnam during the 1960s soured the relationship. American support for Britain's unequivocal response after the Argentine invasion of the Falklands Islands in 1982 cemented the new closer relationship. With Mrs Thatcher at the helm, and with Eastern European countries and finally the USSR itself crumbling, Britain enjoyed a minor renaissance as a world power. Britain's support for the United States during the Gulf War in 1991 and its attacks on Iraq in the late 1990s confirmed the continuing importance of the special relationship. But the 1990s were to prove a more difficult decade in which to show resolute leadership. The Balkans in particular seemed impervious to any clear-cut response.

Britain's departure from the Crown Colony of Hong Kong on 1 July 1997 closed a chapter on British history that had stretched back over the centuries. Here was Britain's last great

ABOVE *A stony-faced Chris Patten is handed the flag during the handover ceremony in Hong Kong, 30 June 1997.*

ABOVE *Chris Patten waves his farewell to Hong Kong. Prince Charles stands behind him.*

colony, with six million inhabitants and a dynamic economy being handed over without protest to the last major communist power in the world, the People's Republic of China.

For five years, Hong Kong's last governor, Chris Patten, battled to secure the rights and freedom of its inhabitants under the new regime. At the final handover the British party, led by the Prince of Wales and Tony Blair, witnessed the British flag being lowered for the last time before a world television audience of many millions. Although still three years short of the century's end, it proved a more defining moment than anything that was to be thrown up by the Millennium celebrations. Here the centuries of British domination were being peacefully concluded, with good relations opening up the possibility of growth and new roles in the future.

THE FCO IN THE 21ST CENTURY

One thing we can say for certain about the future Foreign Office is that it will not be immune to change. And it will always have its critics as well as its admirers. In 2000 the Foreign Policy Centre, a New Labour think-tank, proposed replacing traditional ambassadors and diplomats, businessmen and foreign nationals by computers. That same year Robin Cook, the Foreign Secretary, voiced his desire to see the Foreign Office staffed by more representatives of ethnic minorities, more women, and fewer products of Britain's elite public schools.

Some have claimed that the renovation of the Foreign Office building was a rash and wasteful exercise, that it should even now be sold off to private enterprise, along with the vast

ABOVE *Robin Cook (second from right) attends a conference on nuclear power in 1998, with Madeleine Allbright second from left.*

ABOVE *Robin Cook speaking at a Human Rights Conference at the Foreign Office in 1997.*

LEFT *The handover ceremony in Wanchai, Hong Kong, 1997.*

majority of the expensive overseas posts, thus raising billions of pounds of revenue in what would be one of the boldest acts of privatisation ever undertaken by any government. Yet there is undeniably still an essential role for the Foreign Office to play, and Scott's magnificent building, now fully adapted for the information age, remains a beautiful and fitting home for it to do so.

The main role of the Foreign and Commonwealth Office will continue to be the running of Britain's foreign relations on a day-to-day basis, and the management of Britain's embassies abroad. The work of the overseas missions – promoting trade, engaging in dialogue with local politicians and advancing British interests, promoting cultural, social and educational links, and engaging in 'public diplomacy' – is unlikely to become redundant. Today's

ambassadors abroad are visible, high-profile figures – Francis Bertie, Ambassador to France in the early twentieth century, gave only one or two speeches in his thirteen years in Paris, whereas Michael Jay, the current Ambassador, appears frequently on French news programmes, speaking fluently in French.

Britain may not have been able to resolve its position with Europe and its place in the world, but it nevertheless remains true that Britain's history and its ambitions ensure it will play a major role in the world well into the twenty-first century.

And of course Scott's building, at the heart of a capital not conspicuous for the grandeur of its public architecture, strikes visitors as just as imposing, and (despite its much-debated Italian influence) just as quintessentially British as when it first opened its door over 130 years ago.

"There was a hellhole down in the cellars smelling of steamed cabbage. No senior member of the FO staff ever went near the FO canteen. It was pretty ghastly. It wasn't a social thing; it really was an appalling place. I never went there if I could help it. Most people went to a sandwich bar or something. And this is not a social judgement; it's a gastronomic one."

DAVID HANNAY

"It was not an uncommon practice for the occupants of the upper rooms facing Fludyer Street to let down strings of red tape from the top windows and haul up pottles of strawberries, which they had purchased from fruit-sellers in the street, and I remember on one occasion a youth in my own department saying to his fellow-clerks, as the pottles were passing his window, 'What fun it would be if someone was to cut that tape!', when one of his colleagues exclaimed, 'I dare you!' 'You dare me?' inquired the youth. 'Yes, I dare you,' the other repeated. No sooner had he said the words a second time than the tape was cut, and down fell into the area below four pottles of beautiful strawberries."

EDWARD HERTSLET,
FORMER FOREIGN OFFICE LIBRARIAN

"Its finest features were its marvellous position overlooking St James's Park and horseguards parade, along Whitehall, next to Downing St, the Treasury, the diplomat's entrance from the Park, and the Ambassador's Waiting Room.

It epitomised British life at that time – slightly casual, uncontrived, not exactly glittering, but with a certain distinction of its own."

NICHOLAS HENDERSON

"Awful Blitz last night (450 machines). Couldn't sleep till all clear at 4.30. Fine morning and warm. Walked by devious way to F.O. Area Piccadilly, St James's Street, Pall Mall, Lower Regent Street pretty well devastated. Cabinet 11.30. Admiralty hit. From his place at Cabinet table, Winston observed this gave him a better view of Nelson's Column. Quite true."

DIARY OF ALEXANDER CADOGAN,
THURSDAY 17 APRIL 1941

"Lansdowne is chief expert, 'Lamps' Sanderson, was a survival from the mild hilarities of nineteenth-century Punch. He had thick glasses and thin legs, was a great listener to the great, a well-stored official of noted and unoriginal ability, who became suddenly formidable when he fussed into a Department."

ROBERT VANSITTART

"An Englishman was walking down Whitehall looking for the Foreign Office, where he had an appointment, on a foggy night in the black-out during the Second World War, when he bumped into another Englishman.

'Excuse me,' he said, 'could you tell me which side the Foreign Office is on?'

'I don't know, mate,' came the answer, 'but I believe in the last war they were on our side.'"

The Foreign Office as perceived in popular mythology – a familiar after-dinner story

"I hosted a party [in the Grand Locarno room] when it was reopened. I didn't know if, when Thatcher came up the stairs, she would say 'what a monstrous waste of money' but she took me aside and said, 'Douglas, we've got to keep all these buildings in first class condition,' as if I was about to destroy it. Fill it with pigeon shit again or something."

DOUGLAS HURD

"I joined the Foreign Office on the 31st May 1880 and was put in what was then called the German Department. The head of it was Sir Percy Anderson, a very genial official with only one eye. The second in the Department rejoiced in the name of "Beauty" Stephens, who prided himself on his good looks, his success in Society and partly also on his incapacity to do any serious work. He was very amusing but a very bad bargain for the Government."

LORD HARDINGE OF PENSHURST

"an ambassador is an honest man who is sent to lie abroad for the good of his country"

SIR HENRY WOTTON, BRITISH AMBASSADOR –
ITALY, 1604

FORMER FOREIGN SECRETARIES

since 1868

STANLEY, Lord, Edward Henry; (later 15th Earl of Derby)
JUL 1866–DEC 1868

CLARENDON, 4th Earl of, George Viliers
DEC 1868–JUL 1870

GRANVILLE, 2nd Earl, George Leveson Gower
JUL 1870–FEB 1874

STANLEY, Lord, Edward Henry; (later 15th Earl of Derby)
FEB 1874–APR 1878

SALISBURY, 3rd Marquess of, Robert Cecil
APR 1878–APR 1880

GRANVILLE, 2nd Earl, George Leveson Gower
APR 1880–JUN 1885

SALISBURY, 3rd Marquess of, Robert Cecil
JUN 1885–FEB 1886

ROSEBERY, 5th Earl of, Archibald Primrose
FEB–JULY 1886

IDDESLEIGH, 1st Earl of, Stafford Northcote
AUG 1886–JAN 1887

SALISBURY, 3rd Marquess of, Robert Cecil
JAN 1887–AUG 1892

ROSEBERY, 5th Earl of, Archibald Primrose
AUG 1892–MAR 1894

KIMBERLEY, 1st Earl of, John Wodehouse
MAR 1894–JUN 1895

SALISBURY, 3rd Marquess of, Robert Cecil
JUN 1895–NOV 1900

LANSDOWNE, 5th Marquess of, Henry Petty–Fitzmaurice
NOV 1900–DEC 1905

GREY, Sir Edward; (later Viscount Grey of Fallodon)
DEC 1905–DEC 1916

BALFOUR, Arthur James; (later 1st Earl of Balfour)
DEC 1916–OCT 1919

CURZON, Earl; (later 1st Marquess of Kedleston)
OCT 1919–JAN 1924

MACDONALD, James Ramsay
JAN–NOV 1924

CHAMBERLAIN, Sir Austen
NOV 1924–JUN 1929

HENDERSON, Arthur
JUN 1929–AUG 1931

READING, 1st Marquess of, Rufus Isaacs
16 AUG–NOV 1931

SIMON, Sir John; (later 1st Viscount)
NOV 1931–JUN 1935

HOARE, Sir Samuel; (later 1st Viscount Templewood)
JUN–DEC 1935

EDEN, Anthony; (later Sir Anthony Eden [1954] and 1st Earl of Avon)
DEC 1935–FEB 1938

HALIFAX, 3rd Viscount; (later 1st Earl)
MAR 1938–DEC 1940

EDEN, Anthony; (later Sir Anthony Eden [1954] and 1st Earl of Avon)
DEC 1940–JUL 1945

BEVIN, Ernest
JUL 1945–MAR 1951

MORRISON, Herbert; (later Lord Morrison of Lambeth)
MAR–OCT 1951

EDEN, Anthony; (later Sir Anthony Eden [1954] and 1st Earl of Avon)
OCT 1951–APR 1955

MACMILLAN, Harold; (later Earl of Stockton)
APR–DEC 1955

LLOYD, Selwyn; (later Lord Selwyn–Lloyd)
DEC 1955–JUL 1960

HOME, 13th Earl of ; (later Sir Alec Douglas-Home and later Lord Home of the Hirsel)
JUL 1960–OCT 1963

BUTLER, Richard Austen; (later Lord Butler of Saffron Walden)
OCT 1963–OCT 1964

GORDON WALKER, Patrick; (later Lord Gordon–Walker of Leyton)
OCT 1964–JAN 1965

STEWART, Michael; (later Lord Stewart of Fulham)
JAN 1965–AUG 1966

BROWN, George; (later Lord George–Brown of Jevington)
AUG 1966–MAR 1968

STEWART, Michael; (later Lord Stewart of Fulham)
MAR 1968–JUN 1970

HOME, 13th Earl of; (later Sir Alec Douglas–Home and Lord Home of the Hirsel)
JUN 1970–MAR 1974

CALLAGHAN, James; (later Lord Callaghan of Cardiff)
MAR 1974–APR 1976

CROSLAND, Anthony
APR 1976–FEB 1977

OWEN, Dr David; (later Baron Owen of the City of Plymouth)
FEB 1977–MAY 1979

CARRINGTON, 6th Baron, Peter Smith
MAY 1979–APR 1982

PYM, Francis; (later Lord Pym of Sand)
APR 1982–JUN 1983

HOWE, Sir Geoffrey
JUN 1983–JUL 1989

MAJOR, John
JUL 1989–OCT 1989

HURD, Douglas, (later Lord Hurd of Westwell)
OCT 1989–JUL 1995

RIFKIND, Malcolm
JUL 1995–MAY 1997

COOK, Robin
MAY 1997–

BIBLIOGRAPHY

Balfour, John *Not too Correct on Aureole: The Recollections of a Diplomat,* Wiltshire, Michael Russell, 1983

Barclay, Sir Roderick *Ernest Bevin and the Foreign Office 1932–1969,* London, Published by the Author, 1975

Barnes, John *Footsteps on the Backstairs,* Norwich, Michael Russell, 1992

Brown, George *In My Way,* London, Victor Gollancz, 1971

Bruce, H J *Silken Dalliance,* London, Constable & Co., 1946

Bullock, Alan *The Life and Times of Ernest Bevin,* vol. II, London, William Heinemann, 1960

Butler, Lord *The Art of the Possible: The memoirs of Lord Butler,* London, Hamish Hamilton, 1971

Clark, Alan *Diaries,* London, Orion Books, 1994

Cohen, Yoel *Media Diplomacy: The Foreign Office in the Mass Communications Age,* London, Frank Cass & Co, 1971

Colville, John *Footprints in Time: Memories,* London, William Collins Sons & Co., 1958

Colyton, Henry *Occasion, Chance and Change: A Memoir 1902–1946 ,* Norwich, Michael Russell, 1993

Cooper, Duff *Old Men Forget: The Autobiography of Duff Cooper (Viscount Norwich),* London, Rupert Hart-Davis, 1953

Cradock, Percy *Experiences of China,* London, John Murray Publishers, 1994

Crowe, Sybil and Corp, Edward *Our Ablest Public Servant,* Braunton Devon, Merlin Books, 1993

Dakers, Caroline *Sigismund Goetze and the Decoration of the Foreign Office Staircase: 'Melodrama, pathos and high camp',* The Decorative Art Society Journal, No 21, 1997

Dickie, John *Inside the Foreign Office,* London, Chapmans Publishers, 1992

Dilks, David (ed.) *The Diaries of Sir Alex Cadogan 1938–45,* London, Cassell & Co., 1971

Douglas-Home, Charles *Evelyn Baring: The Last Proconsul,* London: William Collins Sons & Co., 1971

Dutton, David *Austen Chamberlain: Gentleman in Politics,* Botton, Ross Anderson Publications, 1985

Eden, Sir Anthony *The memoirs of Sir Anthony Eden: Full Circle,* London, Cassell & Co., 1960

Enever, T *Britain's Best Kept Secret: Ultra's Base at Bletchley Park,* Gloucestershire: Alan Sutton Publishing, 1994

Garner, Joe *The Commonwealth Office 1925–68,* London, Heinemann Educational Books, 1978

Gore Booth, Paul *With Great Truth and Respect,* London, Constable, 1974

Grenville, J A S. *Lord Salisbury & Foreign Policy: The Close of the Nineteenth Century,* London, The Athlone Press, 1970

Hamilton, Keith *Bertie of Thame: Edwardian Ambassador,* Suffolk, The Boydell Press, 1990

Hayter, Sir William *A Double Life,* London, Hamish Hamilton, 1974

Henderson, Nevile *Water Under the Bridges,* London, Hodder and Stoughton, 1945

Henderson, Nicholas *Mandarin: The Diaries of an Ambassador 1969–1982,* London, Weidenfeld & Nicolson, 1994

Henderson, Nicholas *The Private Office,* London, Weidenfeld & Nicolson, 1984

Herstlet, Sir Edward *Recollections of the Old Foreign Office,* London, John Murray, 1901

Hickman, Katie *Daughters of Britannia: The Lives and Times of Diplomatic Wives,* London, HarperCollins Publishers, 1999

Hinsley, F H and Stripp, Alan (eds.) *Codebreakers: The Inside Story of Bletchley Park,* New York, Oxford University Press, 1993

Hoare, J E *Embassies in the East,* Surrey, Curzon Press, 1999

Lord Home *The Way the Wind Blows,* London, William Collins Sons & Co., 1976

Howe, Geoffrey *Conflict of Loyalty,* London, Macmillan, 1994

Jebb, Miles (ed.) *The Diaries of Cynthia Gladwyn,* London, John Murray Publishers, 1995

Jenkins, Simon and Sloman, Anne *With respect, Ambassador: An Inquiry into the Foreign Office,* London, BBC, 1985

Jones, Raymond A *The British Diplomatic Service 1815–1914,* Buckinghamshire, Colin Smythe, 1983

Knatchbull-Hugessen, Sir Hughe *Diplomat in Peace and War,* London, Constable & Co., 1949

Macmillan, Harold *Tides of Fortune 1945–1955,* London, Macmillan & Co., 1969

Marquand, David *Ramsay MacDonald,* London, Jonathan Cape, 1977

Morrison, Herbert *Herbert Morrison: An Autobiography,* London, Odhams press, 1960

Nicolson, Harold *Diplomacy,* 3rd ed., London, OUP., 1969

Nicolson, Nigel (ed.) *Harold Nicolson: Diaries and Letters 1930–39,* London, William Collins Sons & Co., 1966

Nicolson, Nigel (ed.) *Harold Nicolson: Diaries and Letters 1939–45,* London, William Collins Sons & Co., 1967

Parkinson, Cosmo *The Colonial Office from within 1909–1945,* London, Faber and Faber, (1945)

Platt, D C M *The Cinderella Service: British Consuls since 1825,* London, Longman Group, 1971

Robbins, Keith *Sir Edward Grey: A Biography of Lord Grey of Fallodon,* London, Cassell & Co., 1971

Roberts, Andrew *The Holy Fox: A Biography of Lord Halifax,* London, Weidenfeld & Nicolson, 1991

Roberts, Andrew *Salisbury: Victorian Titan,* London, Weidenfeld & Nicolson, 1999

Rose, Kenneth *Superior Person: A Portrait of Curzon and his Circle in late Victorian England,* London, Weidenfeld & Nicolson, 1969

Rothwell, Victor *Anthony Eden: A Political Biography 1931–57,* Manchester, Manchester University Press, 1992

Satow, Rt Hon Sir Ernest *A Guide to Diplomatic Practice,* vol. I, London, Longmans, Green & Co., 1917

Smedley, Beryl *Partners in Diplomacy,* West Sussex, The Hartley Press, 1990

Smith, Michael *Station X: the Codebreakers of Bletchley Park,* London, Macmillan Publishers, 1998

Stamp, Gavin (ed.) *Personal and Professional Recollections: The Autobiography of the Victorian Architect Sir George Gilbert Scott,* Lincolnshire, Paul Watkins, 1995

Swinson, Arthur *Beyond the Frontiers: The Biography of Colonel F M Bailey Explorer and Special Agent,* London, Hutchinson & Co., 1971

Tilley, Sir John and Gaselee, Stephen *The Foreign Office,* London, G P Putnam's Sons, 1933

Toplis, Ian *The Foreign Office: An Architectural History,* London, Mansell Publishing, 1987

Ure, John *Diplomatic Bag,* London, John Murray Publishers, 1994

Lord Vansittart *The Mist Procession,* London, Huchinson & Co., 1958

Walden, George *Lucky George: Memoirs of an Anti-Politician,* London, The Penguin Group, 1999

Williams, Francis *Ernest Bevin: Portrait of a Great Englishman,* London, Hutchinson & Co., 1952

PICTURE CREDITS

Pages 2, 6, 10, 34, 53(left & bottom right), 70-1, 72, 80-1, 82, 84, 86, 88-91, 95-6, 101 (bottom), 103-4, 108, 121, 122(right), 132-42, 198, 218 © Kim Sayer

pages 4, 31, 69, 87, 100, 102(right), 107 © HOK International Ltd/Adam Woolfit

page 12 © RAF Museum Hendon (FA10107)

pages 13, 33(top), 43, 62, 97(bottom left & bottom right), 112, 113(right), 118, 120, 131, 200-7, 209(top), 220-5, 230-1 © Popperphoto

page 14 © Château de Versailles, France/ Bridgeman Art Library

pages 15, 172 © Public Record Office

page 16 © National Gallery, London

pages 17, 49(left & bottom right), 50, 64, 75-7 © HarperCollins*Publishers*

pages 18, 48(bottom), 55, 74, 79, 83, 160(top), 161, 168 © Peter Cook/View

pages 19, 20, 21 (top right, bottom right) © British Library

pages 21(top left), 23, 26-30, 32, 42, 48(top), 57-8, 63, 78(left), 97(top), 113(left), 114-18, 119(top), 122(left), 123-8, 155, 226, 228(bottom), 229(top left) © Hulton Getty

pages 22, 144, 152-3, 159, 166, 169, 187 © Topham Picturepoint

page 24 © Courtesy of the Director, National Army Museum, London

pages 25, 145-51, 160(bottom), 162-3, 170, 176(bottom), 178-81 © FCO Library Photographic Collection

page 33 (bottom) © Imperial War Museum

pages 36, 37 (bottom) © Guildhall Library/ Corporation of London

pages 37(top), 38-9 © Aerofilms Ltd

pages 40, 154(top left) © by courtesy of the National Portrait Gallery, London

pages 41, 59-60, 61(bottom), 66-8, 78(middle & right), 98, 105, 107(left), 110-11, 167, 208, 209(bottom) © FCO Historians Reserve Collection

pages 45-7, 49(top) © by courtesy of the British Architectural Library, RIBA, London

pages 52, 54, 101(top) © Illustrated London News

page 53(top) © HOK International Ltd/Peter Cook

page 56 © Indusfoto Ltd

page 61 (top) © The Royal Archives © 2000 Her Majesty Queen Elizabeth II

pages 92-3 © Mrs Marina Rainey

pages 99, 102(left) © Pat Foley

page 106(bottom) © Crown Copyright/NMR

page 119(bottom) © courtesy of Sothebys, London

pages 129-30 © Central Office of Information

page 154 (bottom left & bottom right), 156-7 © Crown Copyright/UK Government Art Collection

pages 164-5 © John Freeman

page 171 © Architectural Association/Basil Spence

pages 173-5, 176(top), 177 © Jim Hoare

pages 182, 188-91, 194, 196-7 © Pitkin Unichrome by Peter Smith of Newbery Smith Photography

pages 184-6 © Country Life Picture Library

pages 210-11 © Crown Copyright Material reproduced with permission

pages 212(top), 213(top), 214(bottom), 216 © NMPFT/Science & Society Picture Library

pages 212(bottom), 214(top), 215(top), 217, 227, 228(top), 229(top, middle & bottom right) © PA News

page 213(bottom) © Bletchley Park Trust

page 215(bottom) © Jason Hawkes

INDEX

The location of pictures are shown in *italics*. FCO has been used in some sub-headings for Foreign and Commonwealth Office.

abdication crisis (1936) 190
Aboukir Bay (1798) 16
Acland, Antony *127*
    Ambassador to Washington (1986-91) 148
    Permanent Under Secretary (PUS) at FCO 129
Act for the Better Government of India (1858) 17
Adams, John 200
Addington, Henry Unwin 41
Addis, John, Ambassador to China 176
Admiralty 38
aeroplanes 217
Afghanistan 19, 99
Africa, Empire building (1880s and 1890s) 22-3
Afrikaners (Boers) 23, 29
Akers-Douglas, Viscount Chilston (Aretas) 113
Albert Memorial 68, 88
Albert, Prince 42, 155
Alexandra, HRH Princess 151
Allbright, Madeleine *231*
American colonies (July 1776) 14-15, 27
American Electromatic Proportional Spacing Typewriters 208
American War of Independence (1774-83) 15-16, 22
Anglo-Chinese (First Opium) War (1842) 173
Anglo-French, entente (1904) 114
Anglo-French and Anglo-German summit meetings (1990s) 105
Anglo-Persian Agreement (1919) 114
Anne, Princess *159*
ANZAC troops 29
Arab-Jewish problem 122
The Architect 58
Argentine, Falkland Islands (1982) 128, *227*, 229
Armstead, H H, portrait medallions and symbolic figures 76
Armstrong, Robert, (PPS) (1970-75) 110
Ashcroft, Peggy 60
Asquith, H H, Prime Minister (1908-16) 29, 93, 115
Attlee, Clement, Prime Minister (1945-51) 123-4, 138, 166, 220
Australia 24, 27, 28, 29-30, 33
Austria-Hungary, nineteenth century modern economy and navy 27
Austrian Succession (1739-48) 15

Baden-Powell, Robert 24
Balam and Nicholls (quantity surveyors) 46
Baldwin, Stanley, Prime Minister (1935-37) 33, 76, 115-17, 146
Balfour, Arthur 93-4, 110, *112*, 113-15
Balkans 27, 131, 148, 229
Banks and Barry plans for Public Offices 44
Banqueting House 36, 76
Barbados 13
Barber, Anthony, Foreign Secretary 191, *226*
Barclay, Roderick 138
Barrie, J M 186
Barry, Charles 46, 56, 76
Battle of Britain 219
Bearstead, Lord 136
Beaton, Cecil, portraits *119*, *156*

Beauchamp, Lord 93
Beijing, China 173-6
    Boxer Rising (1900) 27, 173-4, *174*, 176
    British Embassy compound *172-4*, 173-6, *175-7*
Belgium, European Community 226
Bengal 16-17, *17-18*, 19
Bentinck, Lord, Governor-General of Bengal (1827-33) and first Governor-General of India (1833-5) 17
Berlin 201, 203
    airlift (1948-49) 221
    British Embassy 144, 160-1, *160-1*
    Conference (1884) 24
Bertie, Francis Leveson, Ambassador to France (1905-18) 158, 231
Bevin, Ernest (1881-1951)
    Foreign Secretary (1945-51) 111, 121-4, *122*, 136, 138, 220-1
    busts 88, *110*, 111, *121*, 134, 141
Bevin, Mrs 123
Biggin Hill 217
Bishop, Freddie, (PPS) (1956-59) 110
Blackhouse, John (1827-42) 28
Blair, Tony, Prime Minister 148, 181, 228, 230
Bletchley Park and GCHQ 211-17, *212-15*
    Nazi invasion of Russia (1941) 165
Blücher, Gebbard Leberecht von, Prussian forces 16
Board of Trade offices (1820s) 38
Boer War (1899-1902) 23-4, 24, 27
Bonaparte-Borghese, Pauline 152
Bonham, Samuel George, Governor of Hong Kong 178
Bonn
    British Embassy 160-1
    Conventions (1952) 160
Bormann, Martin 117
Bramante, Donato, *cortile* 85
Bratby, John 96
Briand, Aristide (French Foreign Minister) 117
Brighton, Royal Pavilion 134
Britain 12-13, 16, 220, 222, 228
    colonies 14-15, 27, 222-3
    Commonwealth of Nations 27, 110
    Dominions 24-7, 33
    foreign policy 33, 226
    global power 11, 30, 33, 219-20, 229
    isolation, end of 27-9
    Labour Government 220
    overseas missions 221, 231
    relations with Soviet regime 162
    Soviet Union alliance (1941) 165
    support for US during Gulf War (1991) 229
    telegraph cable 201-2
Britannia 181
British
    Army, Western Front (Belgium and France) 29
    Broadcasting Corporation 99
    Embassies and ambassadors 143-81, 207, 230-1
    Empire *8-9*, *12*, 105
    Library, India Reading Room 96
    Library (new) 63
    Marines 173
    Navy, battleship *Prince of Wales* 33
Brize Norton 217
Brooke, Peter 168
Brown, David 65, 141
Brown, Eileen (wife of 7th Earl Stanhope) 190

Brown, George (1914-85)
    Foreign Secretary (1966-68) 110, 121, 124-6, *125*
    In My Way 125
Brown, Gordon, Chancellor of the Exchequer 228
Brown, Thomas 200
Bruce, Frederick 173
Brunel, Isambard Kingdom
    The Great Eastern 203
    Paddington Station 48, 81
Brussels, influence of 110
Bryce, Lord, Ambassador to Washington (1907-13) 151
Buccleuch, Duke of 44
Buchanan, James, cable messages 203
Buckingham Palace 115, 134-5, 138
The Builder 44, 85
Burma 186, 220
Burn, William 44
Burnham Beeches *see* Dorneywood
Burns, Terry 195
Burton, Decimus 41-2, 92
Bush, President 151
Butler, Rab, Foreign Secretary (1963-64) 62, 97, 118, 183

Cabinet
    foreign policy 221
    Intelligence Committee 211, 214
Cable and Wireless Company 203
Caccia, Harold, Ambassador to Washington (1956-61) 98, 147
Cadogan, Alexander 97, 98, 232
Cairo, telegrams to 207
Calais, préfect and mayor 217
Calcutta, India 17, 19
Callaghan, James (now Lord), Prime Minister (1976-79) 111, 127, 186
Campbell, Lady 158
Campbell, Ronald Hugh, Ambassador to France (1939) 158
Canada, Dominion of (1867-) 27, 29, *29*, 33
Canning, George, Foreign Secretary 40, 200
Canning, Lord (Charles John), first Viceroy of India 17
Canterbury, Archbishop of 195
Cape Cod, US 14, 147
Cape Colony 24
Cape of Good Hope 22, 24
Carlton Gardens *38-9*, 131, *132*, 133-41, *134-41*, 183, 333
    bomb damage (1940) 136, 141
    Douglas Hurd 141, 195
    Ernest Bevin 122, 136, 138
    Geoffrey Howe 128
    Louis Napoleon 202
    Ministry of Works 136, 138, 141
    Nash, John 134-5, 141
    1990s refurbishment 141
Carlton House 134-5
    Terrace 134, 134
Carrington, Lord *111*, 195
    Foreign Secretary (1979-82) 94, 128, *128*, 141, 158, 195
Castlereagh, Lord (1812-22) 40
Cenotaph 56, *57*, 105, 146
central government, dispersal outside London 62
Chagall, Marc 152
Chamberlain, Austen (1863-1937)
    Foreign Secretary (1924-29) *30*, 99, 116-17, *117*, 208, 217
    Nobel Prize 116
    Secretary of State for India (1915-17) 116

Chamberlain, Joseph 23, 28, 105, 116
Chamberlain, Mrs Austen 117
Chamberlain, Neville, Prime Minister (1937-40) 33, 116-7, 120, 126, 217
Channel Tunnel 115-16
Chaplin, Charlie 169
Chappe, Claude 201
Charles Edward, Prince (Young Pretender 1745) 15-16
Charles I, King 13
Charles II, King, King's Messengers 200
Charles, Prince 54, *71*, 181, 191, 195, 230, *230*
Charles Street 44, 46
Cheese, Anne (housekeeper at Foreign Office) 200
Cheltenham
    Benhall site *210-11*, 211 *see also* Government Communications Headquarters (GCHQ)
Chequers 122, 184-5, 188, 195
Chevening 183, 186-91, *188-94*, 195-7, *196-7*, 217
    Board of Trustees 188, 197
    bomb damage (1941) 190
    church 195
    Foreign Secretaries 184, 191-3, 195-7
    Geoffrey Howe 128, 192-3
    nominated occupants 191
    Prince Charles 191, 195
Chevening Estate Act (1959) 190-1
Chiang Kai-Shek (Jiang Jieshi) 174
China, People's Republic of 19, 27, 105, 173-6
    return of Hong Kong (1997) 179, 181, 229-30
    see also Beijing
Churchill, Clementine 166
Churchill, Winston
    Home Secretary 107
    Prime Minister (1940-45 & 1951-55) 120, 126, 146, 158, 179, 190
        Bletchley Park 211
        bronze statue in Washington 152
        Dorneywood 185-6
        meetings with Stalin 165-6
Civic Trust 63
Civil Service 41, 129
Clarence House 134
Clarendon, Earl of 43, 88
Clayton and Bell 68, 88
Cleopatra's Needle 56
Cleveland Row (next to St James's Palace 39
Cleverly, Charles St George 178-9
Clinton, Bill, President (1992-) 148, 228
Clive, Robert, Governor-General of Bengal (1764-73) 16-17, *17*
Clive Steps *17*, 82
CNN 207
Coe and Hofland plans for Public Offices 44
Cold War 166, 168, 216, 220
Cole, Henry, South Kensington Museum 81
Coles, John 97
Colonial
    hotels 169, *169*
    service 22
Colonial Office 54, 56, 76, *104*, 105, 200
    completion (1874) 56
    Entrance Hall *104*, 105
    and Home Office 76, 105, *105*
    moved to Church House (1947) 60
    (old) in Downing Street 41, 105
        library *see* Foreign and Commonwealth Office (FCO) library
    portraits of Nelson and Wellington 105

restoration (-1995) 71, 105
Colville, Jock, (PPS) (1951-55) 110
Committee of Imperial Defence, Channel Tunnel 115-16
Commonwealth, lowering the flag 219-32
Commonwealth Relations Office (later Commonwealth Office) 60
Congress of Berlin (1878) 112-13
Congress of Vienna, cipher used 207
Conrad, Joseph 169
Constantinople 22, 200, 203
Cook, Captain James 24
Cook, Robin (1946-), Foreign Secretary 94, 96, 131, 131, 141, 196, 217, 217, 230, 231
Cooper, Artemis 156
Cooper, Duff, Ambassador to Paris (1944-) 156, 158
Cooper, Lady Diana 156, 156-7
Coote, Eyre, marble statue (1788) 82
Cornforth, John 86
Cornwallis, Lord, Govenor-General of Bengal 15, 18, 19, 82
Council of India 79
County Hall 94
Court of St James, diplomats 54, 230
Courtauld-Thomson, Lord, Dorneywood 136, 185-6
Coward, Noel 169
Cowley, Lord, Ambassador to France (1852-) 155
Coxhead, Charles, Foreign Office death 58
Crawford and Balcarres, Earl of 94
Crimean War (1854-56) 22, 42, 112
Cromwell, Oliver 12, 36, 186
Crosland, Tony (1918-77), Foreign Secretary (1976-77) 126, 127, 186
Crowe, Eyre, Permanent Under Secretary (1920-25) 116
Crown Estate Commissioners 135
Crystal Palace, Great Exhibition (1851) 48, 81
Cuban Missile Crisis (1962) 147
Culloden (April 1746) 16
Curzon, Lord (1859-1925)
    Foreign Secretary (1919-24) 92-4, 97, 110, 114-15, 115, 200
    Viceroy of India (1898-1905) 21, 21, 114
Cyprus 124
Czechoslovakia, seizure of 33

Daily Telegraph 131
Dakers, Caroline 94
Dalhousie, Lord (1847-56) 17
Danish Red Cross 162
Davidson, Randall, Archbishop of Canterbury 92
de Charost, Duc de 152
de Chevening, Adam 188
de Gaulle, General Charles (later President) 136, 226
de Zulueta, Philip, Secretary for Overseas Affairs (1957-63)   110
Dean, Patrick 124, 147
Defence, Ministry of 144, 216
Delhi, India 17, 20
    imperial 'durbar' (1903) 21, 32, 114
    (New) Viceroy's Palace 146, 149
Denmark, joined the European Economic Community (1973) 226
Denny, John 66
Derby, Lord
    Ambassador to France (1918-) 158
    Prime Minister (1852 & 1858-59 & 1866-68) 45-6
Diplomatic Wireless Service 216
diplomats 167-8, 167, 201
Disraeli, Benjamin
    Prime Minister (1868 & 1874-80) 27, 54, 54, 94
    Congress of Berlin (1878) 112-13
Disraeli, Mrs 54
Dominions Office 60
Dorneywood 183-6, 184-87, 191
    fire (1910) 185
    foreign secretaries 184, 186, 197
    Lord Courtauld-Thomson 136, 185-6

Trust 185
Douglas, Lord Alfred 94
Douglas-Home, Elizabeth 195-7
Douglas-Home, Sir Alec see Home, Lord
Dover 217
Downing, George 36
Downing Street 36, 39-40, 42-6, 47, 51, 73-4, 186
    House of Commons select commttee to consider future 41
    houses 36, 38, 46, 51
Drake, Francis 13
du Maurier, Daphne, Rebecca 186
Dublin, Easter Rising (1916) 32, 32
Dulles, John Foster 124
Dumas, Roland, France's Foreign Minister 196
Dunkirk, evacuation (1940) 33, 158
Dunlop, Mr (Head of the King's Messengers and Communications Department (1941) 97
Dyer, General 32-3

Earle, Lionel 94
East and Central Africa 24, 223
East India Company 13, 16-17, 22, 48, 81-2, 82-3
East India House, Leadenhall Street 48, 51, 81-2
The East offering its riches to Britannia 19
East and West Indies 13
East-West relations 131
Eastcote in Pinner, GCHQ 211
Eastern European countries 229
Eden, Anthony (1897-1977) 88, 88, 217
    Another World 1897-1917; 120
    Foreign Secretary (1935-38, 40-45, 51-55) 88, 120-1, 120, 124, 146, 186
    Lord Privy Seal, visit to Moscow (1935) 162
    Prime Minister (1955-57) 120, 147, 224
Edward the Confessor (1042-66) 36
Edward VI, King, accession (1903) 21
Edward VII, King 52, 105, 155
Egypt 24
    see also Suez
Eire, World War II 32
electric telegraph 29, 201
The Electric Telegraph Company 203
Elizabeth I, Queen 12
Elizabeth II, Queen 96, 129-30, 151, 176, 181
Elizabeth, Queen (Queen Mother) 60, 61, 99
Elliot, Captain 178, 181
Elliot, Walter MP 62
Empire
    Marketing Board poster (1929) 15
    'Tennis Party' 20
encryption and descryption 216
English Heritage 71
Environment, Department of the 62-3
Eton College 185
Eugénie, Empress 80-1, 155
Europa Nostra medal of honour 104
Europe
    claims in West and Central Africa 24
    commerce 28
    discussions between France; West Germany; Italy; Belgium; Luxembourg; Netherlands 226
European Community (EC)
    Britain's attempt to join (1961 & 1967) 159, 222, 226
    initial members 226
European Economic Community (EEC)
    Britain's entry (1973) 110, 126, 170, 226
    Britain's Presidency (1992) 104
    budget 196, 226
    talks in Paris (November 1972) 226
European Union (EU)
    relations with 131
    UK Representative to 144
Euston station 63
Eversley, Viscount 44
Exchange Rate Mechanism (ERM), Britain's entry (1990) 226

facsimile equipment (fax) 211, 216
Falklands War (1982) 68, 147, 195, 229
Far East 27, 33, 220-1
Fergusson, Ewen, Ambassador in Paris (1987-92) 158
Fergusson, Sara 158
First Lord of the Treasury (Prime Minister), Downing Street house 36
Flameng, François, Moscow Embassy 164
Florence, telegraph communication established with 203
Fludyer Street 40-1
Foley, Pat, furnishing schemes 99, 162
Foreign and Commonwealth Office (FCO) 60-1
Foreign and Commonwealth Office (FCO) 40, 61, 67, 67, 74, 107, 201, 202, 231-3
    bombs 107
    building 35-71, 66, 71, 98
        today 73-107, 231
    computer systems 216-17
    Downing Street 19, 39, 40
    facades 38, 71, 75, 76-7, 77, 78, 79
    great renovation (1980s-90s) 65-71, 67, 131, 230
    importance of 110
    Information Centre 105
    internet protocols 217
    inventory of furniture 71
    Library 106-7, 106-7, 200, 207
    London Open House weekend viewing (1997) 71
    portable satelite terminals 216
    Print services and Reproduction Centre 208
    relations within 127-8
    relationship with Number 10; 64-5, 110, 128-30, 146, 221
    St James' Park elevation 74
    staff restaurant 71
    statues 16, 17, 71, 78, 78, 82, 84
    use of entire Public Offices 61
    word processors 216
    see also Bletchley Park and GCHQ; King's Messengers
Foreign Office 50
    aerial photographs (1939 and 1995) 38-9
    Ambassador's Waiting Room 97
    archways 71, 76-7, 76-7
    Britain's changing post war importance 221
    building 22-4, 45-6, 51, 58, 60-2, 232
        completion (1868) 51, 54, 56, 63, 204
        interiors 86, 90-2
        public competition 44-5
        styles, battle of 46-7, 51, 54-7
    communications outside 216
    computers 216
    Conferences 217
    copyists 208
    courtyards filled with huts 58, 60
    Departments
        Ciphering 60, 204, 207, 207
        Communications 97, 203, 204, 216
        German 82
        Librarians 15
        Slave Trade 15
    Downing Street
        facade 76, 78, 78
        houses 46, 51
    early nineteenth century 40
    elevations 74, 76
    engine room in 1941; 13
    entrance 48
        from King Charles Street 79
    Entrance Hall 90
    established as separate department (1782) 15, 38
    establishment of 200
    floor plan 68, 90
    Foreign Secretaries 109-31
        engagements 95, 97, 131
        lift 124
        Room 54, 94, 95, 96-8, 96, 122, 128, 208
            painting of Nepalese prince 96, 128

private bathroom 97
Government Code and Cipher School (GC & CS) 211-12
Grand Staircase 54, 54-5, 60-1, 71, 88-9, 88-91, 94, 99, 104, 113, 130
    bust of Ernest Bevin 88, 110
    murals 55, 89-93, 92-4, 92-3
Gurkha Staircase 19, 67
'Hardinge reforms' (1904-6) 28-9
Heath government announcement (1971) 63
and India Office buildings, proposed use as trade and conference centre dispersal outside London 62
Lady Typewriters 208, 209
lifts 97, 113, 124
Locarno Rooms (1952) 65
    repainted (1926) 60, 71, 99, 101-2
Locarno Suite 98-9, 117
    Cabinet Room 42, 60, 94
        see also Locarno Suite, Dining Room
    Ciphering Department 60, 204
    Conference Room 60, 102, 104-5, 205
        original paintwork 101
        restoration completed (1990) 102
        view from Dining Room 70, 103
        see also Grand Reception Room
    design and craftsmanship on walls and ceiling 70, 103
    Dining Room 102, 102
    dinners for foreign dignitaries 99
    floor plan 90
    Grand Locarno Room 30-1, 98
    Grand Reception Room 58-9, 70, 100-1, 101-2, 204
        above false ceiling 66
        engraving of ball (1878) 101
        Lord Salisbury 101, 113
    King's birthday celebrations 99
    official and other functions 104-5
moves
    Pembroke House in Whitehall Gardens 51, 54
    plans to (1950s) 62
    temporarily into India Office (1947) 60
    need to impress visitors 56
    and Number 10 Downing Street 64-5
    officials 110-1, 120, 129
    (old) in Downing Street 19, 40, 41, 43
    fireplaces 96, 102
    printing presses 208
    openings cut to India Office 60
    outbreak of World War I 28
    overseas posts 200, 217, 231
    Permanent Under Secretaries (PUS's) 97-8, 109, 111
        Room 97-8, 208
    printing, and copying 201, 208
    Private Secretary's Office 97, 111, 128
        portraits of previous foreign secretaries 97
    promoting commerce 28, 96
    quadrangle 48, 57, 58, 63, 66, 74, 74, 78, 78, 90
    reform (1840) 41
    Resident Clerk 204
    restoration work (1987-90) 71, 104
    search for new building (1870s-1940s) 40-4
    speaking tubes 208, 209, 211
    State Rooms 54, 90
        World War I 58, 60
    statues and bas-reliefs 76
    statues representing overseas powers 78
    street plan on completion (1870s) 56, 56
    switchboard 208-9, 209, 211
    taken from the south (1870-80) 36
    telegram from Paris (1852) 155
    telegrams 207, 217
    telephone lines 208-9, 209
    tower 74, 76
    transferred to Downing Street (1793) 39
    and Treasury, replacement plans 62
    Treasury building from aerial photograph (1747) 37
    Tube Room 209

typewriters 43, *208*
work began (September 1863) 51
see also Scott, George Gilbert
Foreign Policy Centre (New Labour think-tank) 230
Foreign Princes, need for reception rooms 41
Foreign Secretaries
   Chevening 184, 191-3, 195-7
   Dorneywood 184-6, 197
   see also Foreign Office, Foreign Secretaries
Formosa Straits 124
Forsythe, Frederick 131
Fox, Charles James, Secretary of State for Foreign Affairs 15, 38-40, 200, 217
France 13, 23, 27, 112
   'entente cordiale' (1904) 28, 155
   European Community 226
   fall of (1940) 216, 219
   Free French government 136
   relations with 115, 152, 155
   Revolutionary Wars (1793-1799) 39
Francis I, Emperor of Austria 152
Franco-Prussian War (1870-71) 88
Franks, Oliver 146
Frederick I, King of Prusia 196
French Supreme War Council 120
French-Canadians, World War I 29, *29*
Frink, Elizabeth 152
Frith, W.S. sculpture details 76
Fujimura, Seichi 179
Fulcher, Miss Sophia 208

Gainsborough, Thomas, portrait of Phillip, 4th Earl of Chesterfield (1769) *190-1*
Gallipoli (1915) *28*, 29
Gambia 13, 22
Gandhi, Mahatma 32-3, *33*
Gaselee, Sir Stephen (Librarian) 59, *106*, 200, *200*, 209
general elections
   (1900) 'khaki' 113
   (1951) 124
   (1992) 71
General Strike (1926) 7, *57*
Geneva 217
George II, King, province of Hanover 15
George III, King 14, 96, 122
George IV, King, Paris ball 153
George IV, King (1820-30) 134
George Street 43
George V, King 117, 168
George VI, King 60, *61*, 99, 166, *190-1*
Germany 23, 27, 30, 33, 158, 211, *216*
   relations with 113-15
   Ruhr, French occupation (1923) 115
   unification (1871) 22, 160
Ghana 13
Gielgud, John 60
Gilbert, Martin 120
Gillmore, David 98
Gilmour, Ian, Lord Privy Seal 141
Gladwin, Cynthia 158
'Glorious Revolution' (1688-9) 15
Goderich, Lord 135
Goerge III, King 36
Goetze, Sigismund 92
   murals *55*, *89-93*, *92-4*
Gold Coast 22, 24, 223
Gorbachev, Mikhail 168
Gordon, General 24
Gordon Walker, Patrick, Foreign Secretary 186
Gore-Booth, Paul, Permanent Under Secretary (PUS) 124
Goulden, Richard, statue of a Gurkha (1929-30) 71, 81, 82
Government
   Code and Cipher School (GC & CS) 211-12
   Communications Headquarters *see* Bletchley Park and GCHQ
   of India Act (1919) 32
   of Ireland Act (1920) 32
   Stationery Office, monopoly (1823) 200
Governor-Generals 16-17, 19
Grant, Sir Alexander, Carlton Gardens 135

The Great Eastern 203
Great Reform Act (1832) 38
Great Western Railway, Paddington to West Drayton 202
Greenwich, meridian for longitude and time zones 11
Grey, Earl (1764-1845), Prime Minister (1830-34) 40, 111
Grey, Lord of Falloden (formerly Sir Edward Grey) (1862-1933)
   Foreign Secretary (1905-16) 29, 76, 78, 93, 96, 110, 114, *114*, 208
   inscription on plaque 76, 78, *78*
   memoirs *Twenty Five Years: 1892-1916*; 96
   Secretary of State for the Colonial and War Departments 178
'Group of Five' (now G8) 110
Guernica, Spain, bombing 60
Gulf War (1990-1) 68, 148, 207, 229, *229*

The Hague, British Embassy 151
Hailsham, Lord, Chevening 191
Halifax, Lord (1881-1959) 78, *118-19*
   Ambassador to Washington (1941-46) 120, 151
   Chancellor of Oxford (1933) 117
   Foreign Secretary (1938-) 117-20
   Viceroy of India (1926-31) 117
Hall, Benjamin 43-4
Hamilton, Sir William (Ambassador in Naples) 140
Hammond, Edmund PUS 41, 88, 203-4
Hannay, David 232
Hansard parliamentary reports 96
Hanslope Park 216
Hardinge of Penshurst, Lord (Charles)
   'Hardinge reforms' (1904-6) 28-9
   Viceroy of India 97-8, *97*, 114-15, 232
Hardy, Thomas 186
Harmsworth, Alfred C W (later Lord Northcliffe) 135
Harrison, James 208
Hastings, Warren, Governor-General of Bengal (1773-85) 17
Hatfield station 217
Hawkstone Chapel, Shropshire 47
Hayter, William, Ambassador to Moscow (1953-57) 60, 166, 168
Healey, Denis 127
Heath, Edward
   Prime Minister (1970-74) 126, 129, 138, 147, 159, *226*
   application to join European Community (1972) 226
   Chevening nominations 191
   FO was not to be demolished (1971) 63
Heathrow 217
Henderson, Arthur 116
Henderson, Lady (wife of Nicholas) 151
Henderson, Mary 158
Henderson, Nicholas 111, 122, 124, 184
   Ambassador in Paris (1975-79) 158
   Ambassador in Washington (1979-82) 94, 146-8
Henry VII, King 12
Henry VIII, King 12
Hepworth, Barbara 152
HMS *Hermes* 228-9
Hertslet, Edward, former Foreign Office Librarian 41, 232
Highton, Cecil Denny (CDH) 66, 68
Hitler, Adolf 33, 117, 120, 126, 131
   Operation Barbarossa (1941) 165
   Rome Embassy 170
Hoare, Jim 174
Holland 22
Home, Lord (Alec Douglas-Home) (1903-95) *226*
   Commonwealth Secretary (1955-60) 187
   Foreign Secretary (1960-63; 1970-74) 114, 126, *126*, 176
   Secretary of State for Commonwealth Relations (1935-60) 126
Home Office (1882-1878) 42, 54, 56, *57*, 61, 63, 71, 76, 105, *105*

Home Secretary's Room 107
Local Government section, explosion (1883) 107
   move to Queen Anne's Gate (1978) 61, 65, 68, 105
   sculpture representing British cities 78
Hong Kong 128, 131, 169, 178-81
   Government House (1855-97) 175-6, 178-81, *178-81*
   returned to China (1997) 179, 181, 229-30, *230*
Hope, Alexander Beresford MP 86, 90
Hopkinson, Henry 144, 146
Horse Guards Parade 38, 74
House of Commons 51
   bill to purchase remaining plots between Parliament Street and Foreign and India Offices 54
   bombing (1941) 62
   restored Chamber 62
   select committees 41, 58
Houses of Parliament 76
   Big Ben 56
   destroyed by fire (1834) 41
Howard, Sir Esme, Ambassador to Washington (1924-30) 151
Howe, Elspeth 128, 195
Howe, Geoffrey (1926-) (now Lord Howe of Aberavon)
   Carlton Gardens 141
   Chancellor of the Exchequer (1979-83) 129, 195
   Chevening 128, 192-3, 195
   downfall of Margaret Thatcher (1990) 228
   Foreign Secretary (1983-) 71, *127*, 128-9
Hoyer-Millar, Frederick, Ambassador to Germany (1955-) 160
Human Rights Conference at Foreign Office (1997) *231*
Hurd, Douglas (now Lord Hurd of Westwell) (1930-)
   Carlton Gardens 141, 195
   Chevening 195
   Foreign Secretary 65, 71, 97-8, 102, 104, *111*, 128-9, 129-31
      Foreign Office building 232
   Political Secretary at Number 10 (1970-74) 129
   Scotch on the Rocks 131
   The Smile on the Face of the Tiger 130-1
   Third Secretary of Beijing Embassy 175
Hurst, Mr *30*
Hussey, Christopher 76, 90

Illustrated London News 54, 94
Inchcape, Lord 135
India 16-21, 24, 30, 32-3, 203
   independence (1947) 33, 60, 220-2
   London Act (1935) 33
   Moghul emperors 13
   World War I & II 32-3
India Acts (1784 & 1858)) 19, 48
India Board of Control on Cannon Row 48
India Office (1858-1947) 17, 19, 48-9, *49-50*, 51, 54-7, 60, 74, 77, 79-82, *79*, 86, 203
   catalogue of works of art 85
   Council Chamber 17, *18*, 52-3, 82, *83*, 85
   Durbar Court 52, *52-3*, *61*, 65-6, 68-9, *79*, 82, *83-4*, 85, 88
   entertainment for President Lebrun of France 60, 99
   glass roof 71, 85
   entrance 71, 81, 82
   Library and Records, Digby Wyatt's notes 78
   Muses' or Naiad stairs *80-1*, 82, 86, 155
   restoration work (1984-87) 71
   Secretary of State's office 86, *86-7*
   statues 77-8, 82
   Sultan's Court (renamed Durbar Court) 52
   see also Wyatt, Matthew Digby
Indian
   Army 29, 114
   Civil Service created 17
   Mutiny (1857) 17, 21, *21*, 45, 48, 78-9, 82

National Congress, first meeting in Bombay (1885) 21
Round Table Conference (1931) 33
Intelligence Services Act (1994) 214, 216
International Monetary Fund 65
IRA mortars (1991) 107
Iraq, mandate 30
Ireland 12, 27, 32, 131, 226
Irish Free State (Eire) 32
Isaacs, Jeremy 192
Islamic Mahdist regime 24
Isogai, Lieutenant General, Governor of Hong Kong 179
Israel 221-2, 224
Italy 22, 33, 115, 226

Jackson and Shaw, tender for Colonial Office 56
James I, King (James VI of Scotland) 12, 14
Jameson Raid (1895) 23
Jamestown, military settlement established (1607) 14
Japan 27-8, 33, 219
   World War II 33, 179, 220
Jay, Michael, Ambassador to France 231
Jebb, Cynthia 158
Jebb, Gladwyn, Ambassador to France (1954-60) 158
Jekyll, Gertrude 151
Jerusalem, King David Hotel 169, *169*
John, King (1199-1216) 188
Jones, Inigo 36, 76, 188

Kaye, William 200
Kelk and Co. 46, 51
Kennedy, John F, President (1961-63) 147, 229
Kent, William 38
Kenya, independence (1963) 223
Kenyatta, Jomo 222
Kerr, John 98
Keyes, Roger 174
Kharitonenko family 162
Kharitonenko, Parvel Ivanovitz 168
Khrushchev, Nikita, British Embassy visit 168
Kimmins, Lt Col John 201
King Charles Street 63, 74
King Street 36
King's Cross station 217
King's Messengers/Queen's Messengers 90, 200-1
Kipling, Rudyard 186
   Feed at Raffles 169
Kirk and Parry 46
Kirkpatrick, Ivone 120, 124
Kitchener, General 24, *24*, 114
Knatchbull-Hugessen, Hughe, Ambassador to China 174-5, 208
Knight, J P, painting of Wellington and Nelson (about 1840) 105
Korean War 221
Kruger, Paul, Boers' President 23
Kuwait, British Embassy 229

Labour government
   International Monetary Fund (1976) 65
   referendum of EEC membership 226
Lancaster House Conference (1980) 226
Lansdowne, Lord, Foreign Secretary 28, 114
Lausanne Conference (1923) 114
Law, Dick 123
Lawford, Valentine 118
Lawson, Nigel (now Lord Lawson of Blaby) 228
Le Havre 158
League of Nations 33, 110
Lebrun, President of France 60, *61*, 99
Lee of Fareham, Lord, Chequers 184
Leon, Sir Herbert 212
Lindsay, Sir Ronald 146
Lisbon, British Embassy 151
Litvinov, Maxim, Deputy Commissar for Foreign Affairs (Soviet Union) 162
Livingstone, David 22, *22*

Lloyd George, David, Prime Minister (1916-22) 94, 110, 114-15, 162
Lloyd, Selwyn (1904-78), Foreign Secretary (1955-60) 124, *124*, 128
Local Government, Department of 58, 68, 107
Locarno 116-17
  Conference (1925) *30*
  Treaties (1925) 30, *30*, 32, 60, 99, 116-117, 211
  see also Foreign Office, Locarno Suite
Lombard Street, post office 201
London
  Heston airport 217
  Lord Mayor of 185
  Open House weekend, FCO viewing (1997) 71
  University, analysis of paint scrapings from FCO 68
Lorenz code 214
Lossiemouth, Scotland Ramsey MacDonald 116
Low, Ivy (wife of Maxim Litvinov) 162
Lucknow *see* Indian Mutiny (1857)
Luftwaffe 211, 219
Lutyens, Sir Edwin
  Cenotaph 56, 146
  plaque to Lord Grey of Fallodon 76, 78, *78*
  Viceroy's Palace, New Delhi 146, 149
  Washington Embassy 144, *144-5*, 146, 149, *150*, 151
Luxembourg, European Community 226
Lyons, Lord (British Ambassador in Paris 1867-87) 155, 158

Macaulay, Lord 42
McC Mathias, Charles, Jr 192
MacDonald, Ramsay (1866-1937)
  Foreign Secretary 115-16, *115*
  Prime Minister (1924; 1929-35) 33, 116
Maclean, Fitzroy 165
MacLehose, Murray, Governor of Hong Kong (1971-82) 181
Macmillan, Harold
  Foreign Secretary (1955) 217
  Prime Minister (1957-63) 110, 124, 126, 147, 168, 222-3, *226*, 228
Madras and Bombay, India 19
Maitland, Donald, (PPS) 121, 124
Major, John *111*
  Foreign Secretary 71, 130, 197
  Prime Minister (1990-97) 110, 131, 141, 148, 228
Making, Roger, Ambassador to Washington (1952-56) 147
Malaya, Japanese take over 33, 220
Mallaby, Christopher, Ambassador to Germany (1988-93) 162
Malmesbury, Lord 41
Manchuria 27
Mao, Chairman 175
Maoris, New Zealand 24
Maratha War (1818) 17
Marconi, wireless telegraphy stations 203
Marshall Aid 122
Martin, Sir Leslie, report on future of Whitehall (1965) 62-3, 107
Mary, Queen 60, *61*, 99
Massachusetts, Salem 'witch' trials (1690) 14
Maugham, Somerset 169
Maw, tiles 85
Mayflower 14
Mayo, Viceroy of India 19
Mazin, Antoinne (French Embassy 1720) 152
Messina conference (Sicily) (1955) 226
Metropolitan Police 54
Meyer, Christopher, Ambassador to Washington 148
MI5 Security Service 107, 211, 214-15
MI6 Secret Intelligence Service (SIS) 131, 211, 214-16, *215*
  Moscow Embassy 168
Michael Wilford and Partners 160
Middle East 30, 221

Middleton, Peter 195
Millennium celebrations 230
Minister of Defence, Dorneywood 185
Ministry of Works, Carlton Gardens 136, 138, 141
Minsk, Russia 144
Minton, Della Robbia ware 85
Minton-Hollins, floor tiles 88
Mitford, Bertie (diplomat in Japan) 51
Molesworth, William 42-43
Mond, Alfred (Commissioner of Works) 94
Mons and Marne, French and British Expeditionary Force 158
Montevideo, British Embassy 101
Moran, Lord 124
Morrison, Herbert (1888-1965) 117
  Foreign Secretary 123-4, *123*, 138
Morrison, Peter 159
Mortimer, Edward 158
Moscow
  Bolshevik Ministry for Foreign Affairs 162, 168
  British Embassy
    Kharitonenko mansion (1931-2000) 162-6, *162-6*, 168
      Stalin visits 165-6, 168
    new (2000-) 168, *168*
  Communist coup (1991) 131
  KGB 168
  Kremlin 132, 165
Mountbatten of Burma, Lord 186
Mugabe, Robert 223
Munich 126
Murmansk and Archangel, British troops landing (1918) 162
Mussolini, Benito *30*, 33, 117
Mysbrack, Michael, overmantel relief in India Office 82, *83*

Nanjing, China, Japanese invasion 175
Napoleon Bonaparte *16*, 153
Napoleon III *80-1*, 155
Napoleon, Prince Louis 135, 202
Napoleonic Wars (1793-1815) 16-17, 22, 39
Nash, John 46, 62, 134-5, 138
Nasser, Gamel Abdul 224
Natal, South Africa 24
National Maritime Museum, Greenwich 101, 190
National Telephone Company 208
National Trust 186, 191
NATO (1940-) 82, 110, 122, 221
Nazi-Soviet Pact (1939) 165
Near East 128
Nelson, Horatio 16, 56, 105, *107*
Netherlands 22, 226
New England, settlers 14
New Zealand 24, 27
  World War I & II 29, 33
Newfoundlanders, World War I 29
Nicholas II of Russia 168
Nicholson, Harold 123, 144
Nicosia, Ledra Palace Hotel 169
Nigeria 13, 24, 223
Nine Years' War (1689-97) 15
Nkomo, Joshua 223
Normanby, Lord, Ambassador to France (1852) 155
North Africa, World War II 33
North Atlantic Treaty (1949) 146
  Organisation *see* NATO
North, Lord, Prime Minister (1770-82) 15
Northcote-Trevelyan Report, modern Civil Service 41
Northern Department (prior to 1782) 38
Northern Ireland 148
Number 10 Downing Street 58, 138, 211, 216
  Cabinet Room 101, 185
  and FCO 64-5, 110, 128-30, 146, 221
  Political Secretary 129
  Secretary for Overseas Affairs 110, 129
Office of Works 41, 44, 47, 51, 94
Old Public Offices 73
  see also Public Offices

Old War Office 38, 66
Omdurman, battle of 24
Operation Barbarossa (1941) 165
Orange Free State, South Africa 22, 24
Ormsby Gore, David, Ambassador to Washington (1961-67) 147
Osborne, Mr 46-7
Ovey, Esmund, Ambassador to Soviet Union 162
Owen, Deborah 127
Owen, Dr David, Foreign Secretary (1977-79) 110, *111*, 127-8, 186

Pacific War (1941-45) 175
Paddington Station 48, 81, 85
Pakistan, independence (1947) 60, 220-2
Palestine 30, 221-2, *221*
Palliser, Michael, Permanent Under Secretary (PUS) 17, 98, 127
Palmerston, Lord (1784-1865)
  Foreign Secretary (1830-34; 1835-41; 1846-51) 22, 40, 111-12, *113*, 208
  Gilbert Scott, second design in Byzantine style 46-7, *51*
  Home Office (1852-55) 112
  Prime Minister (1855-) 43-4, *43*
  Secretary at War (1809-29) 111
Paris 56, 152, 217
  British Embassy 22, 144, 152-5, *152-5*, 156, *156-7*, 158-9
    Austen Chamberlain and Eden 217
    Britain's attempt to join EC 159
    Duff Coopers 156
      Library 152, 156, *156*
      first telegram to Foreign Office (1852) 203
    George Brown 124
    Queen Victoria 155
    restorations 155, 158
    WWI & WWII 158
  Communard uprising (1971) 155
  Conference on Security and Cooperation in Europe (1990) 159
  Franco-Prussian War (1870-71) 155
  German Spring Offensive (1918) 158
  Peace Conference (1919) 114
  Swiss Consulate 158
Parliament Street 36, 56
Parliamentary Committee (1858) 203
Parliamentary Intelligence and Security Committee 214-15
Parminter, Vye 155
Parsons, Anthony, UK Representative at UN in New York 148
Patten, Christopher, Governor of Hong Kong (1992-97) 131, 181, 230, *230*
Patten, Lavender 181
Pauncefote, Lord 144
Peace of Aix-la-Chapelle (1748) 16
Peace with Spain (1604) 14
Pearl Harbor, bombed by Japanese 179
Pembroke House in Whitehall Gardens 51, 54
Penn, William, Pennsylvania 14
Pennethorne, James 42
Percival, General (British Commander at Singapore) 220
Persia 19, 30
Peter the Great 13
Pevsner, Nicholas 76
Philip III of Spain 12
Philip IV of Spain 12
Philip, Prince, visit to Beijing 176
Phyffers, Theodore, reliefs in Indian Office 85
Piccolo, teleprinter-based high frequency radio system 216
Pitt, India Act (1784) 19
Plain English 94
Poland, German invasion (1939) 33
Pompidou, President George 159
Port Said *224-5*
Portland stone 51, 85
Portugal, civil war 112
Post Office 204, 208-9, 211
Powell, Charles, Secretary for Overseas

Affairs (1984-91) 110, 129
Powell, Jonathan 148
Prince of Wales battleship *33*
Princess Royal 155
Principal Private Secretary (PPS)
  to Foreign Secretary 217
  to the Prime Minister 110
PRODROME (telegraphic address) 204
Property Services Agency (formerly Ministry of Public Buildings and Works) 65
Proust, Marcel 152
Prussia, foreign minister 13
Public Buildings and Works (successor to Office of Works) 62
Public Offices 58, 60-5
Public Record Office, Scott and Wyatt original drawings 68
public telephone network 216
Punch magazine 112
Pym, Francis (now Lord Pym), Foreign Secretary *111*, 128, *129-30*, 141, 146, 195

Queen Anne's Gate, Home Office building 61, 65, 68, 105

RAC Club, Pall Mall 136
radio 203, 216
RAF 211, 217
Ransome, Arthur 162
Reagan, Ronald, President of US (1981-89) 147, 228
Rees, Merlyn, Home Secretary, Dorneywood 186
Registry 60
Reid Dick, William 76
Reilly, Lady 124-5
Renaissance 12-13
Rennie, Dr 173
Reuters 207
Rhodes, Cecil, Consolidated Mines Company 23
Rhodesia 127, 223, 226
Richards, John Inigo, view of Moreville Hall, Shropshire 127
Ridley, Captain (of MI6) 212
Rifkind, Malcolm, Foreign Secretary (1995-97) 196
Rippon, Geoffrey, plans to demolish Foreign Office (1963) 62-3, 107
Roberts, Andrew 113, 120, 217
Roberts, David RA 44
Rockingham, Marquess of 38-9
Rome
  Bramante's *cortile* in the Palazzo della Cancelleria 85
  British Embassy 170, *171*
  customs authorities 201
  old Embassy *170*
  Villa Wolkonsky 170
Romeo and Juliet 60
Roosevelt, F D 146
Ross, Sarah and Nick 192
Royal
  Academy, Gilbert Scott 81
  Air Force 115
  Fine Art Commisssion, Locarno Rooms 60
  Navy 22, 33, 115, 190
Rusca, Dr (Mayor of Locarno) *30*
Rusk, Dean, US Secretary of State 152
Ruskin, John 47, 51
Russia 22, 27-8, 30, 112, 114-15, 162, 165

Sackville-West, Vita 123
St James's Park 41-2, 45, 49, 73
St Michael's Church, Cornhill in the City of London 47
St Pancras station 63
  Midland Grand Hotel 68, 71
St Peter's church (later Westminster Abbey) 36
St Petersburg 162, 200
Sakai, Lieutenant General Takashi 179
Salisbury, Lady 113
Salisbury, Lord (1830-1903) 114
  Foreign Office 88, 101, 113
  Foreign Secretary 28, 94, *112-13*, 112-14,

217
  Prime Minister (1885-92 & 1895-1902)
    28, 101, 110, 112
  Secretary of State for India (1866-67);
    1874-78) 112
Saturday morning work ended (1956) 124
Saudi-Arabian desert, British soldiers 229
Scharf, George, drawing of Foreign Office
  (old) 40, 40
Schofield, Paul 168
Scotland, Parliamentary union (1707) 12
Scott, George Gilbert 43, 48, 90
  Albert Memorial 68, 88
  churches 47
  Colonial and Home Offices 54, 76, 105
  Foreign Office 19, 58, 62, 90
    beam technology 104
    competition 44-7, 51
    completion (1868) 54, 56, 63
    drawings of tower 76
    Gothic design 45, 46-7, 58, 71, 81
    Grand Staircase 88
    interiors 86, 104
    Locarno Rooms, original colouring 71
    Locarno Suite decorations 99
    materials used 96
    second design in Byzantine style 46, 47,
      51, 78
    successful Italianate design 47, 47, 51,
      78
  Home Office elevations 76
  professor of architecture at Royal Academy
    81
  Public Offices 19, 61, 73-107
    and Digby Wyatt 74, 76, 78
  study of Classical buildings 51
Scott, Giles Gilbert, restored Chamber of
  House of Commons 62
Secret world 199-217, 207
  telegrams 155, 201-7, 204, 206
  see also Bletchley Park and GCHQ
semaphore masts 201
Senegal 13, 16
Seven Years' War (1756-63) 15
Seymour, Horace 97
Shanghai, China 60, 175
HMS Sheffield 228
Shekhtel, Moscow Embassy Grand Staircase
  164, 164
Sheridan, Richard Brinsley 15, 39
Shuckburgh, Evelyn 126
Sidney Street crisis (1911) 107
Sierra Leone 22, 222-3
Simpson, John 193
Sinclair, Sir Archibald 126
Singapore 169, 169, 220
  Japanese take over (1942) 33, 219-20
Single European Act (1983) 226
Sino-British relations 176
Skidmore's Art Manufacturers Company of
  Coventry 88
slave trade 22
Smith, Ian 226
Smith and Taylor 51, 54
Soames, Christopher (now Lord Soames)
  223, 226
  Ambassador to France (1968-72) 158-59,
    159
Soames, Emma 159
Soames, Mary 158
Soames, Nicholas 159
Soane, John 38, 40, 74, 138
Somerset House, government offices
  (1776-96) 74
Somme, Battle of the (1916) 211
South Africa
  Kimberley, diamonds discovered (1867)
    23
  Republic (1961) 222
  South West Africa 30
  Union of (1910-61) 24, 27, 29, 33
South Georgia, raising Union Flag and White
  Ensign (1982) 228
South Kensington Museum 81
South West Africa (later Namibia) 23, 30
Southern Africa 23, 128

Southern Department (prior to 1782) 38-9
Soviet Union 115, 126, 128, 165
Spain 22, 112
Spanish Armada (1588) 12
Special Operations Executive (SOE) 216
Spence, Basil 61, 170-1
  see also Queen Anne's Gate
Stalin, Joseph 162, 165-6, 168
stamp duties imposed (1765) 14
Stamp, Gavin 63
Stanhope, 1st Earl (James) 188, 196
Stanhope, 2nd Earl 188, 196
Stanhope, 3rd Earl 188
Stanhope, 4th Earl 188, 197
Stanhope, 5th Earl 188
Stanhope, 6th Earl 190
Stanhope, 7th Earl 190
Stanhope, Earl of 44
Stanhope, General James 196
Stanhope, Lady, (wife of 5th Earl) 188
Stanley, Sir Henry and David Livingstone
  meeting 22
State Paper Office 74
Stationery Office 200, 208
Statute of Westminster (1931) 33
Stephens, Mrs Winifred 176
Stewart, Michael, Foreign Secretary 126
Stirling, William MP 44
Stuart, Sir Charles 152-3
Submarine Telegraph Company 203
Sudan 24
Suez
  cable connections 203
  Canal (opened 1869) 19, 24, 225
  Crisis (1956) 120, 124, 147, 223-4,
    224-5, 228
Sunday Times, reference to Foreign Office as
  'magnificent slum' (1967) 65
Surrender of British Fores at Yorktown (1781)
  14
Sydney, Australia 25

Tait, T.S., purposed Colonial Office building
  60
Tanzania (Tanganyika) 23, 222-3
Tate Britain, London 149
Teignmouth, Lord 53, 84
telegrams 203-4, 207
telegraph cables 201-3
10 Downing Street: The Illustrated History 78
Thackeray, William, marriage to Isabella
  Shaw 152
Thames 36
Thatcher, Denis 148
Thatcher, Margaret, Prime Minister
  (1979-90) 110, 128-30, 128, 147-8, 159,
    168, 226, 228
  Chevening nomination 195
  European integration 226, 228
  FCO restoration 66, 232
Thompson, Arthur B, tender for Colonial
  Office 54, 56
The Times 43-5, 47, 92, 99, 125, 202
Togo 23
Touraine, French government 158
Trafalgar
  battle of (1805) 16
  Square, Nelson's Column 56
trains and boats and planes 217
Transjordan 30
Transvaal 22-4
Treasury
  building 73
    (1730s) (now Cabinet Office) 38
    (old) refronting by Barry 76
    to complement the Foreign Office 58
  Cabinet War Rooms and work of Number
    10; 60
  foreign policy 221
  telephonic communications in Foreign
    Office 208
  and Trade departments 144
Treaty of Allahabad (1765) 16
Treaty of Nanjing (1842) 173
Treaty of Paris (1763) 16
Treaty of Rome (1957) 226

Trelawney, Sir John 45
Truman, President Harry 146
Turing, Alan 211
Turkey, Sultan of, ball for (1867) 52, 52, 82,
  85
Tyrell, Lady 158
Tyrell, Lord, Ambassador to France
  (1928-34) 158

Uffizi in Florence 92
Uganda, independence (1962) 223
Ulster 32
United Nations 110
  Security Council 220
  Suez Crisis (1956) 224
United States 27, 184-5, 219-20, 223
  Falklands War 229
  post WWI isolationism 30, 144, 146, 221
  Presidents 110
  relations with Britain 126, 144, 147-8,
    220, 223, 226, 228-9
  World War I & II 29, 144, 146, 158
USSR 229

van Blarenberghe (1716-94), Surrender of
  British Fores at Yorktown (1781) 14
Vansittart, Robert 97, 98, 114-15, 232
Venetian blackamoors, Dorneywood 185
Versailles
  peace treaty (1781) 15
  Treaty of (1919) 30
Victoria, Queen 42, 54, 85, 112-13, 155,
  203
  declared 'Empress of India' (1876) 21
  Diamond Jubilee (1897) 27, 27
  Golden Jubilee (1887) 26-7, 27
  insignia on Foreign Office Grand Staircase
    floor 88
Victoria station 217
Victorian
  railway stations 63
  Society 63, 71
Vienna 203, 217
  Convention on Consular Relations (1963)
    201
Vietnam War (1956-75) 147, 228-9
Villiers, George, statue in Foreign Office 88
von Bismarck, Chancellor Otto 23

Wales 12
Wales, Prince see Charles, Prince
Wales, Princess of 54
Wallace Collection 101
Walpole, Robert 38
War Office 42
War of the Spanish Succession (1702-14) 15
Wars of Jenkins' Ear (1739) 15
Wars of the Roses (1455-85) 12
Washington
  British Embassy 144-52, 147-51
    British Embassy showcase (1982) 151
    Lutyens creation (1930 photos) 144-5
  Conference (1922) 144
Waterloo, battle of (1815) 16
Wedgewood Portland vase 140
Wellesley, Arthur see Wellington, Duke of
Wellesley, Richard (later Lord Mornington)
  17, 19, 82
Wellington, Duke of 16-7, 82, 105, 107,
  111, 141
  Ambassador to France (1814-15) 152
Wells, H G 162
Welsh Nationalists 94
West Africa (Gold Coast and Nigeria) 13, 22,
  24, 223
West Germany, European Community 226
West Indian islands 16
Western Europe, urbanisation of 28
Westminster 36, 37
  Hall 44, 62
  Hotel 51
  Palace of 41, 56, 76
  Statute of (1931) 33
Whistler, Rex 185, 186
White House, National Security Advisor 110
Whitehall 36, 38, 56, 76, 77, 79

departments 110, 221
  Martin report on future (1965) 63
  officials 113
  Palace 36, 39
Wilberforce, Bishop 54
Wilhelm II, Kaiser (1890-) 28
William of Orange (William III) and Mary 15
Williams, Francis 123
Wilson, David (later Lord Wilson of
  Tillyorn), Governor of Hong Kong 181
Wilson, Harold, Prime Minister (1964-70 &
  1974-76) 126-7, 147, 176, 191-2, 226
Wilson, Horace 120
Windsor Castle 185
Wireless Corps 136
Wooton, Sir Henry, Ambassador to Italy
  (1604) 232
World War I (1914-18) 19, 29, 29, 32-3, 93,
  211
  Public Offices 58
  run up to 28, 203
  United States 146, 158
World War II (1939-45) 29, 32-3, 62, 120,
  220
  United States 146, 158
Wright, Patrick 98
Wyatt, Matthew Digby 49
  Commissions of Crystal Palace 48, 81
  Foreign Office, Secretary of State's office
    86
  India Office 48-9, 51, 79, 81
    Durbar Court 88
    exterior elevation 49, 49, 74
    interiors 90
    Italianate tower 49
    Library and Records notes 78
    researching original intentions and
      designs 68
  Paddington Station 81, 85
  Rennaissance of Italy 81
  Slade professor of fine arts at Cambridge
    University 81
  South Kensington Museum 81

Yamashita, General 220
Yeltsin, Boris 131
Yorktown, British forces surrendered (1781)
  14, 15
Youde, Edward, Governor of Hong Kong
  (1982-86) 181
Young, Mark, Governor of Hong Kong 179
Yugoslavia, crises (1990s) 68

Zambia, independence (1964) 223
Zimbabwe settlement 128

North Atlantic Council Deputies

PASS No. 146

VALIDITY EXTENDED TO 31 JUL. 1952

VALIDITY EXTENDED TO 3.1.DEC. 1952

SECRETARY GENERAL

СОВЕЩАНИЕ МИНИСТРО
ИНОСТРАННЫХ ДЕ

Берлин, 195

В ЗАЛ ЗАСЕДАНИЯ

Фамилия **Sir F. Hoyer-Millar**

Должность

Делегация **United Kingdom**

Делегация СССР

TRIPARTITE MEETING
FOREIGN MINISTERS OF FRANCE, UNITED KINGDOM, UNITED STATES
NEW YORK, NEW YORK, SEPTEMBER, 1950

174

NAME **Sir F. Hoyer-Millar**

OF **United Kingdom**

TITLE **Adviser**

SIGNATURE

CHARLES W. YOST
SECRETARY GENERAL

BY
SECURITY OFFICER

Period Pass No. 13520

Admit. MR F. HOYER-MILLER.

Expiring on

31 JAN 1945

For duty in connection with

DE (CA)

COUNCIL OF FOREIGN MINISTERS

Lancaster House · London SW1

SEPTEMBER 1945

VISITORS' GALLERY
INTERNATIONAL MILITARY TRIBUNAL

SEAT NO 2
SESSION 175

No. 106

NINE-POWER CONFERENCE
LONDON, SEPTEMBER 1954

DELEGATE'S PASS

Name Sir F. Hoyer-Millar

Delegation United Kingdom

245

PEACE CONFERENCE
Paris, July 1946

Admit the Bearer of this Pass to the Offices
of the United Kingdom Delegation

Bearer's Signature

NOT TRANSFERABLE